KATE FELUŚ is a garden historian and historic landscape consultant. She researches and writes about designed landscapes of all periods, specialising particularly in eighteenth- and early nineteenth-century parks and gardens.

'In these pages the gardens of William Kent, "Capability" Brown and Humphry Repton spring to life. So along the paths we glimpse people from the great house walking or sweeping by in their carriages. Boats in the guise of men o'war or Chinese junks take them on pleasure trips on Capability's newfangled lakes. On the banks they can be spotted fishing rod in hand or, if water takes a more covert role, they might be caught swimming stark naked in a cold bath.'

SIR ROY STRONG

'Kate Feluś has unmasked the Georgians – caught them in their garden indulgences, fabulous beyond the realms of even their clothes or their interiors. The book is wittily scripted through morning, noon and night, with fascinating illustrations, many rarely seen.'

JANE BROWN, author of *The Pursuit of Paradise* and *Lancelot 'Capability' Brown: The Omnipotent Magician, 1716–1783*

Office; the Somerset Record Office; the Buckinghamshire Record Office; the West Sussex Record Office; and the Henry E. Huntington Library. Also the librarians at the Somerset Local Studies Library; the National Monuments Record; the staff in the Rare Books, Manuscripts and Map Rooms at the British Library; the librarians of St Johns College Library, Cambridge; the West Sussex library service for their county store, the rich depths of which I have regularly plundered; and the ever-helpful staff at my local library.

Particular thanks for numerous contributions also go to Dianne Barre, Oliver Jessop, Philip White and Min Wood, who when the mountain of my Ph.D. seemed unsurmountable persuaded me not to give up. I am grateful to Jenny Simmons, Cees Roos and Kay Morgan for reading early drafts; to Mike Kleyn and Susan Campbell for their encouragement, hospitality and wisdom; and to Jane Crawley for helping me to see how an up-cycled Ph.D. thesis could work as a book. Thanks to everyone at I.B.Tauris, especially my editor, Philippa Brewster, for her patience and enthusiasm for the subject.

For helping me to keep at least one foot in the present and real life while I was writing, I am grateful to Fiona Barrett, Louise Dignand and Rosie Simmons, and to their families for taking in my refugee children. Sue Slade, my parents Gillian and Anthony Feluś and my sister Aimée have all been a constant support. My final debt is to those closest to me, my sons Hal and Ivo, who have tolerated this cuckoo in their nest, and to Jon Edgar, sometimes frustrated but always supportive, who has still managed to plough his own furrow, while enabling me to plough mine.

Acknowledgements

O NE SUMMER'S DAY, in the final year of the last
   millennium, I sat on the rear seat of a coach heading back
to York after a day at Castle Howard. I had just met Professor
Timothy Mowl and on that journey we discussed the question
of how the Georgians actually used their gardens. He suggested
that it would make a suitable subject for a Ph.D. thesis, and
that is how this book began. It is therefore fitting that my first
acknowledgement is to Professor Mowl, my supervisor and
friend; I thank him for his patience, generosity and regular wise
counsel. Also at the University of Bristol, Michael Liversidge
has always been encouraging, and I am grateful to the GNS
Foundation for funding my studies there.

Living at Stowe was an invaluable experience and thanks
must go to all my friends from that period, for helping to
recreate goings-on in the garden, from sailing on the lake to
music in the temples. My next debt is to Nick Owen and John
Phibbs for teaching me to read landscape, to really understand
how it worked, and for their unstinting generosity with nuggets
of evidence and the benefit of their long experience in analysing
Georgian parks and gardens.

The evidence on which this book is based comes from a wealth of disparate sources, and that is reflected in the length of the list of people to whom I owe a debt. No matter how seemingly small or insignificant, their contributions have been invaluable and I am grateful to them all: Rosemary Baird, Andrew Barber, Harry Beamish, Ian Berry, Michael Bevington, Ray Biggs, Simon Bonvoisin, Kate Bostock, Jane Bradney, Jane Brown, Cynthia Gaskell Brown, Mike Calnan, Penelope Cave, Jane Clark, Alexia Clarke, Adrian Cook, Abigail Coppins, Fiona Cowell, Rachel Cowgill, Mike Cozens, John Culverhouse, Mel Czapski, Stephen Daniels, Duncan Davidson, Ivan Day, Steve Desmond, Jo Dixon, Andrew Eburne, Caroline Egar, Patrick Eyres, John Forster, Amy Forster-Smith, Basia Furmanik, Susan Gordon, Andrew Hann, Elain Harwood, Sandy Haynes, Clare Hickman, Matthew Hirst, Christine Hiskey, Gareth Hughes, Sally Hughes, Phil Hudson, Kate Johnson, Sir Henry Keswick, Elizabeth Knight, Tim Knox, David Lambert, Kim Legate, Karen Lynch, Richard Mabey, Ian Mackintosh, Laura Mayer, Jennifer Meir, Joanna, Ned and Clare Mersey, Susan Middlemas, Mark Newman, Richard Oldfield, Tom Oliver, Francesca Orestano, Elizabeth Owen, James Peill, Jill Plater, Martin Postle, Cristiano Ratti, Jean Reader, Michael Richardson, Michael Rudd, Sarah Rutherford, Sue Shephard, Steffie Shields, David Standing, Caroline Stanford, Mike Sutherill, Michael Symes, Peggy Synge, Nick Tomlinson, Martin Towsey, Gary Webb, Richard Wheeler, John White, James Collett-White, Liz Whittle and Tom Williamson.

Additionally, I am grateful to the search room staff at the Bedfordshire and Luton Archive; the West Devon Record

The
SECRET LIFE
of the
GEORGIAN
GARDEN

BEAUTIFUL OBJECTS & AGREEABLE RETREATS

KATE FELUŚ

I.B.TAURIS
LONDON · NEW YORK

For my parents,
Gillian and Anthony Feluś

Published in 2016 by
I.B.Tauris & Co. Ltd
London · New York
www.ibtauris.com

ISBN   978 1 78453 572 8
eISBN   978 1 78672 007 8
ePDF   978 1 78673 007 7

A full CIP record for this book is available from the British Library
A full CIP record is available from the Library of Congress

Library of Congress Catalog Card Number: available

Designed and typeset in Monotype Fournier by illuminati, Grosmont
Printed and bound in Sweden by ScandBook AB

MIX
Paper from
responsible sources
FSC
www.fsc.org   FSC® C007584

Contents

ACKNOWLEDGEMENTS   vii

FOREWORD   xi

ONE   Introduction   1

TWO   Setting the Scene   8
Georgian Landscapes and Georgian Life

THREE   Morning   31
Tours – Refreshments en route – Boating – Bathing

FOUR   Afternoon   82
*Fishing – Study – Curiosity – Amorous Liaisons
– Games & Recreation*

FIVE   Evening   145
Food – Drink – Music

SIX   The Night-time   190
Moonlight – Fêtes – Illuminations – Fireworks

AFTERWORD   214

NOTES   222

SELECT BIBLIOGRAPHY   241

LIST OF FIGURES   248

INDEX   252

Foreword

I T IS FORTY YEARS since the publication of Mark Girouard's landmark book *Life in the English Country House*. In the preface the author wrote:

> Even the most knowledgeable country-house enthusiasts tend to think in terms of architects, craftsmen or family history, but to know surprisingly little about how families used the house which the architects and craftsmen built for them.

In that book gardens hardly get a mention, for it was published in 1978, the year before *The Garden* exhibition at the Victoria and Albert Museum, which signalled that the garden was about to enter the mainstream of scholarship. In the decades that followed there was an outpouring of major books on garden designers and on the gardens themselves. Garden history itself entered the halls of academe and garden aerial photography, archaeology and re-creation took off.

Even with this sustained burst of activity little was explored in the Girouard sense of what we might call 'Life in the English Country House Garden'. This is what makes this book so pertinent. Here, for the first time, we have a lively evocation of what the Georgians used their gardens for, a subject as valid and as interesting as it is to know how the rooms in their houses functioned. In these pages the gardens of William Kent, 'Capability' Brown and Humphry Repton spring to life. So, along the paths we glimpse people from the great house walking or sweeping by in their carriages. Boats in the guise of men-o'-war or Chinese junks take them on pleasure trips on Capability's newfangled lakes. On the banks they can be spotted fishing rod in hand, or, if water takes a more covert role, they might be caught swimming stark naked in a cold bath. Others would find an eye-catcher into which they could retreat to contemplate or read, for libraries often played a role in these seemingly fairy-tale buildings scattered across such aristocratic domains. And then there were sports of archery, quoits, cricket or bowls. When we visit these buildings today we have to exercise our imagination to place in them what is caught in so many contemporary paintings: gentlemen sitting in country chairs leaning back glass in hand, ladies more genteelly sipping tea, others about to go off on horseback or in a phaeton to view what Miss Austen referred to as the 'improvements'.

The visual material gathered here presents us with an English Arcady, for all of us know that any activity in the garden is subject to that curse of the island, the English weather. That has been and still is the imponderable factor about life in the garden: will it be too hot or too cold, too windy or belting down with rain. But here for the first time has been gathered everything that the Georgians got up to in their gardens – weather permitting.

Sir Roy Strong

Buildings probably were first introduced into gardens merely for convenience, to afford refuge from a sudden shower, and shelter against the wind; or ... to be seats for a party, or for retirement: they have since been converted into objects; and now the original *use* is too often forgotten in the greater purposes to which they are applied; they are considered as objects only: the inside is totally neglected; and a pompous edifice frequently wants a room barely comfortable. Sometimes the pride of making a lavish display to a visitor, without any regard to the owner's enjoyments; and sometimes too scrupulous an attention to the style of the structure, occasions a poverty and dulness within, which deprives the buildings of part of their utility. But in a garden they ought to be considered both as beautiful objects, and as agreable retreats...

THOMAS WHATELY,
Observations on Modern Gardening, 1770

ONE

Introduction

ALMOST TWENTY YEARS ago I was lucky enough to
live and work at Stowe in Buckinghamshire, one of the
finest of all Georgian gardens and a creation on so vast a scale
that Horace Walpole described it as 'that province that they
call a garden'. The National Trust had not long begun their
epic restoration and it still had the magic of a forgotten place,
with secrets to be discovered. As a budding garden historian I
noticed that most visitors to the gardens route-marched from
one building or monument to another, noses in guidebooks,
absorbing dates and names of architects, only glancing up to
mentally tick that feature off the list before tramping on to the
next. I knew, almost instinctively, that there must be more to
experiencing the garden than that. The plethora of temples and
other eye-catchers had surely lent themselves to leisure and
enjoyment, but when I asked the question of how they, and
their counterparts in other such gardens, had been used when
they were in their prime, the only answers I found were of the
vaguest sort: perhaps for picnics, maybe for tea, possibly the
odd musical soirée?

Interest in historic gardens is relatively new. It was only in the late 1960s and 1970s that historians tentatively started to think designed landscapes worthy of investigation. This gained momentum following the Great Storm of 1987, when an understanding of these designs was necessary to their restoration, after the extensive damage wrought that October night. Since then probably more has been written on gardens and parks of the Georgian period than any other in the history of designed landscapes in Britain. This is because the Landscape Style, the predominant fashion through the era, has been seen as the most important British contribution to European art, and as the one occasion on which this island race, on the windswept periphery of Europe, innovated rather than followed their Continental cousins.[1] The French christened the style the *jardin anglais* and the English landscape garden was imitated from colonial America to Imperial Russia. But in all the acres of print written about such creations over the last five decades, the picture of how life was lived in these designed landscapes has been obscure and fragmented; at best information has been limited to a snippet here, a paragraph there. So, the story of the social use of these great designs has remained untold. Here the landscape garden reveals its secret life for the first time. It is a secret that has been in plain view, but until now the disparate pieces of the picture have never been brought together.

The traditional view of landscape parks and gardens is that they were artistic compositions painted using a three-dimensional palette of landform, trees, grass and water. They were seen as attempts to emulate the landscape paintings of the seventeenth-century masters such as Claude Lorrain and

Nicolas Poussin. Like these artists' depictions of the Roman Campagna, they were dotted with temples and ruins. But the taste of the British was broad and eclectic, and, in reality, once this aesthetic was translated to the British countryside the styles of the buildings that punctuated the views in parks and gardens were myriad: a classical temple here, a Gothic tower on that hill, a Chinese seat by the lake, and a range of hybrids in between. Their small scale also lent itself to architectural experiments; in garden buildings styles were tried out before being used in the more extensive architecture of parent houses.[2] However, they were not just visual statements. Thomas Whately, one of the great commentators on the development of the Landscape Style, acknowledged the compositional importance of these buildings in his *Observations on Modern Gardening*, but he warned against 'the pompous edifice', the folly of grand visual shows without use and function, saying that 'in a garden they ought to be considered both as beautiful objects, and as agreable [*sic*] retreats'.[3] Whately's concern, though doubtless born out of the observation of a trend, was in fact exaggerated. The stories of life in the garden recounted here demonstrate just how important use and enjoyment of their gardens was to the Georgians and how often this took place in buildings that were both 'agreeable retreats' and 'beautiful objects' in the landscape. These eye-catchers, as they were known, were the focal point of so many activities that they present us with a lens through which a picture of life in the garden can be focused.

Parks and gardens had, of course, been used for leisure pursuits before. In fact they always have been, and there are strong echoes of both classical Rome and Elizabethan

England in how the Georgians used their gardens. However, in the period covered by this book – the eighteenth and early nineteenth centuries – the scale, layout and position of garden buildings in relation to the house changed. Landscape parks and gardens had become generally more extensive than those of previous ages, now taking in hundreds of acres. The Georgian equivalent of the Tudor banqueting house, which had previously been located at the corner of the walled court adjacent to the house, or even on the roof, was moved further away from the mansion, often up to a mile or two.[4] The detached and sometimes remote quality of these 'retreats' allowed them to become an escape from the bustle of the country house.

The period explored here is 'Georgian' in the widest sense. The time frame covers the whole of the Hanoverian dynasty from the accession of George I in 1714 to the death of William IV in 1837. It therefore includes the period often known as the Regency, which in strict political terms ran from 1811 to 1820. The 123 years from the death of Queen Anne to the accession of Queen Victoria encompasses the passing of almost five generations. Society inevitably evolved during this period. Gardens echoed fashions and changed from the geometric and formal, with roots in the decades after the Restoration in the late seventeenth century, through the naturalistic style of Lancelot Brown and his imitators, against which the followers of the savage Picturesque rebelled, to the rebirth of formality, albeit in a more limited form, often combined with naturalistic parkland beyond. But through the ebb and flow of styles, patterns of use remained fairly constant.

It is from the highest echelons of society, the aristocracy and sometimes royalty, that most stories of the social use of garden come. These were the people with the resources to create the most innovative, most extensive parks and gardens and the leisure to use them. However, there are many clues to suggest that the garden-using habits of the upper classes filtered down the social scale to at least the lower middle classes. A cast of characters from all strata of the literate classes appear repeatedly thorough this book. They are the voices that have spoken loudest to me, those that have stood out among the wealth of evidence. But they are the tip of the iceberg. Every large estate and quite a few smaller ones have a story of use and happenings in the garden, sometimes one that has become almost a myth, possibly based on real events and handed down from generation to generation, so it has become embroidered and the hard truth impossible to distinguish in the narrative – a meeting place for lovers here, a gambling den there. Such stories often appear in isolation, the only anecdote on real life in the garden in that particular place. There are too many of these stories to be included here, but their frequency bears out the more solid facts that are harder to come by, and in turn the evidence often shows that these stories are likely to be based on truth. There are, therefore, many great gardens, with plenty of 'agreeable retreats' that are not mentioned here and I trust readers will excuse these omissions.

We know that many leisure activities and scholarly pursuits took place in the garden, but pictorial sources, especially those depicting real events, are a rarity. This is particularly true of people doing things inside their garden buildings on a day-to-day basis. It is likely that more everyday goings-on were not the subject of artists because they were just that, everyday. There was nothing out of the ordinary in a lady writing letters in her ornamental cottage or a gentleman practising his flute in his summer house. But where the lack of evidence is felt most keenly is in views of fêtes or grand entertainments in the pleasure ground. There are a few notable examples that do show hundreds of diners on long benches under the trees, but almost nothing that shows this use of the garden at night, which happened frequently. Although Jean Claude Nattes, then drawing master at Stowe, made several sketches of the temporary architecture erected for the celebration of the visit of the Prince of Wales in 1805, he does not seem to have returned with his easel at night-time when the buildings were part of the entertainment. So we have no visual record of the excitement of the fireworks, or the effect of the thousands of lanterns strung in the trees. It is possible that this was because he was too busy enjoying himself.[5] This omission, however, is compensated for by two vivid and complementary diary entries written by a pair of sisters who were guests at the entertainment. Their accounts of the whole evening perhaps tell us more than the snapshot that would be given by a watercolour, which could only capture one moment in time.

Almost any activity that took place within the house in the Georgian period could also take place outside, and when it did so was frequently tinged with increased enjoyment. This sort of pleasure seems timeless; after all, who has not observed that picnic food, enjoyed in beautiful surroundings, seems to taste better than food eaten at home? Every meal of the day that could be served in the house was also eaten outside. Georgian parks and gardens were used at all hours, from sunrise to sunset and beyond. All the activities that took place in the garden are described here during the hours when they most frequently took place. So the main chapters of the book deal with each of four phases of the day: morning, afternoon, evening and night-time. Consequently it describes a hypothetical day in the life of the Georgian garden, ending with the excitement of music and fireworks, and a night late home to bed. In reality, of course, things were not so rigidly structured. Different people had different habits. Not everyone sailed on their lake in the morning or retreated to their garden building for peace and quiet in the afternoon. Furthermore, the arrangement of the day and the activities that took place within that time frame were necessarily different if the family were at their country seat quietly on their own, as opposed to hosting a grand house party, with large numbers of guests to be entertained. It was on such occasions that the garden and its buildings really came into their own and became the playground for pleasure-seekers of all sorts, as is revealed in the following chapters.[6]

TWO

Setting the Scene

Georgian Landscapes and Georgian Life

WHEN JANE AUSTEN's most popular heroine, Elizabeth Bennet in *Pride and Prejudice*, confesses to her sister that she is not exactly certain when her feelings towards Mr Darcy started to change from disdain to love, she tells Jane: 'I believe I must date it from my first seeing his beautiful grounds at Pemberley.' Significantly she does not identify the grand mansion, but his verdant acres. In fact, in encouraging her to visit Pemberley in the first place, her aunt tells her persuasively: 'If it were merely a fine house richly furnished ... I should not care about it myself; but the grounds are delightful.'[1] Elizabeth is admittedly an outdoorsy type of heroine, but these sentiments were common during the Georgian period. Parkland, gardens and the ornamental buildings within them regularly received higher praise than the great house. At times, even the garden building – that 'agreeable retreat' – had a higher status than the house, especially during grand entertainments.

Jane Austen was born in 1775, exactly halfway through the period covered by this book, into an England which had seen, over the previous half-century, a revolution in landscape design. From the 1720s, not long after the accession of George I, garden design evolved apace. Charles Bridgeman, William Kent, Lancelot 'Capability' Brown and Humphry Repton rank among the greatest ever designers of landscape. These are the iconic names of the era. There were many others besides: less well-known designers, followers or pupils of the greats, theoreticians, professional gardeners lent to other estates, or owners themselves who designed their own grounds and bestowed their taste on friends and family for the improvement of their respective landscapes. Brown was the most prolific of all these men and advised at well over 200 sites, from the far north-east of England, almost on the Scottish border, down to Devon in the south-west. Many of his creations were so extensive in their acreage that it is not much of an exaggeration to say he transformed the face of the English countryside.[2]

The reign of George I (1714–1727) saw the first tentative steps towards a less formal style, loosening the straitjacket of geometry that had dominated gardens up till that point. Charles Bridgeman inherited the mantle of Henry Wise, royal gardener to Queen Anne, but he started to move away from the established straight lines, clipped evergreens and gravel walks, introducing the snaking serpentine into his designs. This loosening picked up momentum in the 1730s. Around this time, William Kent, carriage painter turned artist–decorator–garden designer, 'leapt the fence and saw all nature is a garden', as Horace Walpole tells us. Although the significant innovation of the ha-ha, the sunken wall which allowed designers to dispense with visual barriers, had been used for a couple of decades, especially by Bridgman and the architect John Vanbrugh, it was

Kent who opened gardens up to their wider landscapes, calling in the surrounding countryside and allowing the long vistas that were to become the norm, as at Rousham (Oxfordshire). Then along came Lancelot Brown, the lad from Northumberland, not yet known by his nickname of 'Capability', literally walking in the footsteps of Bridgeman and Kent as head gardener at Stowe (Buckinghamshire) and proving himself as engineer, designer and project manager.[3] He went on to become the pre-eminent designer of his day. Jane Austen was seven when he died and many of the great houses she knew, including Godmersham and next-door Chilham (Kent), sat in parks either created by Brown or adapted in his style. That is to say, naturalistic in appearance, characterised by lawns, water, woods – what has become the archetypal setting of the English country house. Austen went on to mention Repton, Brown's self-proclaimed heir, in *Mansfield Park*, as the improver Mr Rushworth hoped to consult on the fate of his old-fashioned avenue and his promising prospects.[4] She was also well aware of the aesthetic movement of the Picturesque, championed by the clergyman William Gilpin, which reacted against Brown's smooth lines, being instead attracted to wilder scenery, rocky outcrops and ruined castles.

Repton provided designs for his clients bound in red Morocco leather. Known as 'Red Books', they became almost his trademark. He promoted himself as the successor to Brown, but his approach took a slightly different direction and, particularly towards the end of his career, he reintroduced an element of formality close to the house, with terraces, pergolas and flower gardens. This more intricate, more floriferous style continued to the end of the period discussed here. What all these designers and arbiters of taste had in common, and what set the tone for the age, was the opening up of the long view thanks to the decline of walled courts and the innovation of the ha-ha. Now viewers could appreciate extensive vistas, these scenes were often punctuated with ornamental buildings, the 'beautiful objects' so loved by Whately and his contemporaries, and these objects could also become 'agreeable retreats', places to go for privacy, quiet contemplation or to entertain on a small scale. Consequently the ways of using parks and gardens subtly changed from how they had been used in the past.

As with any movement, there were exceptions to the rule. Brown is often, sometimes unjustifiably, accused of 'sweeping away' the designs of previous generations, but in many places old-fashioned gardens remained, or were even created. Delaford, the home of the hero Colonel Brandon in *Sense and Sensibility*, published in 1811, clearly had been fossilised a century or so earlier; it was 'quite shut in with great garden walls' with 'delightful stewponds and a very pretty canal'. Austen, who knew such gardens, described it in a positive light as a 'nice old fashioned place' with 'an old yew arbour' where one might be diverted by viewing the traffic on the road. Incidentally, traffic in the eighteenth and early nineteenth centuries was seen as an animation to the scene, not as a polluting nuisance as it might be today. Delaford is symbolic of Brandon, old-fashioned perhaps, but with many other merits. Delaford is fictional, but many such gardens did survive unchanged. It was also not unknown for new designs to be executed in outmoded styles, like Leigh Park (Hampshire). Here, in the 1820s and 1830s,

Sir George Staunton laid out what was essentially a rococo landscape, complete with a chinoiserie (oriental style) boat, some 70 years after that style had ceased to be in vogue.

In garden buildings, as in gardens themselves, form followed function.[5] It is hard to say whether the aesthetic imperatives of the far-flung eye-catcher (like classical temples or Gothic towers, for instance), which are so characteristic of the landscape park and garden, led to their dual purpose as retreats, or whether the reason for the proliferation of such buildings was due to their suitability for escape from the country house during a period that increasingly valued privacy.[6] In truth it is likely to be a bit of both. Likewise, with the creation of ornamental lakes, for which Brown was so famed. Their role was visual certainly; in places it was also highly practical in the management of water in times of flood and drought; but such lakes were created for leisure too. There are enough accounts of boats being built at the same time that lakes were extended, or rivers dammed, to imply that the enjoyment of boating was a reason for their construction.[7]

A designed landscape that rolled out from the house across hundreds of acres of the surrounding countryside was an expression of ownership. Far-flung lodges and eye-catchers 'appropriated' the landscape to the house, as Repton observed, forming markers of possession. While the landscape inside the park boundary mimicked elements of the countryside, it could be read in a glance as different from it. However, just as aesthetics is only one element of the attraction of the style, so was such aggrandisement. Those rolling acres of parkland and woodland were also functional, even profitable. The country estate with the house at its centre acted as an individual economic unit, perhaps not quite self-sufficient, but largely so. The timber and underwood, in parkland clumps and perimeter shelterbelts had use and value. The planting of trees was a long-term investment on the part of landowners who expected to hand their property down to their heirs. John Evelyn had first urged the planting of timber, ostensibly for the patriotic purpose of providing wood for the navy. His *Sylva: A Discourse of Forest Trees* was first published in 1664, but regularly reprinted in the subsequent decades, and was still consulted as a manual for tree planting by estate owners until at least the early nineteenth century. Timber was actively managed, felled and replanted. In certain places, under the timber trees there would be coppiced underwood, cut by the estate woodmen on a rotation of 10 to 20 years, the produce of which would be used as fuel and for a multitude of other functions, from handles for the rakes that kept the paths of the pleasure ground looking neat to hurdles for sheep pens and building materials.

Parks had, of course, existed before the Georgian period; the first deer parks are recorded even before the Norman conquest in the eleventh century, and a boom in creation followed in the thirteenth and fourteenth centuries.[8] However, during the aesthetic revolution of the eighteenth century, parks became less synonymous with deer. While venison was still a prized meat (and sometimes a luxury eaten on a picnic) and many great estates retained their herd (the fallow deer still grace Brown's masterpiece at Petworth, West Sussex, today, for example), deer are not really compatible with the raising of young trees. So, though some of the aesthetics of the earlier deer park were retained in the Georgian parkland, deer were often replaced by sheep and cattle. This was the time of the agricultural revolution, and these parklands were a good place to show off one's improved breeds – beasts that produced more meat to feed owner and household, and also to be sold for profit. John Lawrence noted in 1801: 'there cannot be more interesting objects of view, in a park, than well chosen flocks and herds.'[9] Many landowners took up the new ideas, some of which were developed at great estates hand in hand with the development of their designed landscapes. Thomas Coke at Holkham transformed the productivity of his estate on the poor

FIGURE I   The Queen's Temple at Stowe, after Thomas Medland, 1797. Previously known as the Ladies' Temple, it was dedicated to female friendship and contained a fine room decorated with murals of ladies engaged in shellwork, needlework, music and painting by Francesco Sleter. Marchioness Grey said this was the only building she would choose to sit down in. Note the horse pulling the roller.

FIGURE 2   A detail from *Haymaking at Sandleford Priory*, by Edward Haytley, 1744. The Montagu family are stationed on the edge of the ha-ha, from where they can watch the rural ritual of haymaking. They have the additional amusements of a telescope to view the landscape and a game of bowls.

soils of north Norfolk in the 1770s and 1780s, at the same time expanding and improving the park. He was influenced by an earlier landowner and pioneer of agricultural improvement, the satisfyingly alliterative 'Turnip' Townshend, at nearby Raynham Hall. The 6th Duke of Bedford continued the improvement instigated by his predecessor at Woburn (Bedfordshire) at the end of the eighteenth century and hosted agricultural shows known as 'shearings', which ran for a week and were held at the model farm in the heart of the park.[10]

As well as a place to graze sheep and cattle, where they could be seen and admired, the parkland was also necessary for grazing horses. As John Phibbs has pointed out, the country house needed lots of equine power to keep it functioning, from carriage horses and hunters, to the gardener's nag that towed the mower or roller (FIGURE 1).[11] Moreover, these required hay as well as fresh grass, and hay meadows were an integral element of Brown's parklands. The making of the hay happened in summer, at a time when most landowners could be guaranteed to be at their estates in the country. This was a rural ritual that could be a spectator sport (FIGURE 2) or a more interactive entertainment. While some landowners were content to watch from a distance, no doubt enjoying the weather and the view, there was an element of 'all hands on deck' about it. Getting the hay in before the weather turned was of great importance and gentlemen might roll up their sleeves and muck in with their workers. Nor was it uncommon that genteel ladies would dress up, or perhaps dress down, in rural garb and 'toss hay about a little'.[12]

A measure of the attractiveness of the rural ritual of hay-making survives in a gossipy anecdote from Horace Walpole, who described how Lady Sarah Lennox, fourth daughter of the Duke of Richmond, made hay in the park at Holland House (now West London), close to the road where she could be seen by passers-by.[13] Her labours, enticingly dressed in rustic garb, were timed to coincide with the daily ride of the young, and then unmarried, King George III. He was already clearly taken with her, and her ambitious brother-in-law, Henry Fox, saw the advantage of such a match. The haymaking may even have been part of his scheme. In the end, the hoped-for marriage was scotched by Lord Bute, who feared Holland's influence, but the story was well known (FIGURE 3).

To dress in rural garb and make hay may seem like a novelty, but Sarah Lennox's rural attire reflected a trend through the

FIGURE 3   An engraving of *Palemon and Lavinia*, by John Raphael Smith after William Lawranson, 1780. The scene alludes to Sarah Lennox's haymaking exploits. Any contemporary would have been able to identify the couple as Sarah and the king – Holland House in the background being a not-too-subtle hint.

FIGURE 4   *The Wedgwood Family*, by George Stubbs, 1780. The potter Josiah Wedgwood, on the far right, is wearing typical, practical country clothes. His daughter Susannah, in the centre, wears a fashionable riding outfit, de rigueur even when not on horseback. The family might be ready for taking a circuit of the grounds, the older children riding, the parents on foot and the youngest child pulled in a typical garden chair. The round tripod table on which Josiah is leaning is also typical of furniture easily transported outdoors.

eighteenth century. As gardens became less formal and mimicked the countryside around them, the elite started to adopt adapted versions of working clothes. By the time the Landscape Style had reached the height of its popularity in the third quarter of the eighteenth century, as Brown was crisscrossing the country visiting client after client to discuss improvements, the coats of his male clientele became less full in the skirt and were swept back allowing freer movement, the heels of their shoes were lower and they had discarded their fine silks for everyday use, instead opting for more hard-wearing broadcloth, in muted country colours of browns and greens. These were more practical garments for spending long hours walking or riding round one's park. In parallel with the development of the Landscape Style, ladies' dress too started to become more functional. By around the 1760s fashionable women wore feminised versions of men's riding clothes, and these would be used for riding, walking and travelling (FIGURE 4). As Nicola Shulman has pointed out, such outfits were more conducive to these activities.[14]

The vogue of the landscape garden was not merely limited to the nation of its origin. The style was widely emulated in Europe and even in the rebellious colonies of America. No one embodied the mania for the *jardin anglais* better than Catherine the Great. She was such an admirer that, as well as laying out the great park of Tsarskoe Selo outside St Petersburg in the 1770s, she commissioned Josiah Wedgwood to create what has become known as the Green Frog dinner service. Made up of 952 pieces, it was decorated with scenes of contemporary English landscapes, including the most famed places of the day: Stowe, Stourhead, Mount Edgcumbe and Studley Royal.[15] Although the English invented these gardens, they were more conservative in their use of them than their continental counterparts. In mainland Europe, landscapes could be even more vast, buildings could be more extravagant and their use more exclusive. At Wörlitz in Germany, Prince Leopold Friedrich Franz of Anhalt-Dessau had a miniature volcano, which appeared to erupt during pyrotechnic entertainments. He also had a substantial Gothic garden pavilion, constructed of gingerbread-coloured brick and edged with icing-like white stone. This confection of a building housed both his art collection and his mistress.[16] Catherine the Great had coasting hills, the progenitors of the modern roller-coaster, in both her parks of Oranienbaum and Tsarskoe Selo.[17]

These large-scale novelties and extreme exclusivity in the garden, along with such extravagancies as Marie-Antoinette's Petit Hameau, a purpose-built rustic village at which she could escape the formality of court and pretend to be a humble country girl, were far beyond anything seen in England. Ornamental dairies, elegant and functional, were sometimes built for the mistress of the house to dabble at making butter in attractive surroundings, but there was nothing like a whole make-believe village. This is probably due to the vast social gulf between the upper and lower orders in the pre-revolutionary societies of France and Russia, which was not so marked in England, where revolution had already been experienced not once but twice in less than half a century. While there was undoubtedly great hardship for some sectors of the lowest classes in England, they were not serfs as they were in Russia, and perhaps the English did not feel the need to remove themselves from their servants so comprehensively. Furthermore, in Europe the most extravagant garden buildings could be expected to be those of royalty, who tended to set fashions in gardening and architecture. In England, royal extravagance on such a scale did not happen, especially towards the beginning of our period, as the early Hanoverians were relatively insecure. While Queen Caroline was a great patron of the arts, and commissioned some remarkable garden buildings at Richmond, which will be discussed later,

George I and George II were both renowned philistines. Although the British monarch was more than a figurehead, real power was, after the Glorious Revolution of 1688, in the hands of the aristocracy. So it was the upper classes who laid out the trend-setting parks and gardens of the age and who enjoyed using them.

By 1820 the nobility consisted of just 350 families out of a population of 18 million, and it is from this level of society that much of the evidence here derives. This might suggest that the book therefore only tells the story of life in the gardens of those at the pinnacle of society, but the picture is wider than that.[18] Typical uses of upper-class gardens actually filtered a long way down the social scale. The innate pleasure of being in a garden may have been experienced at times by the workers – the weeder woman and the gardener's boy – but even if they were literate their voices have not been recorded by history. However, those of the genteel and middling sort, the polite classes, even down to those who were not owners of property, are recorded and we know that they emulated those higher up the social ladder in their pleasure and leisure in the garden.[19] The scale of their gardens was smaller; the number of buildings within them would perhaps have been a handful at most and some might be temporary like tents. Though few middle-class garden buildings have survived, the voices of the users have, mainly in letters and diaries. Clergymen, doctors and farmers all enjoyed their gardens; they worked in them, played in them and entertained there too. Their garden-using habits are woven through the following chapters, alongside those of the upper classes.

One fundamental difference between the middle-class house and the upper-class country house set in gardens and parkland was in the sheer number of people contained within it.[20] The country house was a busy place, with droves of servants, guests and often a variety of hangers-on, from the poor relation to the friend of a friend, on his way somewhere with a handy letter of introduction in his pocket.[21] 'My house is an inn' was an expression used by more than one master of a great house. Lord Coventry at Croome (Worcestershire) alluded to the tail end of a tradition dating back to medieval times, when he wrote of this circumstance being due to 'the hospitality my ancestors exercised for some generations at Croomb, [which] makes it impossible for me to effect any privacy or retirement'.[22] It is no coincidence that he erected a number of garden buildings to which he could quietly slip out.

Even in the early years of the eighteenth century the aristocracy was surprisingly peripatetic, considering the discomfort of carriages and how bad roads were. They travelled a lot, dividing their time between London and their country estate, or in some cases estates, plural. During the 123 years covered by this book, however, the roads of England improved immeasurably. It was the greatest period of road building since the Romans. The development of a turnpike network took off in the 1750s and the 1760s, reaching its peak in the 1830s. Carriage design likewise saw many innovations with the equipage becoming lighter, faster and better sprung. Summer was the time when the majority of people travelled most frequently; as well as spending time at their own house, they might visit friends and relations. Once on the road, they would often string visits together, stopping at private houses of acquaintances in preference to inns.[23]

With new, improved roads, tourism boomed too. Many private gardens and houses were open to polite strangers, and travellers would stop on their tours to admire them, just as Elizabeth Bennet did at Pemberley. At some places guidebooks were available. The most popular destinations imposed opening times, and Horace Walpole even sold tickets for entry to his house at Strawberry Hill (Middlesex). While the tourists' experience of the pleasure ground was of a less intimate kind than that of the house guest, gardens and parks excited their comment, both praise and censure; their accounts provide valuable social evidence. However, the line of definition drawn between tourist and guest should not be too precise; the tourist might be rather grand yet enter as an ordinary member of the public, as Marchioness Grey of Wrest Park did at Stowe in 1748. She later commented scathingly on the proliferation of structures: 'The Temple of Friendship is reckoned the Best, but that to Female Friendship is the best Room, indeed the Only good One, for everything ... is Outside, and in all these Buildings there is hardly a Room you would chuse to set down in' (see FIGURE 1). The Marchioness's judgement is telling; she was an enthusiastic user of her own garden. We will continue to meet her throughout the book.

Lord Coventry's complaint about his house being an inn sounds rather misanthropic, but there is no evidence to suggest he was particularly anti-social. Of course some owners were more hospitable than others, many positively encouraging guests and revelling in entertaining them. During this period the idea of the house party in the country was born. The tradition has been traced back to Sir Robert Walpole's 'congresses' at his palatial Houghton Hall (Norfolk).[24] The notoriously venal Walpole, who is considered the first British prime minister, used his hospitality to cultivate political friends and allies. Walpole was a contemporary and political rival of Lord Cobham, first creator of the gardens at Stowe. At his Temple of Friendship (which did not live up to Marchioness Grey's expectations), Cobham gathered together his political cronies. The building was equipped with a cellar kitchen. He also had a temple dedicated to Bacchus. The inside was decorated with paintings of the god of wine, the model for which was the then vicar of Stowe. This says something about both the tone of the building and the men, both Cobham and the clergyman. However it was his heir, Earl Temple, who was particularly zealous about his summer gatherings at Stowe. He was quite put out when the weather did not cooperate with his plans. His ideal house party was economically summed up in a letter to his sister Hester, wife of another prime minister, William Pitt: 'Delightful weather the whole week! Chaises, Grotto, Fishing all in perfection...'[25] The chaise driving and fishing were naturally garden- and park-based activities, and the grotto is a reference to his favourite garden building for parties.

William Beckford, Pitt's godson, was said to have been the richest commoner in England. On the one hand he hosted spectacular parties and on the other he shunned crowds at his estate of Fonthill (Wiltshire). While trying to persuade his friend Sir Isaac Heard and his wife to come and stay in July 1799 he satirised the typical summer house party:

Now, my dear Sir Isaac, exert yourself to second these Pius
intentions... Show Lady Heard that she shall not be worn to
death with seeing Sights, nor crammed to satiety with French
Ragouts, nor pressed into rumbling Carriages, nor drenched
with unwholesome dews by Evening Excursions, nor worried
out of bed in the Morning to drive to Kitchen or Flower
gardens, Alms-houses or Pigeon-houses, Farms, Temples
or Plantations. At my University no such proceedings are
to be dreaded. I read no Lectures, I go no Rounds, I try no
Experiments, I go my own way, and wish everybody that
comes to me to do the same.[26]

As Amanda Vickery has so aptly put it, the huge Palladian
houses so favoured in this period were 'suited to the sunshine
of the Veneto', but 'ill adapted to the damp of Albion'.[27] Stowe,
Fonthill and Houghton were palaces, sumptuous and certainly
more modern than any residence of the King at the time. The
fine apartments inside these houses, and others like them,
were grand spaces, designed to impress the visitor, but cold
impersonal rooms in which to live. Through the eighteenth
century the country house, its floor plan and its internal
spaces evolved for entertaining on a large scale, with suites
of rooms that could form a circuit, which Mark Girouard
considers to parallel the circuit drives and walks of gardens.[28]
These rooms were primarily for show, not for living in. In
contrast, garden buildings were necessarily smaller; the largest
tended not to have more than three modest-sized rooms, one
of which could be a simple kitchen or servery. In contrast to
the cool sophistication of the interior of the house, it is easy
to see why such retreats were popular on more than a mere
aesthetic level.

Owners of great houses wanted to impress both their equals and their inferiors. One consequence of this was that many country houses were virtual building sites for long periods of time, with adaptation of facades or redecoration of rooms.[29] Although some of this work could take place while the family was away, summer would have been favoured for many building projects and this was exactly when they would be in the country. So, during these times too the garden building was the first-choice resort of escape. At Holkham the Coke family retreated to the temple, their servants bringing dinner to them in a specially adapted wheelbarrow.[30]

The summer was the time of year when all the great landowners were most likely to be at their country estates. The annual calendar was in part dictated by Parliament, as many landowners sat either in the House of Commons or in the Lords. Since the Glorious Revolution of 1688, parliamentary terms had been longer, and this led to a burgeoning cultural scene in the capital, with its attractions of the opera, plays and shopping. Parliamentary sessions generally began in late October or November, but many of the upper class preferred to remain at their seats until the start of January, at which time the household decamped to London, usually returning around June, therefore being there for the warmest months and when their gardens were at their best. Earl Temple, despite his position as a political power-monger, disliked London, which he described as an 'abyss of Fog, Sulphur, Fever, cold and all the excretions on this side of the Styx', and longed for his beloved Stowe.[31] The Ilchester family at Redlynch (Somerset) and Melbury (Dorset), and their Digby cousins at Sherborne (also Dorset) were keen sportsmen and therefore reluctant to leave the country when there was fine hunting and shooting to be had between September and January. They would then head for London to escape the cold and the high chance of being snowed in.[32] The middle classes, while likely to visit London once in a while, were often, by their professions, such as doctor or clergyman, more tied to their locale. Even among the upper classes there were exceptions. Lady Susan O'Brien, daughter of the Earl of Ilchester, impoverished by an imprudent though ultimately long and happy marriage, lived constantly in the country with only occasional trips to London. One of her comforts was her garden.

The phases of the day, as well as the time of year, influenced how the garden and park of the country house were used. A day in the Georgian period was punctuated, as now, by meals, but the names and times were somewhat different. Through the period they evolved, so that by the coming of the Victorian age meal times and their titles were more or less what we know today. Back in the sixteenth century the leisured classes had taken their main meal, dinner, at eleven o'clock in the morning, with a supper in the later afternoon.[33] By the seventeenth century the routine of three meals, one on rising, another at midday (dinner) and a lighter early evening meal (supper), had evolved.[34] During the eighteenth century the times of taking dinner became increasingly later. For example, in high-society circles in the 1720s dinner would be served at 3 o'clock; by the end of the century it could be as late as 7 or 8 o'clock. This was partly due to the times of parliamentary sittings, and habits of mealtimes spread from the city to the country. However, by this date the situation was actually rather complex, with some more conservative people retaining a mid- to late-afternoon dinner hour; they would then have a mid-evening supper. For most of the eighteenth century at Melbury, Redlynch and Sherborne, dinner was usually served at 3 o'clock, though after shooting it was slightly later at 5 o'clock.[35] As fashionable society started to eat their main meal much later, nuncheon, or luncheon, usually a cold snack, developed to bridge the gap between breakfast and an early evening dinner. Likewise, as the dinner hour continued to become later and later, tea as a light refreshment in the afternoon was introduced to sustain the upper classes through the long hours before their main meal.[36] Tea, the drink, might also be served in the early evening, after a late afternoon dinner. Finally, they might also have a supper served at night, before bed or at the end of an entertainment. At the end of his day out at Esher Place (Surrey) in 1763, Horace Walpole was given supper at 12.15 a.m. and returned home by moonlight.[37] The term 'breakfast' was usually used as we do, to indicate the first meal of the day, but also might mean a celebratory meal served at an entertainment, in a manner akin to our use of the term 'wedding breakfast'.

With the punctuation given by times of meals through the day changing during the Georgian period, the arrangement of the hours either side of the meals must also have changed. But it is interesting to note that the terms 'morning', 'afternoon' and 'evening' seem constant. Given this, especially with the main meal moving from 1 o'clock in the afternoon to the early evening, and even allowing for individuals' habits being different, there are still some general observations we can make about how the Georgians of the upper and middle classes spent their time, and when and how they used and enjoyed their gardens. However, the daily routine of the country house would be different at times when just the family was in residence from when there was a house full of guests to be entertained. At quiet times the morning would be the time for the master of the house to transact his business with his steward. Likewise the mistress might meet her housekeeper to give instructions for domestic arrangements such as meals. A lady like Jemima, Marchioness Grey – an intelligent, level-headed woman – might even do this before breakfast and certainly before her leisure time. In contrast the trend-setters of the beau monde like Georgiana, Duchess of Devonshire, a generation later, might be served their breakfast in bed and not get up until eleven, perhaps because they had been at the gaming table until the small hours. As their parents carried out their tasks in the morning, so the children of the house would have lessons before whatever the early afternoon meal was.

In contrast, when there was a house party to entertain, the tempo of the day might shift from the upbeat excitement of boating in the morning to more *piano* pursuits in the afternoon, like fishing. Guests would come together again for dinner and some form of entertainment in the evening, perhaps a dessert in the garden. If the party was especially grand, or there was something particular to celebrate, then as darkness fell strings of lamps might be lit and the whole night end with a grand finale of music and fireworks. On such occasions commentators often compared the entertainments with the diversions to be had at the famous London pleasure garden of Vauxhall.

So let us pass into the pleasure ground, as such creations were frequently called. It is fine summer weather, the plants in the shrubberies are in bloom and scent, and life and leisure are played out on the stage of the garden. Let us walk down the winding gravel path through the shrubbery until we gain the view of the lake, with its boat at anchor, and the temple on rising ground beyond. Let us seek out the people about to board for a morning sailing on the water, or on their way to discover the refreshments laid out earlier by the servants in the fine room of the temple, and follow them on their journey through a day in the life of the Georgian garden.

THREE

Morning

Tours —— Refreshments en route ——
Boating —— Bathing

My garden is at present in the high glow of beauty,
my cherries ripening, roses, jessamine, and pinks in
full bloom, and the hay ... complete[s] the scene. We
have discovered a new breakfasting-place under the
shade of nut-trees, impenetrable to the sun's rays in the
midst of a growth of elms, where we shall breakfast
this morning; I have ordered cherries, strawberries and
nosegays to be laid on our breakfast table, and have
appointed a harper to be here to play to us during our
repast, who is to be hid among the trees. Mrs Hamilton
is to breakfast with us, and is to be cunningly led to
this place *and surprised.*

MRS DELANY, Delville, June 1750

IN HIGH SUMMER when the garden was beautiful and
bountiful, like that of Mrs Delany, these attractions might
draw people outside even before they had broken their fast.
At Penrice Castle (Glamorgan), in the first decade of the
nineteenth century, Thomas Mansel Talbot sometimes 'took
a glass of spa water soon after getting up ... and then took a
walk before breakfast'.[1] To go for a stroll in the garden was

the most basic manner of experiencing it. Carefully contrived drives and walks, both using the gently winding serpentine line and taking the garden-user to specific features and viewpoints, were fundamental to the aesthetics of the Landscape Style. Even a relatively modest house, with a pleasure ground on a small scale, would have a circuit walk around the shrubbery (FIGURE 6). In grander designs there would be a combination of walks to be taken on foot and drives for carriages and riding on horseback. In the most extensive estates these could go for miles. Brown's client the Duchess of Northumberland was said to have 98 rides on her estate at Alnwick, both near the castle and through the detached Hulne Park.[2]

The dry gravel walks of the pleasure ground were of great importance, particularly for ladies wearing dainty shoes who, especially earlier on in the Georgian period, would not be expected to walk long distances. As the eighteenth century progressed, walking and riding were considered important exercise, especially for women. In 1774, Dr John Gregory published *A Father's Legacy to His Daughters*. He wrote: 'I would particularly recommend to you those exercises that oblige you to be much abroad in the open air, such as walking and riding on horseback. This will give vigour to your constitutions, and a bloom to your complexions.'[3] By the early nineteenth century a new generation of young ladies were becoming more adventurous; Gregory's attitude towards exercise, it seems, was more common, and Elizabeth Bennet in *Pride and Prejudice*, with her cheeks full of colour and her 'fine eyes' enlivened by the exercise of a brisk walk, might be seen as a model for that, although Mr Bingley's sisters were still shocked by what they perceived as her impertinent independence, arriving with boots covered in mud from her walk. For them a gentle amble in the Netherfield shrubbery would have been the norm. Although fictitious, Austen's Bingley sisters were voicing an attitude that prevailed in some quarters – but not all. Around the time of the publication of Jane Austen's novels, the daughters of the 2nd Earl of Ilchester enjoyed fresh air and exercise, being both gardeners and energetic walkers. In 1811 a friend wrote to Mary Talbot to tell her that her sister, Lady Charlotte, looked 'so well, enjoying her garden ... working hard in it [and] walking four and six miles without fatigue.'[4]

When Brown provided walks in his designs, the paths were gently cambered and topped with gravel for drainage. At about 7½ to 8 foot wide they were just right for the sociable number of two or three people walking side by side.[5] However, as Elizabeth Bennet found in the Netherfield shrubbery, such paths were not wide enough for four and she was again shut out by the Bingley sisters.[6] In 1766 Lancelot Brown's men were working at Temple Newsam (Yorkshire) and making something of a mess. While the 'Brownifications' were happening during fine April weather, Lady Irwin was keen to get outdoors despite the mud and she took solace in her untouched, pre-existing gravel walk, where she could walk without fear of dirt: 'I am out of doors all day long, Mr Brown has put us in a wo[e]ful dirty pickle, but my gravel walk is always a resource and very much made use of.'[7] In winter these paths were especially valued. In February 1825 Lady Susan O'Brien noted in her diary: 'Walked on the gravel walk. Crocuses in great beauty.'[8]

FIGURE 5   The Palladian Bridge at Stowe, Seeley after Medland, 1797. The
Palladian Bridge at Stowe differed from others in this style in allowing vehicular
traffic. In this view the garden chaise driven by a lady, probably the Marchioness of
Buckingham.

A walk in the pleasure ground or a drive around the park
was a typical morning activity, especially when the family had
guests to entertain. Lady Mary Coke was part of the company,
along with Princess Amelia, second daughter of George II,
at Park Place (Oxfordshire) in June 1770. In her diary Lady
Mary describes how she drove one of the 'little chaises' and
'the Princess let Lady Aylesbury drive her' in another. Horace
Walpole was in a third and Henry Seymour Conway, their host,
walked. The following week many of the same party were at
Stowe, where every day they breakfasted at 9.30 and the guests
spent the morning either walking or driving in the garden. By
this time an outer circuit of the gardens was around 2½ miles,

FIGURE 6   *The Garden of the Deputy Ranger's Lodge, Windsor Great Park*, by Paul
Sandby, *c.*1790s. The artist's brother Thomas, also a painter and architect, was
appointed Deputy Ranger of Windsor Great Park by the Duke of Cumberland; these
are the walks and shrubberies of his garden. While the Sandby brothers were well
connected, they were not rich: this could be seen as a garden of the affluent middle
class.

though the many lesser paths gave scope for meanderings on
foot that were far longer. The outer circuit around the top of the
ha-ha, with views into the gardens and out to the parkland and
wider landscape, was particularly suitable for the small carriage
known as the 'garden chaise'. Stowe's version of the Palladian
Bridge differed from its cousins at Wilton (Wiltshire) and
Prior Park (Somerset) in not having steps, therefore allowing a
circuit to be made in a carriage (FIGURE 5). The chaise would

FIGURE 7   A detail from *Riders on an Avenue in the Park at Luton*, by Paul Sandby, *c*.1765. This is a rare depiction of a grass drive, which can clearly be seen crossing the gravel surface of the approach to the house. The grass drive is being enjoyed by a couple in a garden chaise.

also have allowed a variety of experience, giving something different from a walk – the speed could be faster, the viewpoint higher, so the garden was experienced in a subtly different way.

Almost as an antidote to uncomfortable journeys on bad roads, landowners took pleasure in laying out and then driving on private roads on their estates. Although major routes improved through the eighteenth century with the turnpike network, cross-country travel was still fraught with hazards. In Brown's time drives were often grass, as he liked to hide the surface from view, unlike Repton. In Paul Sandby's view of the park at Luton Hoo, we have a rare glimpse of a grass drive as laid out by Brown (FIGURE 7). They were, at this stage of carriage development, more comfortable to travel on, as well as not interrupting the vista. Edmund Burke commented that 'most people must have observed the sort of sense they have had, on being swiftly drawn in an easy coach, on a smooth

turf, with gradual ascents and declivities.'⁹ At Heveningham
(Suffolk), one of Brown's final works, there were 16 miles 'of
a beautiful grassy ride, turfed so that the open horse-carriage
can drive over this superb country ... everywhere there are
views more or less extensive: everywhere there are certainly
fine rich farmlands before your eyes. Sometimes you are under
cover of woodlands; always the ride is arranged so that you get
the most enjoyable perspective.'¹⁰ In Watts's engraving we can
see the open carriage driving over the grass in the foreground,
contrasted with the closed-in travelling coach arriving at the
house on the main, surfaced approach (FIGURE 8). At Blenheim
the guidebook described how, as a visitor travelled round the

FIGURE 8   *Heveningham Hall, in Suffolk, the seat of Sir Gerard William Vanneck
Bartholomew*, by William Watts after Thomas Hearne, 1782. People tour the
landscape in a chaise, on horseback and on foot. Another important element of a
morning's entertainment – the boat – awaits them on the lake.

FIGURE 9 A detail from *North-west View of Wakefield Lodge in Whittlebury Forest, Northamptonshire*, by Paul Sandby, 1767. The gentleman drives the lady on a tour of the park, which was laid out by Brown.

park, 'near and remote objects, open and shut upon the eye like enchantment'.[11]

Just as main roads were improving in the second half of the eighteenth century, so was the design of carriages; they became better sprung and more comfortable. The names used to describe them vary but those used in parks and gardens carried two people facing forward, were open-topped, had four wheels and were pulled by one horse, occasionally two (FIGURE 9). These were sometimes called a cabriolet; sometimes, when specific to the designed landscape, a garden chair or chaise. Towards the end of the eighteenth century the phaeton was developed. These sporty, open carriages featured better springs

and very large wheels, so giving an even higher vantage point for the driver and passenger. Typically they were drawn by one or two horses and could be driven fast. In 1795 they were described as 'the most pleasant sort of carriages in use, as they contribute to health, amusement and fashion more than any other'.[12] The phaeton was eventually overtaken by the curricle as the early-nineteenth-century version of the sports car. Smart, light and two-wheeled, it was large enough for the driver and a passenger. In 1808 Lady Charlotte, daughter of the 2nd Earl of Ilchester, enjoyed 'two or three delicious drives' in her brother's new curricle.[13] At the turn of the nineteenth century, Repton was designing for phaetons and curricles that were able to go much faster than in Brown's day. These were better suited to the gravel drives and rides he provided for his clients.

Artists often portrayed couples in the sort of open carriages that were used in the designed landscape with the gentleman at the reins, but they were in fact frequently driven by women. Joanna Martin, writing about the ladies of the extended Fox-Strangways family, notes several examples: in 1758, at Sherborne, her sister-in-law's estate, Elizabeth Strangways Horner, 1st Lady Ilchester, and a friend 'drove about the park in the chariot'. The Ilchesters' own principal seat was Melbury, the accounts of 1768 for which record the payment for 'a garden chaise and harness for my ladies use'. Two generations later, in 1811 Charlotte Lemon (the now married daughter of the 2nd Earl, whom we met walking 4 to 6 miles every day) told her sister Mary: 'Mr Lemon has got me a very easy gig and the perfect horse, in which I drive myself every day.'

An important reason for getting out into the landscape and making a circuit on foot or horseback was 'to contrive improvements'. There is something of a pleasing circularity about it: you improve to further enjoy; you further enjoy because you improve. Many of the great landscapes of the day were continually tinkered with. Planning improvements to your garden was a major pastime for not just the aristocracy but also the affluent middling sort in the Georgian period. Friends and family who were considered to have a certain talent, interest and taste might be prevailed upon to give their opinions, or even designs. Coplestone Warre Bampfylde designed his own landscape at

Hestercombe (Somerset) and with his friend Richard Phelps, the local painter, sketched out designs for his neighbours. One surviving drawing was even scribbled on the back of an apothecary's business card. The surviving correspondence of Sanderson Miller shows him to have been a much desired guest for his company, musical talents and building designs. His judgement was highly valued in matters of taste in landscape and architecture. In his diary he noted one particular trip to Stowe in November 1749: 'Walking in the garden – with the company and Mr Brown ... five hours.'[14] Even if the party took a meandering tour longer than the 2½-mile circuit, this is quite a long time. Miller's expertise and involvement at Stowe and elsewhere, and the presence of 'Capability' Brown, suggest that improvements were being contrived as the party walked, and discussions and debate lent a leisurely pace to the proceedings.[15]

Brown was engaged in a professional capacity by Admiral Anson when he acquired Moor Park (Hertfordshire) in 1752. One fine morning a 'Council of Taste' was assembled, also including William Pitt (another one of the Stowe circle). Anson's wife Elizabeth described the tour to her sister-in-law, Marchioness Grey, with wry amusement, saying that it

> would have given you great Entertainment. I walked on
> Horseback & was attended by the Gentlemen on Foot, whilst
> we surveyed the Garden, as it is called; afterwards they
> mounted too, to view the Park: – My Lord acted the Part of
> Owner – Mr. Anson of a good Cousin ... to shew and puff
> – Pitt of an Enthusiastic Admirer, & Brown of an Artist who
> scorned to find difficulties in executing any great or beautiful
> Idea, & made nothing of raising or levelling any spot to the

height desired. — This is a short Sketch of what entertained
… me for about four hours…[16]

While Elizabeth Anson merely played the role of an amused observer of this scene, ladies too gave advice. All the 2nd Earl of Ilchester's children were given gardens as children, but it was Mary Talbot who became the keenest gardener. Her judgement was sought by friends and family, for whom she provided plans. A natural disposition against snobbishness gave her a circle of friends of a range of social standing. One such was Ann Fowler, wife of Dr Richard Fowler of Salisbury. Ann was clearly also a keen gardener, but she sought Mary's opinion of her own improvements. Her description of her garden tells us much about middle-class plots:

> These soaking rains have been very good for the garden … how well every thing looks, particularly my American pets, who seem to enjoy themselves very much. But I want you so much you cannot imagine, for Dr Fowler has increased my *territories* quite to the cow's house. All that ground where potatoes were — is not that *very magnificent?* And now I want you to tell me how I shall do it, for I shall not think it right if you don't, so if you can give me a little bit of a ground plan as to the interior, I should be *so much* obliged to you. A thick plantation to hide the cow's mansion of course? And laurels close to the pales? A sweetbriar hedge as the fence? Where shall I put the entrance? Where it is now, or at the further end? … Had not I better leave a sort of shrubbery where my boundary is now?[17]

Walks of 2 or 3 miles which lasted five hours would demand stops for refreshment. Often specific buildings were constructed at the further point of a circuit to cater for such needs, as well as to form objects from views elsewhere in the design. Sometimes such a strategic point would be marked by a tent, or furniture taken ahead and arranged by the servants. Glimpsed from a distance, Robin Hood's Temple at Halswell (Somerset) is a rococo pavilion, but when approached along the circuit drive it is a rustic thatched hut. Here, halfway round a tour from the house, a visitor could take tea, or a more comprehensive meal,

FIGURE 10 A design for a 'Gothick Lodge' from William Halfpenny's *Country Builder...*, 1756. The arrangement of spaces (the open loggia, the parlour, kitchen and passage), the proportions and the materials all closely match that at Halswell.

because a kitchen and fine room for dining were included within its typical three-room arrangement (FIGURE 10). Likewise the Ionic Temple at Rievaulx would have formed the furthest point of a carriage drive from Duncombe Park (Yorkshire), around 3 miles away.[18] The wide grassy terrace running above the River Rye has spectacular views into the valley, reaching a climax with the ruins of Rievaulx Abbey. Here the Temple is a place to stop, get out and stroll, enjoy the vistas and be refreshed. Food could be prepared in the basement kitchen. It is one of the few Georgian garden buildings with an intact interior and original furnishing, and is presented by the National Trust as if awaiting the arrival of the guests for a meal.

At Wardour Castle (Wiltshire) a terrace drive ran from the mansion built in the 1760s to the Old Castle. The keep had been slighted into attractive semi-dereliction during the Civil War, so made both a visual feature and a destination, and a detached pleasure ground was developed inside the medieval bailey, with a bowling green, banqueting house and later a grotto. Taking advantage of an earlier structure, the Banqueting House was built into the medieval bailey wall, with views one way to the hulk of the keep, and the other across the lake and parkland. Its pretty Gothic doorway, Gothic windows with stained glass panels and crenellated roof line are a nod to the medieval archi-tecture of the castle. On the upper level, at the same height as the lawn around the keep, it has one fine, large room, with a smaller anteroom adjoining. This would have been a serving room, and there was originally a kitchen in the basement.[19]

At Hackfall (Yorkshire), William Aislabie went one step further than creating a detached pleasure ground, for here

FIGURE 11 *Hackfall*, by J.M.W. Turner, *c*.1816. The banqueting house of Fisher's Hall can be seen on the knoll above the river in the centre. Mowbray Point was located on top of the precipice in the background.

there is no parent house at all. The design lies 7 miles – then something over an hour's drive – from the main residence of Studley Royal, where the Aislabie family had already laid out a fine garden. But Hackfall, with its steep-sided valley through which the River Eure rushes, its rocky outcrops and smaller side valleys with natural waterfalls, was so ravishing that, though his father had bought the property to exploit its stone and timber, William Aislabie just could not help but lay out a garden here (FIGURE 11). With a long network of paths descending into the valley and some quite steep climbs, there were a number of possible places en route for rest and refreshment. In the depths of the wood was Fisher's Hall, a

FIGURE 12 *The north-east view of Selborne from the Short Lythe*, by Samuel Hieronymus Grimm, 1776. The Hanger is the wooded hill that fills the background of the view; at its left side the Hermitage and Zigzag can be seen. The Wakes stands to the left of the church, separated from it by the trees. The figure explaining the view to the lady and gentleman in the middle may possibly be Gilbert White himself. The tent with blue-and-white striped roof on the right could be the one used to entertain the Battie sisters, thirteen summers before.

small, octagonal banqueting house, and perched on top of a precipice looking into the valley was Mowbray Point, which, like Robin Hood's Temple at Halswell, had three rooms, including a kitchen. The gardener's house was also equipped with a fine dining room. In 1795, it was here that John Henry Michell and his party started their morning tour, where, he wrote, 'we regaled ourselves with a plain breakfast, and were much entertained by the honest intelligent converse of our conductor', who would have been the gardener himself.[20]

Where a bricks-and-mortar structure did not exist as a convenient place to stop and take some refreshment, a tent sometimes served the same purpose. Placed at a strategic point in the landscape, it might even be the destination for a walk or ride. From here a visitor could enjoy carefully contrived views of the landscape. A tent also formed an eye-catcher from a distance. For this reason such tents were often highly designed and brightly coloured. Some were semi-permanent structures, like the Turkish Tent at Painshill (Surrey), but most would be moved around the landscape and were taken down and stored in the winter. Their ephemeral materials – generally canvas on a wooden frame – and lack of permanency means that tents are the least well surviving of garden buildings, though they may have been one of the most popular. Often the only evidence for a tent having existed in a park is a levelled platform with the hint of a path running to it.[21] However, they are well documented in both written and pictorial sources.

As a young man the clergyman and diarist James Woodforde used a tent in the garden of his parents' parsonage in Somerset to find the peace to study the 'Greek Testament'.[22] Gilbert White erected his tent at various points around his landscape, both in his garden and further afield at strategic viewpoints; it can be seen on the edge of one of the views of Selborne by Grimm (FIGURE 12). The group portrait of the Shaw family by Devis (FIGURE 13) is indicative and typical in its detail. The family are shown in their park, with the house, Eltham Lodge (Kent), in the background. The haymakers are busy behind them. The one-horse garden chaise awaits them, suggesting they are about to go off and tour the landscape. In the background is their tent. The canvas, which might once have been cream coloured, is supported by a central pole topped with a golden finial; the entrance is flanked by red poles. Inside

FIGURE 13 *Sir John Shaw and his Family in the Park at Eltham Lodge, Kent*, by Arthur Devis, 1761. The family sit in the park, where haymakers are working behind them. The garden chaise awaits to take them on a tour. On their return they may be served refreshment in the tent, with its two-tier circular table and chinoiserie dining chairs.

the tent is a two-tier circular table and fine-looking chinoiserie dining chairs, perhaps awaiting the refreshments the servants are about to bring.

However, a stopping point, or destination, need not even be marked by a tent. It could merely be a clearing in the shrubbery or an opening off the path with a good view, where chairs and a table had been set up. These would often be Windsor chairs and a tripod table. The chairs were simple and relatively light,

FIGURE 14   *William Berry Introduced as the Heir to Raith*, by Johan Zoffany, 1769. The purpose of this painting was not to depict gentlemen meeting in the landscape to contrive improvements; however, their hill-top meeting place, the grey Windsor chairs, the tripod table and the wine cooler are all typical of such a scene.

usually painted green or grey. The advantage of the tripod table was that the top flapped down, making it more portable. Both chairs and tables are seen in numerous 'conversation pieces' – group portraits – which were so popular from the 1740s onwards. The paintings of Arthur Devis, George Stubbs (for example FIGURE 4) and Johan Zoffany (FIGURE 14), for instance, were created indoors in their studios, not outside in the garden, and many of the garden settings in which they portray their sitters never really existed. However, some were real places, closely observed, and the details they show of the accoutrements and furniture are accurate, and correlate with evidence provided by inventories.[23]

As the eighteenth century progressed the hour of the main meal of the day became increasingly later, so to bridge the gap between breakfast and a late afternoon dinner a light snack might be served. This was at first called 'nuncheon' and later became 'luncheon'. At the end of a walk, or halfway round the circuit, such a refreshment was often served outside. Although many garden buildings had the facilities to prepare warm food, a 'cold collation' was more common. Humphry Repton's view of the scene at Heaven's Gate, Longleat (Wiltshire), illustrates a party about to enjoy some refreshment at a carefully contrived viewpoint (FIGURE 15). The diners are sitting on a blanket, with food and drink emerging out of baskets, in a manner we might recognise today as a picnic. But in the second decade of the nineteenth century this was a term only just coming into use in the sense we know it today. The earliest meaning of the word in English was more akin to the phrase 'ad hoc'.[24] During the eighteenth century, when it was first associated with food,

FIGURE 15 – *The View from Heaven's Gate at Longleat*, by Humphry Repton, from his book *Fragments on the Theory and Practice of Landscape Gardening*, 1816. The party are about to enjoy an ultra-modish 'pic-nic', with eatables and drinkables emerging from baskets.

it was used to describe a 'contributor feast'. This was generally an indoor meal to which each guest contributed a dish from a prearranged menu. At the turn of the nineteenth century, the word was associated with a high-society club, the dealings of which have the undertone of something slightly risqué; they met for shared meals followed by amateur theatricals and concerts. It is likely that the short-lived Picnic Club, which met in 1802 and 1803, brought the word into common parlance. In the following decade, when Jane Austen started publishing her novels and Repton was a well-established landscaper, the word came to mean an outdoor meal shared by two or three families who joined forces to visit a specific site such as a viewpoint.

Exactly contemporary with Repton's view, Jane Austen used the term in a rather disparaging manner in *Emma* (published in 1816).[25] Describing the experience that the visit to Box Hill was intended to be, before Mr Weston tactlessly invited Emma's social rival Mrs Elton, Austen writes: 'everything was to be done in a quiet unpretending, elegant way, infinitely superior to the bustle and preparation, the regular eating and drinking, and the pic-nic parade of the Eltons...' Here the picnic stands for something beyond the simple pleasures, something rather vulgar and full of performance. With Mrs Elton's pretensions to the latest fashion, this is probably an example of the picnic as an ultra-modish experience. Austen was, however, not generally negative about the experience of an outdoor meal. The taking of simple cold provisions for an outing in the designed landscape was also well known to the Austen family themselves. Jane's niece, Fanny Austen Knight, whose father owned both the estates of Godmersham (Kent) and Chawton (Hampshire), mentions several such expeditions in her diaries. In September 1807, while holidaying at Chawton, she described how with her mother, brother and uncle they went to Chawton Park Wood, part of the medieval deer park on the far side of the village, and 'rambled about in it' and ate some 'Sandwiches &c seated upon an old tree. We had the Mule, & Mama & I rode each by turns.'[26] At home, at Godmersham, she sometimes went on expeditions to eye-catchers in the park, equipped with 'a basket of Bread & Cheese & a bottle of Water, some books & work & Paper & Pencil'.[27]

~⋙⋘~

Just as staff of the National Trust today will acknowledge that the three most important things for visitors are 'views, brews and loos', so it ever was. It has been suggested by Mavis Batey

FIGURE 16   A Moss House from the architectural pattern book *Decorations for Parks and Gardens* by Charles Middleton, 1790. This Moss House is designed as a single-seater privy, a little-known but fundamental building in the eighteenth-century designed landscape.

that one of the reasons for the development of shrubberies in the eighteenth century was to hide privies in the garden.[28] These were clearly more than desirable if long hours were spent away from the main house; indeed they were sometimes referred to as 'necessary houses' (FIGURE 16). Often they were simple wooden sentry-box-like constructions, which have not survived, though other more solid structures have.[29] Hidden in the shrubbery, a short distance from the Banqueting House at Wardour, is a rare survivor, an intact privy. This is a fine

FIGURE 17   The
interior of the privy
adjoining the Banqueting
House at Wardour.

example of the type, a three-seater earth closet (the Georgians
did not go in for privacy when it came to this activity in the
garden), set in a simple building with a pitched roof, with
understated wooden panelling and appropriately low-key decorative Gothic plasterwork surrounds to the windows (FIGURE
17). Another example survives at Goodwood (West Sussex). In
the remnants of a shrubbery in the detached pleasure ground
around Carné's Seat is a small octagonal building that was
once also a three-seater, with half-height panelling around

the walls, finished with a Vitruvian scroll-work frieze.[30] An alternative arrangement was to include a privy within a garden building. At Wrest Park, both the Bowling Green House and the grand Archer Pavilion had integrated privies. The latter was another three-seater earth closet set in a semi-basement beneath the grand room.

~~✴~~

The perfect morning in the designed landscape was described by Jane Austen in her first published novel, *Sense and Sensibility*. In it the congenial Sir John Middleton organises a trip to see the park at Whitwell, where

> The grounds were declared to be highly beautiful, and Sir
> John, who was particularly warm in their praise, might be
> allowed to be a tolerable judge, for he had formed parties
> to visit them, at least, twice every summer for the last ten
> years. They contained a noble piece of water; a sail on which
> was to form a great part of the morning's amusement; cold
> provisions were to be taken, open carriages only employed,
> and every thing conducted in the usual style of a complete
> party of pleasure.[31]

The Georgians' perception and experience of boats was rather different from our modern one. Back in the eighteenth century, before the coming of the railway, waterways and the various types of boat that travelled upon them were essential forms of transport. This was especially true in London where most wealthy families, the creators of landscape gardens up and down the country, spent at least half their year. The Thames was the major artery of the capital; it was much easier to negotiate than the crowded, ill-maintained streets. In the eighteenth century there were only two bridges in what we call Central London, so the river was used not only to travel east–west, but also north–south to cross from one bank to another. The Thames was the scene of great ceremonies and spectaculars too.[32] Outside London, goods and people travelled regularly by sea, by river and, latterly, by canal. So knowledge and experience of boats on the part of the general population was far greater than it is today. The wealthy and landed classes also had experience of waterborne transport through their connections with the merchant fleet, but more particularly with the Royal Navy. There was hardly an upper-class family which did not have a son, brother or cousin who was a sailor. In everyday life, boats were a functional necessity; in the landscape garden they were used mainly used for pleasure.

Water was a near-essential aesthetic component of the Georgian designed landscape. On these lakes and pools, vessels came in a wide array of sizes, styles and colours: from the simple rowing skiff to scaled-down men-of-war and highly decorative yachts and galleys, designed to complement the architecture of the garden and park. The prolific designer Lancelot Brown was a master of water engineering; even on the most tricky soils he would provide his clients with a piece of water.[33] There are several examples of boats being built for an estate owner at exactly the same time as his lakes were being created, suggesting that the enjoyment of boating was a fundamental reason for their creation. At Luton Hoo (Bedfordshire), even as Brown was creating a sheet of water from the diminutive River Lea, Lord Bute was having a boat constructed. In 1766 it was

FIGURE 18   *The View from the Head of the Lake at Stowe*, by Bernard Baron after
Jacques Rigaud, 1739. Lord Cobham is enjoying a boating party with friends and
family, with several smaller vessels cluster around his ornate boat. The principal
boat has an open cabin covered with an awning, carved figures on the rear and a
dragon/lion on the prow. The man framed in profile in the centre of the cabin may
be Alexander Pope, distinguishable by his hunched back.

reported that 'the Earl of Bute has lately engaged some Ship-
carpenters to build, from the timber of his estate, the model
of a first rate man of war, with a view to adorn the extensive
canal now making at his Lordship's seat at Luton Hoo'.[34] In
his *Sketches and Hints on Landscape Gardening* (1794) Humphry
Repton expressed the opinion that 'a large lake without boats
is a dreary waste of water'.[35]

One of the finest vessels seen on the Thames during the
eighteenth century was the state barge designed in 1732 by
William Kent for Prince Frederick (often referred to as the best

king the British never had).[36] In its gilded exuberance it was as sophisticated as the most luxurious carriage of the day. Today it can be seen in the National Maritime Museum at Greenwich. Some of the owners of the greatest gardens of the time were supporters of Prince Frederick. They also employed Kent, and the state barge was influential on pleasure craft found on lakes in designed landscapes in the 1730s–1750s. One of Kent's best patrons was Lord Cobham. The boat he had at Stowe, both to adorn his lake and to entertain his friends and family, had similarities with Prince Frederick's barge.[37] Cobham's boat can be seen in all its glory, central to a multi-vessel boating party, in a scene drawn by Jacques Rigaud in 1733 (FIGURE 18).

Cobham's Kentian galley was of its time. When the old lord died in 1749, the estate was inherited by his nephew, Richard Grenville, later Earl Temple. He was the archetypal new broom, and started sweeping away the most out-of-date features of his uncle's garden almost immediately. Not for him this fantastical confection of a boat. Instead he adorned the lake with a scale model of a good, solid man-of-war, the sort of vessel on which the Royal Navy was building an empire. It may have coexisted with Lord Cobham's galley, as both 'the boat' and 'the ship' are referred to in accounts, but certainly upstaged it.[38] The 'Ship', as it was simply known, was always made ready for summer use in May or June and decommissioned in the autumn. She was in a similar class to Lord Bute's 'model of a first rate man of war' at Luton Hoo, the three-masted 'snow' at West Wycombe, *The Lincoln* at Clumber Park (Nottinghamshire) and that at Woburn, which was described in 1762 as 'a fine yacht of thirty to forty tons, carrying ten guns'.[39]

At West Wycombe (Buckinghamshire) lived Sir Francis Dashwood, a contemporary and rival of Earl Temple. He derived his fortune from seaborne trade with Turkey and India, and enjoyed dressing up as an eastern potentate. Beyond the connection with mercantile shipping, it comes as no surprise that the well-known bon viveur and founder of the notorious Hellfire Club numbered among the many diversions in his pleasure ground all the essential elements of a mock-naval battle. Such events were called *naumachia*, a Roman corruption of a Greek word. These battles staged in the parks and gardens of Georgian England were conscious re-creations of Roman events, though never quite as ambitious as their classical predecessors. They were also patriotic gestures and celebrations of British naval supremacy.[40]

West Wycombe was visited, as so many great gardens were, by curious travellers. One such visitor in the 1750s was a Thomas Phillibrown.[41] He described the various vessels on Dashwood's lake, including a 60 ton 'snow' with three masts, writing: 'it is completely rigg'd and carries several brass carriage guns which were taken out of a French Privateer ... a sailor constantly is kept who lives aboard.'[42] He further reported that his party had been taken over her; there was a 'pretty cabin' and everything was neat and shipshape. He continued: 'there is also another 2 mast vessel, a little in the Venetian manner, also a 1 mast vessel like a sloop and also a barge' (FIGURE 19). The whole fleet afforded 'an agreeable prospect'. Phillibrown concluded his description by recounting how there had once been a battery on the side of the lake and that during one sham fight the proceedings had to be suspended after one

FIGURE 19 A detail from *A View of the Walton Bridge, Venus's Temple, etc. in the Garden of Sir Francis Dashwood Bart at West Wycomb*, by William Woollett after William Hannan, *c*.1757. A party disembarks from a small shallow craft near the centre of the view, perhaps the barge referred to by Philibrown, while Dashwood's two-masted ship lies at anchor. The domed Temple of Venus can be seen in the far right of the view.

of the captains sailed too close to the fort and was hit by a blank round, 'which occasion'd him to spit blood and so put an end to the battle'.

Dashwood's lake, which was about the same size as the largest at Stowe, was a little on the small side in comparison to most lakes used for naumachia. If the Grenville family could not stage mock naval battles at Stowe, it seems likely that they did at their other house, Wotton (Buckinghamshire). The vast lake here was ingeniously created by Lancelot Brown, who fed the whole 40 acres with one small drainage ditch. Its extent and a patchwork of other evidence are persuasive that its scale was determined by the desire to play such aquatic war games. There are tantalising mentions in the accounts of a 'ship' and work at 'the Ship Cannons' in the late 1770s and early 1780s. Both a battery on the side of the lake and a dock were marked on an estate plan of 1847. George Moutard Woodward, visiting in 1796, described a 'large vessel' moored at one end of 'the amazing sheet of water'.[43]

At Newstead Abbey (Nottinghamshire), ancestral estate of the poet Lord Byron, the lakes were also extended to give more scope for boating. If he was, as famously said, 'mad, bad and dangerous to know', it was nothing compared to his great-uncle, the 5th Lord Byron. He was also known as the 'Wicked Lord' and the 'Devil Byron' after he killed his neighbour (and cousin) William Chaworth in a duel.[44] While it was expected that a younger son might join the navy, it was somewhat unconventional for the heir to the estate to do so; nevertheless he was a midshipman in the Royal Navy when he inherited the estate in 1736. The family naval connection went even further as his younger brother John was also a sailor. Foul-weather Jack, as he was known for his propensity to attract bad weather, was among Admiral Anson's crew for the famous round-the-world voyage of 1740–44.[45] So both seafaring and unbalanced characters may have run in the Byron blood. It was with some reluctance, it seems, that the 'Wicked Lord' gave up his career at sea. As if to compensate, he carried out a programme of improvements to his park at Newstead Abbey (Nottinghamshire) in the 1740s, which included expanding the lake and constructing a pair of miniature forts on the shore (FIGURE 20).

On the water at Newstead there was a fleet of boats, including a 20-gun schooner that was manned by estate staff as well as professional sailors, assumed to be retired members of Byron's former crews.[46] To put this 20-gun schooner into

FIGURE 20 *A Perspective View of Newstead Abby* [sic] *and Park*, from *The Complete English Traveller* (London, 1771). Here, the rear of one of the batteries on the shore of the lake and two of Byron's fleet of boats can be seen.

context and illustrate the ambitious scale of his boating activities at Newstead, we can compare this largest vessel with *The Trial*, for example, a model of which can be seen in the National Maritime Museum, Greenwich. Built in 1790, she was tough and well-equipped enough to capture privateers with her modest eight guns; twelve fewer than Byron's schooner. The scene at Newstead was described the year after the improvements by

FIGURE 21   The landscape at Batchacre Hall from Stebbing Shaw's *History and Antiquities of Staffordshire*, published in 1801. The view shows Admiral Whitworth's unfeasibly large man o'war and an array of smaller boats, probably around the late 1750s. The islands are dotted with forts and cannon are ranged along the side of the house. Other amusements include archery being practised by a couple in the centre and there are three figures viewing the landscape with a telescope from the roof.

the Duchess of Northumberland (she of the 98 rides), who explained:

> Opposite the House, close to the Water edge, is a fortress and on one side a large extensive Castle [in] which are the Kennel and Hunting stables. At a distance on an eminence in a Wood in the Park, you see a large and very pretty Gothic Tower, at the foot of which, between Towers which form a Gateway, is a Battery of 4 Guns, 9 pounders. There are a great variety of Boats and Ships on the piece of water.[47]

Both the Byron brothers went off to sea as boys. How did these aristocratic lads from landlocked Nottinghamshire fair when aboard their first ships? Even before the enlargement of the lakes at Newstead in the 1740s, had they grown up messing about in boats? Perhaps a major reason for staging these mock naval battles was as a training ground for those younger brothers destined for naval careers. Some paintings recently discovered in a Staffordshire farmhouse strongly suggest that this might have been the case. The landscape at Batchacre (FIGURE 21) was laid out around 1756 by another retired naval officer, Admiral Richard Whitworth.[48] Here he created a series of lakes, with a variety of ornamental buildings, including forts and batteries like those at Newstead and West Wycombe. The lakes have long since gone and the land drained, but a remarkable series of views survive showing a landscape dedicated to nautical pursuits. On the shore and in front of the house, a number of canons were ranged towards the lake. In the lake itself, each of a pair of islands is equipped with a miniature fort. On the water were three sailing vessels, two of which might be described as men-of-war, as well as a smaller boat in which to row out to them. The largest ship was seen in another view; it had three masts and was comparable with the 'snow' at West Wycombe and the ship at Stowe. In the detailed view, the scene is animated by what appears to be the preparations for a naumachia (FIGURE 22). Perhaps the most interesting point about the painting is the pair of boys in the middle of the scene, walking down to the lake with oars slung over their shoulders. Their prominent place in this picture lends greater weight to the theory that such escapades were a way of training – and enthusing – younger members of the family for a naval life.

These testosterone-fuelled antics of taking to the water and firing canons at each other were a far cry from the gentle pleasures of sailing or rowing across a glassy sheet of water on a beautiful, sunny morning. Mrs George Grenville, sister-in-law of Earl Temple, was keen on getting out on the water at Wotton, and on one occasion was particularly annoyed to be 'deprived of the joy of Rowing' by the 'negligence & diso-bedience of the gardener', who let the water out of the lake.[49] (This would have been quite a feat even on the smaller lake.) Mrs Grenville appears to have rowed herself; perhaps it was her way of escaping the busy house, full of the morning bustle of servants cleaning, tradesmen delivering goods, and orders

FIGURE 22 A detail from one of the painted panels surviving in the house at Batchacre (undated, though probably late 1750s or early 1760s; artist unknown). In this view boys are heading for the lake for a morning sailing, or perhaps a naumachia.

to be given for meals for the day or bedrooms for the guests? Humphry Repton, ever keen to please a client, suggested in his Red Book for Holkham that there should be a servant on hand to row ladies when they desired it:

> The man shou'd have the care of the boats and see them properly rigg'd and dress'd in their colours on public days &c, he shou'd lay out nets ... and be at hand to navigate the pleasure boats when any Lady may require it; he ... shou'd always work within hearing of a bell, that he may bring over the Ferry boat to the side on which it may be wanted, and thus he will become a sort of aquatick game keeper; and his house a kind of water Porter's Lodge.[50]

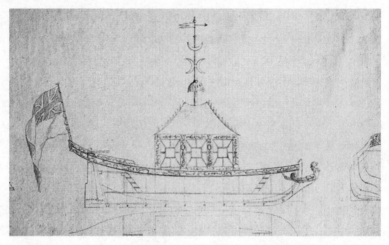

FIGURE 23   A detail from the design for the boat at Wrest, 1765. A 'pretty moving summerhouse', with cabin decorated in the chinoiserie style.

Boats at anchor could form quiet retreats as well as attractive features. Perhaps the most decorative boats on lakes during the eighteenth century were those created in the chinoiserie style. Such vessels often complemented Chinese buildings, but several examples were created before their architectural counterparts, so we might say it was the other way around and the building on land complemented the boat. These types of boat perhaps most clearly conform to the description written by Elizabeth Anson, wife of the admiral, who referred to a flotilla of barges on the Thames as 'pretty moving summerhouses'. Her description of the 'moving summerhouses', along with her suggestion that her sister-in-law Jemima, Marchioness Grey, might retire to the quiet of the cabin of her new boat at Wrest to write letters, tells us much about how she, and probably also Jemima, perceived and used their boats.[51]

A proposed boat on which Jemima might write her letters was the subject of much debate among the Anson circle in the summer of 1750. It may be significant that these discussions came not long after a plan by Thomas Wright (astronomer and garden designer, known as the Wizard of Durham) to start to naturalise the straight lines of the formal canals at Wrest, though it was another decade before this was actually carried out by Brown. The coincidence of works to the canals and plans for boats during the 1750s and 1760s suggests that the adaptation of the water was desired, at least partly, for better boating. In June 1750 Elizabeth Anson consulted her husband on the issue of the Wrest boat. He suggested that a 'galley' would be 'most capable of decoration and ornament'. Perhaps indecision had reigned and this boat was never built, or maybe it started to rot, because fifteen years later a boat was required again. This time, however, the plans were certainly realised and they survive (FIGURE 23). Between 1758 and 1760 Lancelot Brown worked at Wrest; while he respected much of the formal layout of the 1690s–1710s, one of his major innovations was the naturalising of the canal around the outside of the gardens into a long serpentine lake, which would have made for more interesting boating. In 1765 plans were drawn up for a boat with Chinese decoration; like Admiral Anson's earlier suggestion, this was also suitable for rowing. It was 23 feet in length with a central mast (but no sail) topped by three crescents, a cabin with Chinese windows and a tiger on the prow. It may have been constructed to complement the Chinese Temple, which was probably erected in the early 1760s, some time after Brown's improvements. A vivid description of the launch of

FIGURE 24 *The Chinese Junk afloat on Virginia Water*, by Paul Sandby, undated, *c.*1753. As well as the junk, sometimes known as the Mandarin Yacht, Sandby illustrates four other vessels of the Duke of Cumberland's fleet on the lake.

this new boat in July 1766 was written by Marchioness Grey's 15-year-old daughter. (Her other daughter was nine at the time, so perhaps the boat was planned as an amusement for them.)

> This Ship ... had long lain near the water side an object of Admiration to all ... who were we suppose particularly struck with the swan at one end, & the tiger at the other. Having now received her last finishing, it was determined she should be launched the first fair hour. Accordingly at six o'clock in the evening ... she was let down into the water, colours and streamers flying, music playing. Indeed we had no cannons fired, nor cheers given, nor bottle of wine flung at her Head... She came down, literally, Head foremost, & with such a splash ... but recovering instantly, & not sticking in the mud ... she was brought along shore, we embarked under the shade of the Acacias & had a most prosperous voyage. The sun shone ... the water & shores

looked more beautiful than ever... Having passed every
straight & doubled every cape without the least accident, &
being arrived at the open sea behind the pavilion, we landed
under a clump (which I should have called a Wood) & left
the vessel to proceed to its moorings.[52]

The Chinese Pavilion of the Duke of Cumberland (better
known as Butcher Cumberland), favourite and younger son
of George II, post-dated a large boat in the Chinese style at
Virginia Water (Surrey). Like that at Wrest it was highly decorative, with a fine room aboard, though on a somewhat larger
scale. His Mandarin Yacht, as it was called, was converted
from a naval hulk in 1753 (FIGURE 24).[53] It was towed up the
Thames and then hauled overland to Virginia Water, where
it was ornamented with a great winged dragon along the side
of the hull and a fretwork fence around the deck, from which
four ladders descended to the water. Four poles supported
globe lanterns; there were flags at the stern and a central mast,
decorated with crescents and topped by a grasshopper. The
fame of the Mandarin Yacht drew Jane Coke to visit Virginia
Water in October 1753. She described the spectacle: 'Upon this
water are several boats ... what I went particularly to see is
a Chinese ship, which is by far the prettiest thing I ever saw,
with one very good room in it, and no expense spared in the
finishing.'[54]

Unsurprisingly, boating on lakes in the landscape garden was
not without its dramatic, even tragic, incidents. In September
1764 at Sherborne, a party ventured onto the lake in a little
boat. They 'had the misfortune to be overset and thoroughly
ducked'. Unhurt but soaked, the ladies were taken to a nearby

farmhouse and one of the gentlemen 'borrowed the bayley's cloaths, came home and sent the coach with the ladys' servants and cloaths to bring them home dry'.[55] This incident ended happily, with no more than a drenching, but in August 1778 the lake at Grimsthorpe Castle in Lincolnshire was the scene of something far more serious. That summer the 22-year-old composer Thomas Linley the Younger, a musician of such talent that he was called the English Mozart, was staying with his family as guests of the Duke of Ancaster. The party was boating on the lake when a storm blew up and the boat was overturned. Linley drowned while trying to swim ashore. Wolfgang Amadeus Mozart, who had been a fellow student in Florence, said that Linley, 'had he lived, would have been one of the greatest ornaments of the musical world'.[56] Lady Louisa Stuart wrote to ask her sister if she had heard of the news from Grimsthorpe: 'I mean the shocking accident of young Lindley's [sic] being drowned before the windows, and the Duke of Ancaster's death a few days after.'[57]

There was rather less danger of being drowned if the boat your were sailing was no more than a couple of feet long. After moving to his Norfolk parsonage in 1776, James Woodforde adapted his garden with the sort of improvements that were scaled-down versions of what the great landowners were doing to their extensive acres.[58] As well as constructing himself a temple, built of wood and painted pea green, he adapted his horse pond to become his 'Great Pond', and here he sailed his model boats, including one yacht mentioned specifically in his diary, which he called *Anna*.

Another water-related activity popular in the Georgian garden was bathing. Baths were one of the most common garden features and bathing was frequently a morning activity, both for health and for pleasure. Plunge-pool-type cold baths are relatively well known, but the Georgian garden swimming pool has been largely ignored by recent writers. This is probably because, though swimming for leisure in fresh water has had a resurgence in the United Kingdom in recent years, its history has been eclipsed by the story of sea bathing. This started to become popular in the later Georgian period and was by Victorian times so prevalent that it spawned resorts all around the coast.

The Georgians were well aware of, and probably influenced by, the classical precedents for bathing. In 1728 Robert Castell published his *Villas of the Ancients*, which was dedicated to Lord Burlington, whose Bagnio was one of his principal garden buildings at Chiswick (Middlesex). Castell had made a systematic study of primary texts in an attempt to reconstruct the villas of Pliny the Younger. Within the work, there is much explanation of the Roman habit of bathing. By the mid-eighteenth century primitive archaeological excavations were unearthing lost elements of Pompeii and Herculaneum, along with Roman baths there, and were, of course, seen by Grand Tourists. The cold bath built at Wrest in 1770 by Marchioness Grey and her gout-suffering husband, Philip Yorke, was deliberately conceived as a Roman ruin, with the craggy remains of a dome flying over the bath and leaving it largely open to the sky.[59] In Britain, the baths founded by the Romans at Aquae Sulis, better known as the city of Bath, had never been forgotten, and Georgian travellers made their way there in droves both for medical reasons and for leisure.

Two early-eighteenth-century physicians publicised the benefits of cold bathing for health in their writings and influenced the creation of baths in pleasure grounds. The first was Sir John Floyer, who published his *Psychrolousia: or, The History of Cold Bathing, both Ancient and Modern* at the start of the eighteenth century.[60] Floyer built his own bath for public use. It had two pools: the water flowed from the upper one for women into the lower one for men. They were 16 feet by 10 feet and divided by a wall, and beside each there was 'a convenient room … for Undressing'. The bath was filled so that the water came up to neck height.[61] Significantly, Floyer recommended bathing as a pleasurable activity as well as for health.

The second physician-author was George Cheyne, who included a lengthy section on the benefits of regular cold bathing in his *An Essay of Health and Long Life* (1724). Cheyne felt that bathing helped to 'cleanse the ducts', which in turn helped free perspiration. It was also beneficial to stimulate the circulation. He recommended that the plunge into cold water should be combined with exercise. Those wealthy enough should build their own cold bath and use it two or three times a week, in both winter and summer. In winter the bather must be sure to exercise on coming out. Like Floyer, he did not approve of jumping or diving in, for 'it gives too violent a Shock to Nature, and risques too much the *Bursting* some of the smaller Vessels'. The advice was that once a bather was in the water, not to stay long. Patients should submerge themselves several times before getting out and 'rubbing and currying well before they dres'd'.[62] Cold bathing was also used as a cure for mental illness, including depression. Thomas Lennard Barrett, writing to Sanderson Miller in May 1745 from Belhus (Essex, where the landscape was later laid out for him by Brown), told his friend: 'the cold bath which I have gone into for three weeks past has quite recovered my weak nerves and restored me to good Spirits and the Blew Devils are quite gone away, not, I suppose, very well relishing the cold water.'[63]

Secluded settings, with buildings reached through shrubbery and down the sort of winding paths found in wildernesses, were common places for cold baths.[64] If bathers were naked, the reasons for this are obvious. One of the most perfect baths – now as then – is the small octagonal plunge pool at Rousham (Oxfordshire). It is fed by a stone-lined rill of the clearest water, which serpentines down the middle of the path through the shrubbery, in a way that is too tempting not to follow. The bath is set in a small clearing, with a simple, rustic stone alcove in which to change, the whole ensemble utterly hidden from the rest of the garden. On a hot day it must have been extremely inviting. Perhaps it also amused the bathers that they could stand there naked and look down on the decently clothed walkers on the path to the statue of Apollo below, knowing their modesty was protected by the slope and the shrubbery. At Painswick (Gloucestershire), the pool is much larger than that at Rousham and is certainly big enough for more than a plunge. Originally it was likewise of the garden, but concealed from it. It was set in a hedged area, not far from the statue of Pan, the god of woodland revels, with three small structures, two of which are simple arched alcoves, very similar to that at Rousham.[65]

There is no doubt that the pool built by Sir Godfrey Copley at Sprotborough Hall (Yorkshire) was intended as a swimming pool. Copley had an existing interest in waterworks and corresponded with some of the foremost scientists and engineers of the time. He built a technically ambitious pump to bring water up the steep cliff from the River Don into a lead cistern on the top of the house, from which he fed his fountains and canals in the garden and latterly his bath.[66] He described this innovation in a letter to Hans Sloane in September 1707:

> I have succeeded past my expectation in making such a
> bath for pleasure and convenience as I think no one in this
> kingdome hath ye like. It is between 34 & 35 foot long &
> about 16 foot broad with a convenient pair of stairs to go
> down to the bottom & sides lined with lead & holds water
> six foot and four inches deep, but when wee use itt for
> bathing and swimming wee fill it but to 4 foot & half, which
> the water engine will do in less than 5 houre. Two or three
> faggots and a sack of coales doth warm it equall to ye heat
> of your body but we can make it hotter if wee please. I never
> met with any bath more agreable & there is roome enough
> for four or five to swim up and down very well. I have gone
> in severall times and it is very pleasant in [the] morning...
> My wife and some Ladys of her acquaintance have gone in
> together & are much delighted with it.[67]

There is no mention of stimulating circulation or cures for depression here; it was very definitely a bath for the pleasure of swimming and a good example of one being used by ladies as well as men, though at different times it appears. It seems likely, as Sir Godfrey himself supposed, that this was the first of

FIGURE 25   The Boathouse at
Fonthill, today, with the river
god in the background and steps
down allowing swimmers an easy
descent into the clear water.

its kind. What remains puzzling about this firmly documented
heated pool at Sprotborough is that it does not seem to have
been copied by more people.

The dimensions given for Copley's pool allow others to be
measured against it to see how feasible swimming would have
been. That at Sprotborough was about 34 foot long by 16 foot
wide and allowed enough space for four or five swimmers. The
partially open-air pool at Rufford Abbey in Nottinghamshire,
built in 1729, was 12 foot in width, narrowing to 6 foot by 85
foot long; its strange shape and unique dimensions indicating
that the swimming of lengths was anticipated.[68] Here the long,
thin pool ended, unusually, inside the loggia of the summerhouse. This half-in, half-outside arrangement is echoed by
a structure on the edge of the lake at Fonthill (FIGURE 25),

which is now called the Boathouse, but has so many features in common with acknowledged baths elsewhere that its name must be open to question: the circular end terminating inside the building, the double flight of steps down into the water, the eroded sculpture of a nymph or river god behind, and the imitation Roman architecture of the covered section.

The bath in the Grotto at Stourhead (Wiltshire) may not have been large enough to have swum in, but it was certainly used for pleasure. The landscape here and its creator have been largely misunderstood by twentieth-century historians.[69] The tides of time have washed into the valley garden and, as they receded, taken with them most of the smaller, more ephemeral structures, so what we see remaining are the large, solid, classical buildings. Upon these a narrative has been thrust, which it seems lacks any foundation. The creator of the garden, Henry Hoare, a banker with capacious pockets, has been portrayed as something of a morbid pessimist. True, the majority of the landscaping was carried out after the early death of his wife (and he never married again) and against the backdrop of the further loss of his only son. But his letters reveal Henry the Magnificent, as he was called, to have been affectionate and sociable, fit and active. He filled his garden with the same happy hotchpotch of architectural styles we find at Hestercombe or Painshill: he even planned a mosque on an island in the lake, and enjoyed life in the garden.

The Grotto is the most fantastical of the surviving garden buildings, entered through a rocky arch and along a short, dark tunnel. The bath is situated in a central chamber, with a domed roof, pierced by a central oculus that gives definite

Roman overtones (FIGURE 26). The constant running of spring water into the bath might have had a mild jacuzzi-like effect. The building was described in 1757 by Jonas Hanway:

> A narrow path ... leads to the grotto of the nymph, which is formed in rude rock-work, almost level with the water. Here is a marble bason of pure water, which is made use of as a cold bath. In the interior part of the niche, over the bason, is a marble statue of a sleeping nymph, to whom this grotto is dedicated: she is covered with a light garment, which hardly conceals her limbs.[70]

FIGURE 26   The central chamber of the Grotto at Stourhead, by Francis Nicholson, undated. The pool where Hoare enjoyed a 'souse in that delicious bath' is below the statue of the nymph on the right of the view.

As well as the slightly suggestive description of the 'nymph of the grot', Hanway observed, as with a number of other baths elsewhere, a firm visual link between the bath and the water of the lake, which, when in the bath, appeared practically at eye level.

In the hot summer of 1765 Hoare, then aged 60, enjoyed wallowing in his bath. He wrote: 'A souse in that delicious bath and grot, fill'd with fresh magic, is Asiatick luxury.'[71] That last phrase, 'Asiatick luxury', seems a long way from emulation of the Ancients and much more to do with something exotic and indulgent. The following summer he was indulging again: 'I had a delicious souse into the cold bath this morning, to the tune of French horns playing round me all the while, belonging to company who lay at our inn & took advantage of a second view ... before they decamped.' Picture him on the sort of summer day when it would be far too hot to want to wear a powdered wig, wallowing in the refreshing spring water as it tumbled into the pool, the valley resounding with music made by the tourists from across the lake, or in the shrub-beries, adding a further dimension to his experience. (French horns, as we shall see, were the most popular instrument in the pleasure ground as their sound travelled long distances, so worked well in the open air.) Henry Hoare was not the only member of the family who enjoyed a dip in warm weather; his 11-year-old granddaughter was also an enthusiast. In the same letter that has his description of his own wallowing, he wonders: 'I suppose dear Harriot dives like a Di Dapper and there is no keeping her out of the water this hissing hot weather.'[72] 'Di dapper' is an old-fashioned name for the little grebe, which gives a lovely image of her confidence in the water. It is conceivable that Henry had a bed somewhere in one of his many garden buildings, where he could rest after bathing, as recommended by medical treatises, and perhaps as the morning wore into the afternoon he might take himself off there for a quiet nap.

FOUR

Afternoon

Fishing — Study — Curiosity —
Amorous Liaisons — Games & Recreation

Happy the man who to the Shade retires
Whom nature charms, and whom the Muse inspires
Blest whom the Sweets of home-felt Quiet please
But far more blest, who study joins with Ease

Inscription above the doorway of
the Mausoleum at Hestercombe[1]

AFTER THE EXCITEMENT of a morning spent driving at speed over the smooth turf of the parkland, or the thrill of sailing on the lake, quieter, calmer activities might be in order to while away the afternoon hours until dinner time. Fishing was an activity that was widely accessible in parks and gardens, potentially profitable, encouraged quiet contemplation, helped children develop patience and kept them out of mischief. It was something with which to amuse guests and a sport that could be enjoyed in the summer when families were at their country estates and there was no hunting to be had. In the preface to his book *The Experienced Angler* (first published in 1653, but still popular throughout the eighteenth century), Izaak Walton, father of the sport of angling, praised the activity for its calming qualities and opportunities for quiet contemplation, comparing it to hunting and falconry, which led those engaged in these sports to frequently 'bring home more of melanchole and discontent than satisfaction'.[2] In comparison, he wrote, 'the Angler, when he hath the worst success, loseth but hook or line, or perhaps (what he never possessed) a Fish, and suppose he take nothing yet he enjoyeth a delightful walk by pleasant rivers, in sweet pastures.' This was as true of angling on the lake in the garden or park as it was on a river bank.[3]

Angling was a pleasure enjoyed equally by men and women, girls and boys. At the top of the social tree it was enjoyed by the royal family. Princess Amelia was a keen angler. Lady Mary Coke wrote to her sister, Lady Strafford, telling her that 'Princess Amelia is going to have a house upon the Thames, to be at one Month in the Year for fishing, which Her Royal Highness is very fond of.'[4] Lady Mary herself was also a keen fisherwoman. Her diaries include many accounts of her angling excursions, which often took place during summer trips to the country houses of her friends. In July 1768, she was at General Conway's house, Park Place. In her diary she wrote: 'It promised being a very fine day. We breakfasted at the Cottage, but before eleven it rain'd. We had projected fishing, but the fisher Man disappointed Us.' A few days later the weather was fair and she and Lady Ailesbury finally managed to satisfy their desire for an afternoon's fishing: 'We was upon the water till three O'clock, & catched near seven dozen of gudgeon, pope, roach, & one perch.'[5] Lady Mary and Princess Amelia were also among a party at Stowe in the summer of 1770 when fishing was 'in perfection'. They fished together

FIGURE 27 *A View from the Island Seat of the Lake [to] the Temple of Venus and the Hermitage, Stowe*, by J. Course, mid-1750s. The two gentlemen anglers are accompanied by a lady, the cart perhaps carried their tackle to the lake. On the right a rather Venetian-looking barge is emerging from behind the trees. The building in the centre background is the Temple of Venus.

on Eleven Acre Lake (FIGURE 27). Their expedition was highly satisfactory, though more so for Lady Mary than the princess:

> The Princess order'd me to attend her to the great water
> to fish: in two hours I catched three score; two large carpe
> & above twenty considerable perch; the rest small. The
> Princess catched about forty, but none so large as mine, to
> the great mortification of the page who attended her. He
> seem'd to think it a reproach that the Princess shou'd catch
> less fish then mine: his distress made me Laugh.[6]

Perhaps both the Princess and Lady Mary were encouraged to fish as children, as it was often recommended to teach patience and as a wholesome diversion (FIGURE 28). In 1713 Roger North published his treatise, *A Discourse on Fish and Fishponds*, which set down his own experience of the farming of fish and advised on the construction and maintenance of ponds. North was a man who was passionate about fish, above and beyond their value as a staple form of protein. Aside from his advice on management, he particularly recommended fishing as an activity to keep children entertained and prevent them from embarking on more dissolute pastimes. He wrote that anyone who 'aims at an easy and satisfactory Course of Life, must seek that his family, as well as himself, be pleas'd: And if he doth not order it so ... 'tis ten to one they will find such entertainments as shall not be very grateful to him.' So, to distract youth from other temptations he recommended watery pursuits: 'Young People love Angling extremely; then there is a Boat, which gives pleasure enough in summer, frequently fishing with Nets, the very making of nets ... and the Fish, especially upon your great Sweeps, and the strange Surprizes that will happen in Numbers and Bigness.'[7]

At the end of the eighteenth century, angling was still an activity in which children were encouraged. In the summer of 1790 Marchioness Grey at Wrest Park contrived many suitable amusements for her three Robinson grandsons, then aged seven, eight and nine, among which was fishing. The eldest, Thomas, wrote to his uncle, Frederick Robinson: 'Grandmama has bought each of us a fishing rod & we go to that sport every fine day.'[8] Later in the letter he reported that they had

FIGURE 28 *A Family of Anglers: the Swaine Family of Laverington [sic] Hall in the Isle of Ely*, by Arthur Devis, 1749. This conversation piece illustrates all the accoutrements of angling in the mid-eighteenth century and shows it as a family sport.

also fished from the newly launched boat. That same summer at Saltram (Devon), their aunt Anne Robinson, who it appears had not been educated in the sport in her youth, also decided to take up fishing and hoped rather than believed that her niece, Theresa Parker, would also enjoy it.[9] Here the fish are likely to have been marine fish from the tidal Plym Estuary, which formed the setting of the park. She reported to Frederick Robinson's wife:

> I have got a fishing rod and have attempted to catch some Fish out. I am sorry to say I had not a single bite, and am afraid I have very little chance of catching any, but however as I wish to succeed I shall not give the point up, the Child thinks she shall like it vastly but she won't have the patience to try.[10]

Although angling was still very popular at the end of the eighteenth century, the netting of fish, which had been specified as a desirable by Roger North, was dying out. This had played an important role in the designed landscape for centuries, up until the later decades of the eighteenth century. Netting was associated with the ancient practice of farming fish in ponds and lakes. Although such domestic fishponds in England are usually assumed to be monastic and to date from the medieval period, their origins have been traced back to the Roman period.[11] The medieval system of two complementary types of pond, the *vivarium* for the breeding of fish and the *servatorium* for the holding of fish ready for the table, continued into the eighteenth century, though by the second half of the century it was in decline.[12] Utilitarian ponds had already started to be turned into ornamental features in the seventeenth century, but as the eighteenth century progressed it became more frequent for pre-existing fishponds to be transformed into ornamental lakes.[13] As these expanses of water grew ever larger, for their aesthetic qualities and possibilities for more exciting boating, with lakes like that of almost 90 acres developed at Clumber Park, or the 125-acre Virginia Water, for example, it was impossible to drain them, as was necessary for fish farming, and this marks a subtle change in their use from fish farming to boating, with angling continuing to be important.[14]

Both angling and netting are shown in the pair of paintings by Edward Haytley of the Brockman family in their garden at Beachborough in Kent in the mid-1740s (FIGURES 29 and 30).[15] One shows the pool being 'drawn' by two servants on the bank, with another in a boat, presumably helping to move

FIGURE 29   *The Temple Pond, Beachborough, Kent*, by Edward Haytley, *c.*1744.
While this view shows the pool being 'drawn' – fished with a net – its companion
(*opposite*) shows it used also for angling. In the temple the Brockman family watch the
pool being fished, while they can view more distant prospects through the telescope.

the fish towards the net. This a scene that would have been a
familiar one in the Georgian garden, though on a smaller scale
here perhaps than in some other landscapes. Watching the lake
fished had parallels with the rural ritual, the pastoral but essential activity of haymaking. Just as landowners made parties
to watch the haymakers, so the spectacle of the 'drawing' of the

lake was almost a spectator sport. The Grenville family invited guests to Wotton for the event. George Grenville wrote to his sister Hester Pitt in October 1769: 'we expect a house full of company next week at the fishing of our Lake.'[16] In the mid-1760s they were also still netting the lake at Sherborne. One afternoon in November 1766 it was reported in the game book:

FIGURE 30   *The Temple Pond, Beachborough, Kent*, by Edward Haytley, *c.*1744. This is the opposite view. Two of the ladies are angling, while a third draws and the gentleman on the left of the pool carries a book.

began to fish the canals, and made an end about 4 o'clock. It is supposed there was near a ton weight of pikes catched, the largest of which weighed 28 pounds, and several about 15 or 16. There were an immense quantity of fine tench; 40 or 50 brace of exceeding fine carps, but very few large perch. All turned in again, except the pikes and 40 brace of tench and eight of carps.[17]

✴

Angling was such a popular pastime in the Georgian garden that specific buildings were created to serve those fishing. They were often architecturally sophisticated and catered for other related activities such as dining, boating and sometimes bathing too. The fishing lodge built by Charles Cotton in 1674 on the River Dove, within the grounds of his home, Beresford Hall (Staffordshire), may have paved the way for such buildings. Charles Cotton collaborated with Izaak Walton on later editions of *The Compleat Angler*; above the door, the initials of his mentor Walton were entwined with his own. As a building type, fishing pavilions developed out of earlier simple alcoves at ends of canals, which provided shelter from sun, wind or sudden showers, and somewhere to sit near the water, but as the century progressed and perhaps as angling became more popular they moved closer and closer to the water, until they were set right above it. Taken in 1767, Mrs Delany's view of the Water House at Calwich (Staffordshire) built by her brother, Bernard Granville, is a rare depiction of people actually inside a garden building (FIGURE 31). The Water House no longer survives; it was replaced by a classical temple by Mrs Delany's nephew; but it appears to have had three rooms or spaces, one

FIGURE 31 A detail from *The Cascade and Water House at Calwich, Staffordshire*, by Mary Granville Delany, 1767. This watercolour by the sister of the owner gives us a rare glimpse into the inside of a garden building. From the open-fronted room, anglers could lower their rods into the water.

of which flanked the lake or even projected out over it, allowing anglers to sit inside with their lines in the water.

Also in Staffordshire, at Enville, there was another typical waterside building from which anglers could fish. The Boat-house, which makes it sound more humble than it was (for it is now lost), was probably designed by Sanderson Miller in his signature Gothic style. The name was taken from one of its functions, because the fine room sat above a simple barrel-vaulted boathouse, which may have been used to store the small yacht seen on the pond around 1800 (FIGURE 32).[18] A description of 1777 records that 'the boat-house ... is an

FIGURE 32   *The Temple Pool at Enville*, c.1800. Sanderson Miller's Gothic Boathouse is in the far right corner of the pond. Above the boathouse at water level was a fine room from which you could fish.

octagon, prettily ornamented within by festoons of flowers, and medallions in stucco. A curious sliding window ... opens to the water, adorned with painted glass in whimsical groupes of grotesque figures [and] is certainly very ornamental.'[19] The sliding window would have been used for dramatic effect: guests would enter from the land side of the building and the window would be opened to reveal that they were right above the water. The combination of the stained glass and the light reflecting off the water must have made for some pretty, colourful, twinkling effects.

The prime example of this type of multifunctional building is the Fishing Pavilion at Kedleston (Derbyshire), which survives intact and unaltered. An elegant classical building with a central pavilion flanked by half-height boathouses on each side, it was designed by Robert Adam and built in 1772 for the 1st Lord Scarsdale.[20] The pavilion is an easy walk, or an even easier ride, across the park from the house. Originally it was set within its own garden; accounts mention gravel paths and flowering shrubs. Entering the building on the land side, the visitor had a choice, either to continue through the door ahead into the finely decorated fishing and banqueting room, or to descend one of the pair of curved staircases either side of the central door. The stairs from the entrance door led first to each of the barrel-vaulted boathouses that flank the pavilion and then to the central chamber of the undercroft, which contains a plunge bath fed by a nearby spring. As with the cold bath in the Grotto at Stourhead, once in the water the bather would be practically at eye level with the lake. To the rear of the undercroft are two recesses, one for changing and the other an earth closet. The banqueting room is adorned with painted panels depicting various kinds of fish. Opposite the door, over the lake, is a Venetian window that opens, like that at Enville, to allow the casting of a line straight from the room. This is a true multifunctional garden building catering for fishing, refreshments and bathing – a place to escape from the busy house for many hours.

Izaak Walton paralleled the opportunities for quiet contemplation while fishing to those afforded by a gentleman's closet, which in the seventeenth century was his study, a place of

privacy to which to retreat. In the following century the landscape garden and its buildings provided perfect places for
this activity and often performed the same sort of role. Such
garden buildings followed precedents also set in the seventeenth
century, including by the ever-influential John Evelyn. In the
1640s he developed the designed landscape at his brother's
estate at Wotton (Surrey). This may have been as a pallia-
tive for his depression, which was brought on by the trauma
and upheavals of the Civil War.[21] At Wotton he built, in his
own words, '(by my brother's permission) a study, made a
fishpond, Iland [*sic*] and some other solitudes & retirements'.[22]
The study speaks for itself, the fishpond suggests fishing for
its quiet contemplative qualities, and an island is symbolic of
isolation and seclusion. He must have found this both effective
and productive because he later undertook a similar exercise
at his own estate of Sayes Court in Deptford (then Kent) after
the Civil War, in the 1650s. Here he created a two-storey
pavilion which he called his 'elaboratorie', suggesting scientific
experiments, which prefigured some of the most sophisticated
garden buildings of the Georgian period, dedicated to scholarly
pursuits and scientific curiosity.[23]

For Evelyn creating a garden, working in it and simply being
in it were therapeutic. There is something about the combination of nature and art embodied in a garden that is intrinsically
soothing. Many Georgians found comfort and solace this way,
as voiced by William Beckford in 1780. Escaping from the
throng in the house at Fonthill to the solitude of the garden
one fine spring afternoon, he wrote of 'the reviving fragrance
of the vegetation' which was 'not to be described, nor need it

to the Worshippers of Nature: they know the perfume she diffuses when awakened from her Winter's repose'. He continued
in describing the effect on his nervous constitution: 'some
propitious Being seemed to have endowed this spot with the
power of relieving my anxieties [and] the tumult of my spirits,
for no sooner did I breathe the perfume of the flowers which
Blew all around me than a soft delusion stole over my senses.'[24]

Earlier in the century, in 1736, when Henrietta Knight, Lady
Luxborough, was forced into exile in deepest Warwickshire, she
was fortunate that she was already a gardener. After she was
accused of having an affair, her husband sent her to moulder
at his run-down country estate, while he diverted himself
in London with business and mistresses. Separated from her
young children and cut off from the rest of her family, friends
and society in general, she created a garden that must have
been both a distraction and, as her biographer Jane Brown
puts it, a 'solace'.[25] She carved out a life for herself at Barrells, managing the estate, cultivating flowers, choosing the
line of winding paths through her coppice, and contriving
modest buildings to ornament the landscape and also serve
as 'agreeable retreats'. She gradually made friends in the west
Midlands, including with the rather reclusive poet and fellow
gardener-on-a-shoestring William Shenstone. At The Leasowes
(Shropshire) he ornamented the farmland around his modest
house with a circuit walk, punctuated with seats, vistas and
elegiac monuments. Jane Brown describes Shenstone as 'all
politeness and melancholy' and observes that he hated winter,
when he 'sank into a gloomy hibernations, he would not reply
to letters and he certainly could not be dislodged', even by

Lady Luxborough.[26] For him, too, the creation of a landscape was therapeutic.

For those in power, both the garden itself and the activity of gardening provided relaxation and a retreat from 'publick cares'.[27] William Pitt was both a brilliant prime minister and a skilled designer of landscapes, whose opinion was sought by many of his friends. In him, as with John Evelyn, depression and the creation of gardens went hand in hand. He created and adapted gardens at a number of houses he leased or owned, as well as rolling up his sleeves and planting trees in the gardens of his friends, like Sanderson Miller.[28] Others put their energies into their landscapes as a salve to disappointed ambitions or as an occupation of political exile. John Aislabie was disgraced by his association with the scandal of the South Sea Bubble financial crash in 1721. The former chancellor of the exchequer largely created his garden at Studley Royal (Yorkshire) after being re- leased from the Tower of London following the event. Richard, 1st Baron Edgcumbe, put his energy into the development of his landscape at Mount Edgcumbe (Cornwall) after retiring from politics at the fall of his friend Robert Walpole in 1742.

Ladies too were enthusiastic horticulturalists. Lady Mary Coke was directly involved in her modest garden in west London. As well as setting out a new walk with a seat and views to Hampstead and Highgate, she wrote to her sister: 'I am grown a great weeder. I am glad I like it better than my gardener. My garden wou'd otherwise be in great disorder.'[29] The daughters as well as the only son of the 2nd Earl of Ilchester were all given plots in the garden as children and grew into keen gardeners. The keenest among them was Lady

Mary Fox-Strangways, who, when she married Thomas Mansel Talbot and moved to Penrice Castle, created a garden that was one of her chief occupations. Her son wrote: 'gardening was her passion, not her employment for employment's sake, and I do not believe the attraction of all the gaities of London would have induced her to forego seeing the snowdrops or crocuses at Penrice in blow for one single day!'[30] She regularly worked in her flower garden, sometimes with her husband reading to her. Mary missed her garden when she travelled from home; her pocket book records in October 1798: 'Home. Walked to my garden the minute I got to Penrice.'[31] For her, as for Lady Luxborough around 80 years before, gardening was soothing and therapeutic. Mary (by then in her early fifties) wrote to a cousin: 'I have a rose tree at the garden gate, which was dug up by my dear grandmother ... which, with other memoranda ... make my garden more engaging to me than any other spot in the world, and I spend all the time I can get in it, as it mends my health, as well as soothes my heart.'

Joanna Martin has observed that Mary was fortunate in that by the end of the eighteenth century and in the first decades of the nineteenth, ladies' clothes were less restrictive than those of previous generations and she was therefore able to work in them more easily. However, Mary also adopted the dress of the local Welsh countrywomen when in her garden, wearing a 'whittle' and a cloak of red flannel, and recommended this to her gardening friends and relations.[32] Among these was Ann Fowler, wife of the Salisbury doctor, who had requested a plan of the extended garden from Mary when 'contriving improvements'. She drew her husband into her gardening in a hands-on way. Dr Fowler wrote to Mary: 'my employment has been confined to repairing and planting hedges and rooting out weeds.'[33]

~sk~

Once their morning obligations were over, master and mistress might seek solitude in the garden until dinner time. He might retreat to his garden building for some sort of intellectual self-improvement, such as scientific enquiry, and she might take the opportunity to read a book or write pleasurable correspondence. Lady Louisa Conolly, third daughter of the Duke of Richmond (and sister to Sarah Lennox), escaped her house, Castletown (County Kildare), for the refuge of her cottage. Here she wrote letters, including to her sisters. In June 1764 she wrote to Sarah:

> I am sitting in an alcove in my cottage with park before it, in the woods three quarters of a mile from the house, a lovely fine day the grass looking very green, honeysuckles and roses in abundance, mignonette coming up, seringa all out, the bird singing, fresh air all about … my work and my book by me, inkstand as you may perceive, and a little comfortable table and chairs, two stands with china bowls, filled with immense nosegays.[34]

Marchioness Grey, as mistress of a large and important house, found it a relief to escape into the garden for some solitude. She was well educated and scholarly, and was said to never take a solitary walk in the garden without a book in her pocket.[35] At Wrest, the walks and cabinets – formal clearings in the woods preserved from her grandfather's garden – as well

FIGURE 33　*The Misses Van*, by Lady Salisbury, 1791 (formerly attributed to Paul Sandby). A typical scene of a quiet afternoon in the Georgian garden: ladies engaged in reading and needlework.

as the garden buildings, offered ample places for escape from the bustle of the mansion. From her correspondence we know that Jemima Grey, as well as escaping the house to read quietly, also wrote for pleasure in the garden, like Louisa Conolly. A letter from her sister-in-law, Elizabeth Anson, suggests she had several favourite locations in the garden to do this, including the cabin of the boat and the root house (FIGURE 33).[36]

A root house was a form of building often used as a hermitage, with its associations of an ascetic, contemplative life, and this sometimes suggested its use as a place of quiet retreat for reading or writing. Root houses were a popular form of garden building, because they could be made with cheap and widely available materials. They were usually constructed from a framework of gnarled tree branches or roots (hence the name), with woven panels in between. Climbers and other plants were often encouraged to grow through these, or moss might be stuffed into the gaps. Their roofs were usually thatched. As well as hermitages, such buildings also went by the title of 'moss house', 'rustic hut' or 'thatched house', or a combination of those terms.

Both the concept of the garden hermitage and of the rustic, thatched style of the root house were popularised in this period by Queen Caroline, with two of her buildings of the 1730s at Richmond, both designed by William Kent. The first was the Hermitage (FIGURE 34). This was more in the form of a rocky cave, built of rough-hewn blocks of stone. Cave-like structures had long been associated with hermits and contemplatives. The philosopher Jean-Jacques Rousseau's use of the Cave at Wootton Hall (Staffordshire) in the 1760s demonstrates how active that tradition was at the time. Here he wrote at least some of his *Confessions*.[37] All that remains of the Cave, hewn out of the bedrock on which the mansion also sat, is a doorway and a fireplace, which would have been a necessary comfort in what must have been a dark and cold space to sit and write. Queen Caroline's other influential building at Richmond proved a more popular sort of structure. Merlin's Cave was constructed five years after the Hermitage. Somewhat confusingly it was less cave-like, combining Gothic architecture with steep, beehive thatched roofs. Like the earlier Hermitage it had three internal spaces: a central chamber flanked by a room with a bed and a room for books. Describing the building in 1761, the German tourist Count Frederick Kielmansegge said that it had been the Queen's 'favourite reading-place' and that her library was still preserved there.[38]

Like both of Queen Caroline's buildings at Richmond, the root house at Wrest does not survive. Its appearance is

FIGURE 34   *A View of the Hermitage in the Royal Garden at Richmond*, after J. Gravelot, *c.*1730s. Queen Caroline's retreat, which contained a library and a room with a bed.

uncertain, although the name suggests it was at least partly made of tree roots and gnarled branches.[39] Anson's letter which refers to Jemima's root house as a place for letter-writing was written in her own rustic retreat, her 'Hut, on Banstead Downs'.[40] She describes the building as a 'little Thatch-roofed Cottage, in an old chalk pit'. It was a short ride on her 'dun mare' from Carshalton House (Surrey), which she and her husband rented for a short period.[41] However, the family association with Carshalton went further back as some of her childhood had been spent there. The hut in the chalk pit and the nearby 'bench on the top of Banstead Down' may have dated from that earlier period as she said in her letter that her brother Philip, Jemima's husband, will 'certainly recollect' them. The garden at Carshalton was relatively small and contained, and the hut and bench (garden features outside the boundary of the garden) demonstrate that such objects could extend the scope of a designed landscape.

As well as being used for letter writing, and probably reading too, the root house, in its secluded glade at Wrest, evoked a mood of fantasy. In August 1749 Marchioness Grey approvingly reported to her husband that the recently finished building was 'very odd and pretty whilst highly suitable to the place'. Its design and construction were entrusted to Thomas Edwards, a family friend. Even the process of its creation had an element of fantasy about it, as the Marchioness described:

The place really was a picturesque scene while they were at work in it. Mr Edwards was seated under an old oak with a table before him covered with plans and compasses, a book in his hands ... a basket hanging upon a bough by him and

a whistle. The use of this last ornament he pretended was
to call the swans to be fed, but altogether he had greatly
the appearance of a magician... The whistle ... the ensign
of power, was fortunately dropped into the canal or carried
off by a swan as soon as the house was finished so that the
charm cannot now be broken and the building we suppose
may stand for ever.[42]

Root houses, rustic seats and hermitages were often sited in
secluded locations, sometimes by running water. They naturally inspired imagination as well as contemplation. William
Shenstone constructed several root houses in secluded spots
next to purling streams at The Leasowes; the form probably
appealed to him for its simplicity and relatively inexpensive
materials.[43] Their primary purpose was as seats at which to rest
and contemplate the setting, their small scale inviting solitude.
However, here, as at Wrest, there was an element of fantasy
about them, as expressed by Shenstone's own poem:

> Here in cool grot and mossy cell,
> We rural fays and faeiries dwell!
> Tho' rarely seen by mortal eye,
> When the pale moon, ascending high,
> Darts thro' yon lines her quiv'ring beams,
> We frisk near these crystal streams.

As the eighteenth century progressed the serious tone of
solitude, study and contemplation, suggested by the root-house
hermitage became less strongly associated with it. While the
structures endured as incidents in the designed landscape
through the period, the building form gradually became di-
vorced from the association with serious, scholarly uses. They

became more fantastical and even a little gimmicky. Some owners populated them with waxworks or automata, while others tried to employ their own real-life hermit to complete the scene. At Painshill (Surrey) Charles Hamilton engaged a hermit for his hermitage on a term of seven years and under a number of strict conditions, including that he was not allowed to talk to the servant who brought his food from the house. The ascetic life must have quickly been too much for him because, according to some stories, Hamilton had to sack him after three weeks when he was discovered in a tavern.[44]

∗∗∗

Some garden buildings were built primarily to house books. Sometimes libraries and studies were combined with other uses, including dining and places to keep animals or birds. Owners were not always concerned about the danger of their books getting damp, which might be expected in buildings that must have been unheated for long periods, if at all. One example where the dampness of the environment did not seem to be a concern is the spectacularly sited Mussenden Temple, perched on a clifftop at Downhill (County Londonderry), which was built for the Earl Bishop (Frederick Hervey). It was modelled on the Temple of Vesta in Italy and dedicated to the memory of Hervey's cousin Frideswide Mussenden, but used as a study. It was certainly unheated. It was described in 1801:

> The Bishop has built a handsome Grecian temple full of valuable but mouldering books, some on shelves and some piled in disorder on the floor. Since no provision was made for heating, it can only be used in the summer months ... on

occasions the wind on the plateau was so strong that servants could get back to the house only on hands and knees.[45]

Sanderson Miller kept at least some of his books in one of his eye-catchers. In the early 1740s he created a small thatched building perched on the top of the scarp of Edgehill above his house, Radway Grange (Warwickshire).[46] Adjacent to the Cottage, in 1749, Miller built his Castle, a tall octagonal tower with mock-ruined walls; the two structures complemented each other and added to the impression of a decaying ancient edifice, especially when viewed from the house and garden below. Initially the Thatched House was used for a variety of purposes such as serving refreshments and for concerts, but after the completion of the Castle the latter took on this role and the Thatched House became more exclusively used for studious pursuits.

Miller had been a scholarly young man and stayed on at Oxford to study Greek, though he also had long had a fascination with English medieval history, which found embodiment in his designs for his own garden buildings and those for his friends.[47] He used his Thatched House as a retreat, a study and appropriate setting for his collection of antiquarian books. Just as Lord Burlington, gentleman-architect of the previous generation, had had a drawing office in one of the upper rooms of the Bagnio at Chiswick in the late 1710s, it is tempting to think that Miller might also have used the Thatched House as a suitable, and perhaps inspiring, setting to draw the designs of some of the Gothic buildings he created. His surviving diaries do record him reading architectural books here; for example, on 3 August 1750 he went 'up the Hill. Read Vitruvius, two hours'.[48] Other entries note fetching books from the Cottage, or returning them there. As well as using the Thatched House himself as a retreat and study, he also allowed his friends to do so.

Although Miller was not as grand and rich as some of his friends, the buildings he used for scholarly pursuits were far more substantial and ambitious than the little garden building in which William Cowper wrote much of his poetry. At his house, Orchard Side, in Olney (Buckinghamshire), where he lived in the 1780s, he had a summerhouse that he described as being the size of a sedan chair (FIGURE 35). It had previously been used as a smoking room by his neighbour, an apothecary, who also kept bottles under a trapdoor in the floor. In summer Cowper would do all his writing here, the door open to the garden with its pinks, roses and honeysuckles. A small window gave a view into the neighbour's orchard. The summerhouse was just large enough for two chairs and a table, perhaps suggesting that it was not always an exclusively solitary retreat.[49]

One garden building for books was not what it seemed. The aptly named Bono Retiro at Hardwick (County Durham) was constructed in the 1750s for John Burdon, whose money had come from coal mines in the north-east. There was an element of the upstart about him and it has been suggested that he created an elegant landscape to demonstrate his taste and gentility, though in this he was far from unique. At Hardwick there was an eclectic collection of buildings strung along a set circuit and the Bono Retiro was particularly intriguing, especially as not all visitors were allowed in. It was innocuously described in 1803: 'Near the side of the canal is a building called the Library.'[50] Here, despite the moist atmosphere from the canal

FIGURE 35 William Cowper's Summerhouse at Olney in its garden setting with a view of the neighbouring orchard and distant church spire, from *Cowper Illustrated*, by Storer and Greig, 1803.

there was no fear of the books mouldering as they were, in fact, fake. Another author who was clearly better informed wrote: 'Between the windows are book-cases, containing to appearance many elegant books, the works of our most esteemed authors, being a deception of the nicest kind, as they are only of painted wood, but so exquisitely finished, as scarcely to be distinguished from real ones... The windows are all adorned with painted glass, added to which, the situation gives it a sombre shade, peculiarly grateful in a building dedicated to retirement.'[51] What this author did not mention however, was that the stained glass windows had a rather risqué element to them. They were said to display 'The likeness of things so foul to behold / That what they are is not fit to be told', and no visitor seems to have reported the exact nature.[52] So it appears the whole building was a giant joke, perhaps as the expense of those serious, scholarly buildings elsewhere.

⁂

With its height and commanding position, Sanderson Miller's Castle on Edgehill was the perfect place to view the surrounding landscape. There was an element of topographical curiosity about many features in Georgian gardens and parks. Of course views played an important role in the landscape garden for the sake of beauty, but the viewing of vistas was often about more than the appreciation of the composition of a view. Perhaps it is satisfying a natural curiosity and showing a healthy awareness of your environment to be able to gain an extensive view of the surrounding country. In the Georgian period, for young men of a military persuasion, or destined for such a career, an ability to recognise landmarks and assess terrain was an obvious skill to be practised and honed. It might be used in both military strategy and surveying. It is no coincidence that the landscape views of the professional artist Paul Sandby and of the amateur Coplestone Warre Bampfylde are so accurate and full of detail, as they both trained in military draughts-manship.[53] This curiosity to understand topography was also connected to massive cartographic advances in this period, and the Ordnance Survey, established to accurately map the country for strategic reasons, was born in the last decades of the eighteenth century.[54] The desire to view the landscape – both within the physical boundary of the design and beyond – was catered for with the building of belvederes. Such structures had long been known in gardens, and both the standings of the Tudor hunt and roof-top banqueting houses partially performed the same function. As with so many other types of garden building, structures built as belvederes did not always go by that title; some had generic names, others specific to the place or perhaps to other functions the building also had. But they appeared in many gardens and might be simple viewing platforms or more ambitious buildings, like the monumental one at Claremont (Surrey), for example, which was designed by Sir John Vanbrugh. Set on a hill, the central block was on two storeys, but it was flanked by four corner towers of three storeys, with a roof-top viewing platform, and was used also for banqueting and gambling.

Two pieces of equipment with which view the landscape were used by Miller at his Castle: a camera obscura and a telescope. In his diary he recorded on numerous occasions using his camera obscura to see the prospect from the top of the hill.[55] The camera obscura was a very popular instrument used by owners, artists and visitors to Georgian parks and gardens. The optical principles had been known since ancient times, but in the eighteenth century, with the addition of a lens and a mirror, they were utilised as a tool for accurately sketching views and also used for composing and focusing vistas (FIGURE 36). Portable versions were a bit larger than a shoe box and

FIGURE 36   A detail from *Roslin Castle, Midlothian*, by Paul Sandby, *c*.1780.
The lady standing is using a camera obscura to sketch the picturesque landscape.

of roughly the same proportions, though some models folded
down to be disguised as books. Henrietta Luxborough used a
small one, possibly of the book type.[56] At Mount Edgcumbe in
1750 there was one on a much larger scale, made in 'a centry
box, which shuts up' so viewers stood inside it. It was moved
around the landscape and visitors of quality were invited to
use it to view the 'prospects'.[57]

It seems likely that Miller also had a telescope. The telescope
had been invented in the Netherlands early in the seventeenth
century; it was then developed in Italy by Galileo.[58] In 1668, Sir
Isaac Newton designed an improved reflecting telescope, and
there were further significant developments and refinements in

the first few decades of the eighteenth century.[59] The refinement and availability of the telescope, for those with the funds to purchase one, made it a popular prop and diversion for quiet afternoon pursuits in the designed landscape, where there were often already buildings that lent themselves to the use of such devices for viewing the scenery (FIGURE 37). An engraving of the Castle at Edgehill, published in 1767, shows two figures right on the edge of the scarp, viewing the landscape with a telescope (FIGURE 38). While staying with the Lyttletons in August 1750, for whom he had designed another (seemingly ruined) castle at Hagley (Worcestershire), Miller recorded in his diary: 'Seeing the prospects from the Castle with telescope.'[60]

FIGURE 37   *A View of Foots-Cray Place in Kent, the Seat of Bourchier Cleeve Esq.r,* by Woollett, *c.*1760. The group of ladies and gentlemen on the left is viewing the landscape through a telescope, while the gentleman on the right is holding musical instruments and sheet music.

FIGURE 38   Sanderson Miller's Castle at Edgehill, from *Edge-Hill or the Rural Prospect Delineated and Moralized*, by Richard Jago, 1767. On the far right a gentleman views the landscape through a telescope. It is significant that the artist has illustrated important landmarks such as the windmill and church towers in the distance.

Hill House on Cain Hill at Wrest Park was a structure that might have been considered a belvedere. The large pavilion was located in the park to the east of the house. It was built in the 1710s during the formal phase of landscaping carried out by the Duke of Kent, Jemima Grey's grandfather, from whom she inherited the estate. In plan, Hill House was made up of an octagonal central pavilion with four projecting wings. This, combined with its two-storey structure and hill-top location, must have ensured panoramic views across the surrounding landscape. It was an extensive building with a 'great room' on each floor, two staircases and a number of 'closets'. The rooms were well furnished with tables, chairs and couches. Looking glasses and portraits hung on the walls. Other items that were noted in the inventory of 1740, and seem to have been distributed widely across the rooms in the building, are many maps and topographical prints, of both British and foreign locations, suggesting intellectual curiosity on the subject of geography.[61] While Bedfordshire is not a county of dramatic topography, the building was set on the highest point of the park, and though it is not possible to say with certainty that Hill House was ever used as an observatory, the same inventory does list a 'long square telescope' in the Archer Pavilion in the gardens, a far less logical place to keep it. The Shepherd's Lodge at Enville is a later parallel of the Hill House at Wrest, though here the views are more spectacular and long-ranging. One room was decorated with topographical prints of houses, gardens and landscapes, like Hill House, suggesting an interest in geography and topography and perhaps alluding to the building's use as a viewing place. In 1803 it was described as being 'fitted up as a lounging room and observatory'.[62]

The presence of a telescope at Wrest at this date is not surprising considering the family's connection with Thomas Wright, 'the Wizard of Durham'. As well as being a designer of garden buildings Wright was an amateur astronomer of some note; he was the first person to describe the Milky Way. He was connected to Wrest for over a decade from the time he was introduced to the Duke and Duchess of Kent by the cartographer John Senex in 1736.[63] Wright was resident at Wrest for a considerable period of each year, during which time he taught geometry and surveying to the ladies of the house, at that date Sophia Bentinck (the Duke's second wife), Mary Grey (the Duke's youngest daughter by his first wife) and Jemima, later Marchioness Grey (the Duke's grand-daughter). This gives an idea of the intellectual atmosphere in which Jemima

FIGURE 39   A design for a temple at Chartley, Staffordshire, by William Thomas, *c*.1760s. It was to contain a music room, billiard room, kitchen, dining room, hot and cold baths, study and the roof to be used as an observatory.

grew up and shows how well educated the ladies of the Wrest household were. Given Wright's reputation, and the presence of a telescope at Wrest, it is likely that he also taught them astronomy, and Hill House at the highest point in the park would have been a logical place in which to do it.[64]

Another amateur astronomer of some note was Washington Shirley, 5th Earl Ferrers.[65] Ferrers was elected a fellow of the Royal Society in 1761 for his observations on the transit of Venus. He had inherited his estates and title from his elder brother, the 4th Earl, who, after murdering his steward, was the last English peer to be hanged. He was quite possibly insane.

Washington Shirley's coolness and rationality, as expressed in the design for a temple to be sited at his second estate at Chartley Hall (Staffordshire), contrasts with the chaotic, debauched character of his brother.[66] The projected temple of two floors, with a semi-basement, topped by a cupola, with viewing platform, was to be dedicated to 'the Deities that preside over Learning, Music and Oratory' (FIGURE 39). The basement was to contain both a cold bath and a hot bath with changing rooms; the ground floor a refectory, billiard room and music room; and the second floor a study, a room 'for repose' and a 'room for holding mathematical instruments'. The top of the roof would have been used as the observatory.[67] With the serving of food here, the semi-basement is likely to have contained a kitchen. It was probably the scale of such a grand plan that made it unviable as a proposition.[68] Had the building been constructed it would have had parallels with the Royal Observatory in the Old Deer Park at Richmond, built in 1769 for King George III to observe the transit of Venus.[69] Though in style and setting it has similarities with other garden buildings, it is too large to be considered as such.

⁓ᴈᴋ⁓

The pioneering naturalist Gilbert White created his own garden at The Wakes in Selborne (Hampshire). He combined an enthusiasm for hands-on gardening and inventive landscape design with an Enlightenment spirit of enquiry in his close observation of the world around him. In this he is symbolic of his age and the embodiment of interests that were also reflected in many designed landscapes. As well as great collectors of art

and archaeological artefacts, the Georgian period produced collectors of botanical and zoological specimens, and many people
had eclectic interests covering a range of these disciplines. In
the Georgian garden diverse collections of flora and fauna could
be seen alongside architecture that purported to be typical of
buildings from the four corners of the world. Structures and
specific areas of designed landscapes were created to house
these curiosities, as places to study them and as places to be
amazed and amused by them.

Scientific study and classification were in their infancy,
and, with zoological collections particularly, there was still an
element of the seventeenth-century 'cabinet of curiosity' about
them. The most famous of these was gathered in the first half
of the seventeenth century by the Tradescants and exhibited
in the Ashmolean Museum, opened in Oxford in 1683. The
collection, typical in its range but rare in its survival, can
still be seen in the museum; it included, alongside its genuine zoological and geological items, a 'squirrel like a fish', a
'very natural wax hand under glass' and 'many Turkish and
other foreign shoes'.[70] Although the animals making up private
zoological collections housed in Georgian parks and gardens
were often an eclectic mix, this was frequently due to high
mortality rates, partly due to long journeys in less than ideal
conditions and haphazard sourcing. The number of menageries in Georgian designed landscapes that were combined with
rooms for books suggests a definite spirit of scientific enquiry
beyond the cabinet-of-curiosities phenomenon. Sir John Griffin
Griffin's Gothic Menagerie at Audley End (Essex), built in 1774,
had a kitchen, tea room and 'keeping room'. This last either

housed the smaller songbirds in the collection, or provided a room for the keeper.[71] Outside, in an enclosure, larger birds, including gold and silver pheasants, 'exotic fowl' and 'curious pigeons', were kept. An inventory of 1797 notes that along with equipment and furniture necessary for tea making and drinking, the Tea Room also contained a writing case and a number of books, including 'Catesby Carolina ... Complete Grazier, Natural History of Songs of Birds', suggesting the room was a location for relevant and related studies.[72]

The menageries that appeared in many Georgian gardens were associated with some of the prettiest and most ambitious buildings, both executed and unexecuted. As Sally Festing has observed, the term 'menagerie' in relation to the Georgian designed landscape encompassed a number of things; it could mean the collection of animals themselves, the building or area in which they were housed or an associated garden building, and, to add to the confusion, was often used in the sense that 'aviary' would be used today.[73] Menageries in such settings had been known before; the collection of Henry I, initially housed in Woodstock Park (Oxfordshire, across the lake from Blenheim Palace) and later moved to the Tower of London, being the most famous. By the mid-eighteenth century collections of animals were assembled against the backdrop of the development of the scientific classification of species pioneered by Carl Linnaeus. While botanical collections tended not to be associated with the architecture of leisure in the same way as zoological collections, it is likely that – in part at least – the same motivations were working upon landowners who developed menageries as upon those who cultivated collections of exotic plants, and there are many examples of people who were interested in both.

Where there were exotic plants and animals, it was not unusual to find exotic buildings alongside them. The 2nd Duke of Richmond (father to Sarah Lennox, whom we have already met haymaking, and to Louisa Conolly, writing in her cottage) was a collector who brought together flora and fauna on his estate at Goodwood (West Sussex), where they could be seen alongside a wide variety of architecture, supposedly in the style of several different countries. In 1747 Lady Newdigate reported on the varied array of buildings: a Chinese tent, a Gothic tomb, the Stone Dell (also known as the Catacombs) and a 'Lapland House', as well as 'two or three other odd ... buildings'. She also mentioned that 'in ye woods is a building for Macaws wch fly about and add infinitely to the beauty of them'.[74] The Duke planted, among other things, magnolias and cedars of Lebanon, now the staples of the country house landscape, but then amazing curiosities. His desire to have the latest introductions is illustrated by a letter to Collinson: 'The small magnolias are confounded dear butt I must have them.' Lady Newdigate reported that 'the garden is enriched with abundance of curious shrubs and plants particularly ye Magnolia'. A handful of the Duke's extensive planting of cedars survived the 1987 storm and can still be seen at Goodwood.

Though the magnolias were expensive to purchase, the upkeep of the animals was more costly; huge quantities of meat were bought for the carnivores, and bread and grain for the birds. The first reference to the collection was a payment for a coat for the Duke's monkey in 1726. Over the next twenty years it grew and at various times included wolves, lions, tigers, bears, monkeys and racoons, as well as eagles, vultures and owls.[75] An enclosed area of the park was set aside for the menagerie about half a mile's walk from the house. However, it appears that, at times, some of the animals were displayed in tunnels known as the Catacombs, within the Rock Dell, slightly closer to the house. The Dell was ornamented with hermitages, other forms of rustic architecture and fragments of buildings. The ends of the tunnels opened to the Dell. The iron bars across the openings suggest that part of the interest and amusement of the atmosphere created by the space was the frisson of danger given by the appearance of a tiger, or perhaps

FIGURE 40   *Perspective View of the Menagerie and its Pavilion*, after Thomas Sandby, c.1760s. William Chambers' Chinese temple, or ting, sits in the middle of a pool filled with goldfish and surrounded by cages for the animals.

a wolf or a bear. Whether that experience was especially saved for guests is not known, but the menagerie was open to view by tourists, who often came in droves. Despite the thrill of the sight of a savage beast and the eclecticism of the animals and plants, the Duke had a library of the latest texts on discoveries in the natural world, which suggests that his collecting was based on a spirit of scientific enquiry.[76]

A slightly later example of the gathering together of exotic plants, animals and buildings was the garden developed in the 1750s and 1760s by Princess Augusta at Kew. In 1762, Count Kielmansegge described it:

> The house is not large, nor is the garden, in comparison with others, but there is much to see in it in the way of summer-houses, some of which are being built… In these gardens are also fine hothouses and orangeries; an enclosure of wooden lattice-work for pheasants and other rare birds; a large aviary; a temple dedicated to the Sun, after the plans of the ruins of the temple in Baalbec; a Turkish mosque; a Moorish temple; a Chinese pagoda.[77]

Here, alongside the physic and exotic gardens, there was both an aviary and a menagerie, an oval-shaped enclosure surrounded by cages with a Chinese ting in the middle of a central pond (FIGURE 40).[78] The menagerie mainly consisted of birds, but there were also kangaroos, antelopes, 'Algiers cows' and a peccary.[79] The most famous of Augusta's eclectic, exotic buildings at Kew, the 50-metre-high Pagoda, was completed in 1762, and still stands like a beacon over the gardens today.

At Horton (Northamptonshire) the Earl of Halifax built an elegant eye-catcher known as the Menagerie in the late

1750s. It was designed by Thomas Wright (who had taught astronomy to the Duke of Kent's family at Wrest). The building was one of a string of incidents on a circuit drive, and is the best surviving of them, most of the others now being lost.[80] But the building's significance was far greater than that of a mere visual punctuation mark. It was the focal point of Lord Halifax's menagerie, which was housed in a circular enclosure of about 2 acres behind the building. Here he kept a collection of exotic animals, including storks, racoons, eagles, warthogs 'with navels on their backs' (an echo of Tradescant's 'squirrel like a fish'?), a pair of tigers, two 'uncommon martins', 'does

FIGURE 41   *The Menagerie at Woburn* from Humphry Repton's Red Book. It was really more of an aviary.

from Guadaloupe', an ermine and goldfish.[81] As with other such tripartite buildings, the central pavilion contained one grand room, in this case of fairly substantial proportions. On either side it was flanked by screen walls ending in two smaller pavilions.[82] The salon was used for refreshments when visitors went to see the curious creatures. The elaborate plasterwork of the interior has themes that include the passing of time and the fauna of the four continents. A further suggestive element are the festoons of musical instruments, including a violin, a side drum and a French horn, so it would not be surprising if music was played here too. The undercroft of the Menagerie is extensive; it was the original location of the kitchen.

The 6th Duke of Bedford also filled his park at Woburn with rare plants, exotic buildings and unusual birds. A comparison between his interests and those of the 2nd Duke of Richmond illustrate how the spirit of scientific enquiry had evolved over the course of 80 years or so.[83] Humphry Repton's proposals for Woburn included stoves for tender plants and a Menagerie, which, like that at Audley End, was mainly populated with birds (FIGURE 41). The area covered about 2 acres and was described in 1833 as consisting of

> numerous wired compartments ... surrounded with a
> high wire rustic fence ... against which ... are clumps of
> evergreen shrubs, for affording shelter to the pheasants,
> &c. The lower part of the centre, or octagonal building, is
> devoted to a collection of Canaries, and other small birds...
> The upper half of the building consists of a very complete
> Pigeon-house, which is occupied by a numerous collection of
> the most curious varieties of these birds.[84]

FIGURE 42 *Feeding the Ducklings*, by Thomas Rowlandson, undated. A lady attends to her new fowl. The garden setting is clear with ornamental bridge and greenhouse in the background.

As well as affording the pleasure and novelty of visiting and sometimes feeding the animals, aviaries and menageries were probably included in the designed landscape because their inhabitants lent animation to the scene, and also because birdsong was associated with the soothing effects of nature. Although there was certainly a masculine spirit of intellectual enquiry about some menageries, especially those that included larger animals and apex predators, the more common collections of fauna that had a greater emphasis on birds with occasional small mammals were very frequently a feminine domain. Although

FIGURE 43   *The Vinery*, by Thomas Rowlandson, undated. In inclement weather a glass house could be a sociable place as well as one of botanical curiosities.

Lady Coventry's menagerie at Croome included a flying squirrel and 'two American deer', it consisted mainly of birds. A keeper was employed, but she supervised the upkeep herself. He had accommodation attached to the menagerie and there was also a room for taking tea. Lower down the social scale, for middle-class ladies, their poultry collection might include a few birds with ornamental qualities (FIGURE 42). The rearing of fowl was a traditional duty of the mistress of the house, so equally the aviaries in the Georgian garden are a logical, though luxurious, extension to this idea.

Botanical collections seem to have been less closely associated with leisure activities, such as dining or taking tea, than zoological collections were. This may have been because plants were already an intrinsic part of a garden and often collections of exotics were distributed around the pleasure ground rather than in one specific place. They would be viewed, enjoyed and discussed as part of the circuit walk. Princess Augusta had a one-acre physic garden at Kew in which plants were arranged in long rows according to the Linnaean system. This was just one part of her collection, which by 1768, when the first catalogue was published, numbered 3,400 species.[85]

The kitchen garden might also be visited as part of the circuit walk round the pleasure ground or drive through the park (FIGURE 43). While Brown is often accused of banishing them to far-flung corners of the estate, this was not always true, and those that were removed were also connected by the network of drives, so they too became a destination. As Beckford suggested in his parody of the entertainments a host would lay on for a house party, which included taking in the 'Kitchen or Flower gardens, Alms-houses or Pigeon-houses, Farms, Temples or Plantations'. At Wardour Castle there were two kitchen gardens. That near the old castle was used as a nursery and to grow less glamorous, more utilitarian crops.[86] The kitchen garden closer to the mansion was connected with the walks of the pleasure ground by several paths and gateways. It was more ornamental, with an elegant glasshouse as its central feature. This was flanked by pineries built to provide the tricky conditions in which to grow one of the most sought-after items of produce in the kitchen garden – the pineapple. In his Red Book for Woburn, Repton showed visitors admiring the stoves in the kitchen garden in winter, with snow on the

FIGURE 44 *The Forcing Garden at Woburn* as proposed by Humphry Repton in his Red Book, 1805. The elegantly dressed ladies walk through the snow to see what of interest there is in the hothouses with their welcoming warmth.

ground. This must have helped to emphasise how, at that time of year, the warmth and promise of exotic fruit, as well as the element of curiosity about it (especially when there were so few plants to admire outside), would have made the kitchen garden and its various glasshouses an even more desirable stop on the tour of the grounds (FIGURE 44).

❧

The hours many Georgians of the upper classes kept – up all night at the gaming tables; then, if they had responsibilities, rising early to deal with business, or perhaps to hunt – might mean that somewhere quiet to which to retreat for an afternoon nap was desirable. The number of garden buildings that were furnished with beds and bedding testifies to this. Such structures, again, provided a place to escape the busy country house. The prevalence of beds in secluded buildings must have led to temptation, though references to sexual liaisons in pleasure grounds are not specifically related to any known examples, suggesting that a quiet place to sleep might be the primary reason, at least, for their provision. However, that is not to say that amorous liaisons did not take place in gardens, as we shall see (FIGURE 45).

The provision of beds in garden buildings is well documented in descriptions, architectural plans and inventories of contents. For example, the Banqueting House at Drayton (Northamptonshire) had several rooms, one of which was designated as a 'Bed chamber'. It contained a 'Chince bed ... lined with a flowred indian Silk' by 1724, which was still in use in 1779. There was also a 'couch with a white satin cushion and 2 pillows of the same'.[87] An inventory of the Garden House at Southill (Bedfordshire) taken in 1779 illustrates that as well as a bedstead, there were blankets, pillows, a feather bed and a quilt.[88] Other buildings with the provision of a place to lie down in comfort included John Burdon's Banqueting House at Hardwick, which was described as a 'neat retiring apartment'. The Duke of Cumberland's Chinese Pavilion at Virginia Water had a bedroom with an exotic-sounding 'Turkish Sofa'. Plans of both Lord Burlington's Bagnio at Chiswick and Alexander Pope's Grotto at Twickenham also imply the provision of a bed.[89]

At Stowe one of the early garden buildings was explicitly named the Sleeping Parlour. Built in 1725, it was set in the middle of a wilderness known as the Sleeping Wood and reached down winding paths through thick vegetation. It was

FIGURE 45   A detail from *The Seat near the Terrace, with a View of the Adjacent Country to the North-east*, by Paul Sandby, *c.* 1765. The couple animate what is essentially a topographical picture of the Windsor landscape, but Sandby's figures are always well observed and a secluded seat would have been a perfect place for an amorous liaison, though the lady's raised hand suggests she is guarding her virtue.

a fairly simple brick structure, probably consisting of merely one room. The building had creepers growing up its walls, which would have covered the bricks and must have helped it to recede into the verdure of its setting, so as one arrived in the clearing the portico seemed to grow out of the vegetation, rather like later hermitages and moss houses. This accords well with the description of the building found in Gilbert West's poem *Stowe* (1732), which takes the reader on a tour of the gardens. It evokes all the qualities and associations of retreat and rest in the garden: birdsong, water, seclusion, relaxation and escape from the pressures of the worldly life.

However, there is something a little risqué in the inscription above the door that translated as: 'Since all things in Life are Uncertain, Indulge thyself'.[90] Estate accounts give information about the furnishing of the building, and consequently clues suggesting that its primary use was the one to which its title

alluded. In 1750 a payment was made for 'altering the Cush-
eon for the couch in the sleeping Parlour'. There were other
payments for mending leather pillows.[91] So it seems that, at
least by that date, the user of the building was able to lie on
a couch if there was not actually a bed. Lord Cobham, who
had something of a reputation as a philanderer, had died the
previous year, so perhaps a secondary purpose for this temple
of sleep was less relevant by then.[92]

Scandalous goings-on in the garden were even speculated
to have happened at the highest level of society. Princess
Augusta's chief advisor in the development of her botanic
garden at Kew was the Earl of Bute, he who had so carefully
steered the young King George III away from the attractive
aristocratic haymaker Sarah Lennox. Bute also was thought
in many quarters to have too much influence with the young
king, but more particularly with his mother. Perennial gossip-
monger Horace Walpole suggested that Augusta's husband,
Prince Frederick, had encouraged her into Bute's company as
a diversion. When he wanted to be alone with another woman,
'he used to bid the Princess to walk with Lord Bute. As soon
as the Prince was dead, they walked more and more in his
memory.'[93] Given the energies that both Augusta and Bute put
into the improvements of the gardens at Kew, presumably at
least some of their 'walking' was done there. The rumour of
the affair was well known and Bute's political enemies used it
against him. Satirical cartoons also made use of the story, and
one supposed topographical engraving showed a bird's-eye
view of the garden behind the houses on Kew Green with
a secret door and the title 'A View of Lord Bute's Erections

at Kew; with some Part of Kew Green, and Gardens'.[94] The crude double entendre was a reference to the new buildings mushrooming in the gardens, and the Pagoda was clearly the most prominent of them.

The truth of what went on during Princess Augusta and Lord Bute's 'walks' at Kew will never be known, but there is good evidence that a risqué tone was set in a number of gardens, which might either arise from the goings-on there, or even have inspired them. Sexual references were woven into the very fabric of the garden at West Wycombe. Here, when not playing mock sea battles on his lake, Sir Francis Dashwood must have laughed heartily at the wit of his Temple of Venus (see FIGURE 19). It was a rotunda containing a statue of the goddess, a parody of that at Stowe. But at West Wycombe the building was sited on a mount with two curved wing walls either side of an opening below, a very overt reference to female genitalia.[95] Dashwood, with his anything-goes attitude, was famously the founder of the notorious Hellfire Club. Initially the club met at the suitably atmospheric ruins of Medmenham Abbey but latterly transferred its gatherings to West Wycombe Caves. This had started life as a chalk quarry, but Dashwood tunnelled into the hillside to create a network of passages and chambers to provide a variety of spaces for the drinking, dining, dressing up, wenching and practical jokes that characterised their meetings.

At Stowe, the early, western garden contained many buildings associated with love and indeed lust. At the centre of this area was the Rotunda in which was placed a gilded statue of Venus. This area was known as the Garden of Love, both in tribute to the head gardener (conveniently named Mr Love) and for the narrative supplied by the buildings. Close to the Rotunda, situated in a small secluded clearing was Dido's Cave, around which a story was woven that must have been well known to all in Lord Cobham's intimate circle (FIGURE 46). The tale was set down by Cobham's nephew, Gilbert West, in his poetic description of the gardens. As a lengthy aside, he recounts a story involving Conway Rand, Vicar of Stowe.[96] Rand was a colourful character. Tellingly he was the model for the figure of Bacchus in the paintings on the walls of the eponymous temple. While Rand was playing bowls, his interest was excited by a young lady on a swing. He acted swiftly:

Sudden to seize the beauteous Prey he sprung;
Sudden with Shrieks the echoing Thicket rung.
Confounded and abash'd, the frightened Maid,
(While rising Blushes ting'd her Cheeks with red)
Fled swift away, more rapid than the Wind.

West continues by describing how the young lady ran, hoping to lose her pursuer, into a 'thick Covert' that concealed a 'Private Grotto', but 'Alas! too private, for too safely there / The fierce Pursuer seiz'd the helpless Fair.' It was in commemoration of this event that Dido's Cave became known as the Randibus.[97]

This story, together with the interior decoration and furnishing of the Temple of Venus and the suggestive inscription on the Sleeping Parlour, gives an impression of the mood at Stowe under Lord Cobham. Although the Rotunda, built circa 1720, was symbolically dedicated to love, in the early 1730s Cobham

FIGURE 46 Pamela
and Mr. B at the
Summerhouse from
Pamela by Samuel
Richardson, illustrated
by Hubert Gravelot,
1742. When he
accosts Pamela at the
summerhouse, Mr.
B's intentions are
not honourable. The
garden building in
the background of the
illustration from the
novel bears a striking
resemblance to Dido's
Cave at Stowe, where
Conway Rand, the
vicar, caught up with
the 'helpless fair' in
Gilbert West's poem.

added another larger building similarly dedicated, the Temple
of Venus, designed by William Kent. Here, the central pavilion
is formed by one large room. It has two doors, one to enter
from the main body of the gardens and another which opened
into a private garden behind the building. The room is lit by
a pair of windows which flank the rear door but the entrance
front is blind, so no one in the main gardens could see in. Both
this and the secluded garden behind indicate a building where

privacy was an important factor. The room was originally decorated by murals depicting scenes from the tale of Hellenore and Malbecco from Edmund Spenser's *The Faerie Queene*, a tale of a young wife rejecting her older husband for other pleasures with a company of satyrs. All that is known of the furnishings of the room is that there were a pair of sofas, or, as Reverend William Gilpin described them, 'luxurious couches'. Gilpin was disapproving of the tone of the room, commenting in this *Dialogue* that 'this Place is adorned with everything capable of suggesting the loosest Ideas.' His companion was 'not a little moved with Indignation at it', saying 'A Man had need ... of some Philosophy here. This wanton Story, these luxurious Couches and the Embellishments round the Roof, give the Place quite a Cyprian Air – Come, let us leave it.'[98]

The story of an illicit liaison is woven into the fabric of the detached pleasure ground at Stancombe Park (Gloucestershire). Situated in a hidden valley, narrow labyrinthine paths wind on a circuitous course, leading through dark, keyhole-shaped openings to eventually reach the shore of the lake (FIGURE 47). From here it would have been a short row across the water to the Doric Temple, said to have been a trysting place for Bransbury Purnell, who built the garden in the 1810s. The layout was a means of evading his wife, who was too obese to navigate the narrow paths. At the temple he apparently met his lover, said in some versions of the story to be a beautiful gypsy.[99] The tale is unsubstantiated by documentary evidence, but the well-preserved structure of the garden, the Temple and what we know of the use of garden buildings elsewhere suggest that there may be an element of truth to the story.

FIGURE 47   The narrow, sunken paths and keyhole shaped tunnel entrances set the scene for the labyrinthine way to the temple across the lake at Stancombe Park, Gloucestershire.

Although the use of the gardens at Stancombe for amorous liaisons is conjectural, it is harder to refute legal evidence for sexual encounters in gardens. Several cases are documented in which the garden and its buildings took a central role in the events. One case took place at Petton Hall (Shropshire) in the 1770s and led to the divorce of Edward and Hannah Corbet.[100] In the legal proceedings it was stated that Edward Corbet repeatedly met the dairymaid Anne Roberts in his summer house. James Howell, a groom, cited numerous occasions when he had witnessed the couple entering the summer house separately, but on one occasion through the window he witnessed an embrace, before the couple lay down on the floor, not to be seen again for four or five minutes. In neighbouring Herefordshire in 1784, the garden at Stoke Edith was the scene of at least one encounter between Lady Ann Foley and the Earl of Peterborough. They were witnessed in an intimate embrace in the shrubbery near the grotto by an estate worker on his way home. Other witnesses testified to encounters in a carriage near isolated gates to the park. Edward Foley was granted his divorce.[101]

Stockeld Park (Yorkshire) was the scene of an adulterous affair between the lady of the house and her groom.[102] So acrimonious was the divorce case that a wealth of evidence from a range of witnesses, from servants to architects, was compiled that gives an amazingly thorough insight into life in a minor country house in the 1790s. Clara Louisa Middleton was in her thirties and bored by family life after giving her husband eight children in ten years. Her groom, John Rose, was young and handsome with, it seems, a good deal of natural charm so far as women were concerned. The landscape played a central role in the proceedings, with both the shrubbery and the Bathing Well, a pool used by the family for swimming, playing host to their alleged liaisons.

The Bathing Well was surrounded by a high wall, into which was built a changing room. Such buildings, constructed to accompany pools and baths, were often well appointed and could be comfortable rooms. The building does not survive and the case does not relate whether this one was large enough to hold a bed, as some were. The Bathing Well was about a quarter of a mile from the house; Clara Louisa and Rose were witnessed meeting there and disappearing inside the changing room on at least two occasions. On the latter occasion they were challenged by another servant, who had been watching their movements. Other witnesses recounted how Clara Louisa would take walks at night in the shrubbery near the house in winter, where it was presumed she also met Rose. Her maid noted that she returned with a wet and muddy dress. At first

William Middleton did not believe the tales of his wife's infidelity, but when he was finally overwhelmed by the weight of the evidence against her, he became bitter and vengeful. She was banished from the house, separated from her children, including her nine-month-old baby. William had her favourite horse and her dog killed and he shut up the house, never to return. The Corbet, Foley and Middleton cases prove that the seclusion of the garden building was tempting for would-be lovers, but also how little privacy there really was on the country estate.

※

Many Georgian children, like their parents, would have been duty-bound in the morning, unless it were a special occasion or they were given a holiday. Girls particularly might be at lessons, as they were more likely to be educated at home by a governess, while many boys would be sent to school. Boys would, however, be home for holidays, especially those in the summer, when there were ample opportunities for afternoon romps in the garden. The writings of Rousseau were influential on many parents' ideas about raising their offspring. He encouraged gardening and other constructive, physical outdoor tasks such as haymaking, but there were paradoxes too within his writings and many parents were selective in their use of his ideas for the education of their children, still combining ample reading, which Rousseau did not encourage with his back-to-nature call. Although the Duchess of Leinster (Emily, another of the Lennox sisters) failed to persuade the philosopher himself to become her children's tutor, she determined to put many of his ideas into practice and she bought a bathing lodge on the

FIGURE 48 *The Blunt Children*, by Johan Zoffany, *c.*1768–70. These are two little boys, not yet out of petticoats. They are portrayed happily haymaking as the children of the Duke and Duchess of Leinster did at their seaside villa-school at Blackrock, near Dublin, at around the same time as this picture was painted.

Irish coast, south of Dublin, as the perfect place to educate her children in the late 1760s and early 1770s. Here her large brood swam in the sea before breakfast, did their lessons until dinner time, then in the afternoon played croquet or bowls and dug in the garden. The house had its own hay meadows and the children became proficient haymakers (FIGURE 48).[103] It was in line with Rousseau's ideas that the children of the 2nd Earl of Ilchester were all encouraged to garden as children in the 1780s and 1790s. The Ilchester children cultivated flowers, and vegetables too; in the late 1790s Louisa Fox-Strangways, then around ten or eleven years old, wrote to her older sister:

'my garden is the prettiest place in nature. We shall have of our own planting today for dinner, onions, carrots, turnips, lettuce and potatoes.'[104]

In the summers of the early 1790s, Jemima Grey played host to her three young Robinson grandsons at Wrest. All the boys had recently started boarding school (the eldest at a different establishment to the younger two). With three boys – Philip aged seven, Fredrick eight and Thomas nine – she sensibly made much use of her garden, getting them outside and finding interesting amusements for them (FIGURE 49). After their arrival in August 1790, their mother Mary Robinson reported: 'the brothers were glad to meet, & there was a great increase of noise & racket in the evening partly occasioned by producing a tent, kept for [Thomas's] arrival, & which was set upon the Parterre.'[105] Thomas later wrote himself to his Uncle Fritz:

> We are all very well; Grandmama has bought each of us
> a fishing rod & we go to that sport every fine day. We get
> up in the morning about half an hour after six. We have
> got a new tent which we set in every day when it is fine.
> Grandmama has got a great boat which we saw launched on
> Monday.

They clearly had a fine time at Wrest. On his return to school in mid-September Thomas wrote: 'I was very sorry to leave Grandmama and Wrest.'[106] The following summer, he reported to his uncle again:

> Mama told me to write to you to day & to tell you that
> we make ourselves dirty little Pigs by digging a Pond and
> she has ordered each of us a pair of Trousers to keep our

FIGURE 49 *Three Sons of John, 3rd Earl of Bute*, by Johan Zoffany, *c.*1763–4. The artist portrays his subjects engaged in the typically boyish activities of climbing trees, raiding birds' nests and practising their archery, in echoes of the pastimes of the Robinson boys at Wrest over a generation later.

breeches clean. I have some hopes of a horse ... we fish
almost every day & I expect two targets to shoot at with a
Bow & arrows. We have some fireworks to let off tomorrow
night.[107]

Wise Jemima.

Thomas Robinson did not mention bowling as one of the
diversions of his summer holidays at Wrest, but the garden was
equipped with a bowling green, and with the bowling green
house where tea had been taken when Jemima was a girl and
had friends staying at Wrest during the summer.[108] Bowling
had been popular for over 200 years. The national obsession
was so strong in 1541 that the state feared people were playing
bowls rather than practising archery, and a law was passed
allowing bowling greens only in private gardens. In the later
seventeenth and early eighteenth centuries there was hardly a
garden of the gentry class or above that did not have one, and
a neat rectangle of perfectly level grass fitted seamlessly with
the aesthetic of the formal, geometric garden. By the second
half of the eighteenth century that style was in decline and so
were bowling greens. It was while playing bowls at Stowe that
the Reverend Rand's interest was excited by the young lady
on the swing, but by Earl Temple's period the alteration of the
garden meant that it was not one of the diversions he mentions
for his summer guests. Though she may not have been able to
enjoy it at Stowe, it was one of the diversions that Lady Mary
Coke enjoyed during several visits to Park Place (Oxfordshire).
In July 1768 she wrote to her sister: 'After taking a very long
walk, we play'd Bowls, 'tis a great while since I play'd, yet

I think they agreed I was one of the best of the Party.' The family at Park Place may have been particularly fond of the game, and were perhaps rather old-fashioned, because this is a very late reference; the popularity of the game appears to have dwindled in the second half of the century.[109]

As the aesthetic of the designed landscape evolved, from formal to the naturalistic of Brown and his followers, those perfectly level parterres and the fine turf of bowling greens close to the house were easily adapted for another sport, one that was entirely suitable for these more relaxed spaces – cricket.[110] Emily Lennox's father, the 2nd Duke of Richmond, did much to popularise the game of cricket in England, and it was a sport which the Robinson boys played enthusiastically at school, perhaps practising their batting at Wrest in the holidays. Many a mid-eighteenth-century landscape, even today, is home to a cricket pitch, including the Duke of Richmond's Goodwood. During Queen Charlotte's final fête at Frogmore House in Windsor Great Park in July 1817, boys from Eton School played cricket.[111] In his Red Book for Ashridge in Hertfordshire (1813), Humphry Repton suggested the construction of a cricket pitch.[112]

Quoits was a popular outdoor game, often played at inns and on village greens; it was an appropriate amusement for children and also suitable for the levelled ground of the garden close to the house. In July 1759, Caroline Fox wrote from Holland House to her sister Emily, Duchess of Leinster: 'I am sitting in the pretty porch by the hall door in one of the niches ... seeing our four dear boys play at quoits upon the green before the house.'[113] Another game played both inside and outside in the Georgian garden was battledore and shuttlecock; many Georgian children were painted holding shuttlecocks in portraits. It was not yet the competitive sport of badminton that it became, rather a cooperative game, the object of which was for two or more players to keep the shuttlecock in the air as long as possible. Jane Austen played with her nephew William at Godmersham, but did not recount whether they did so outside.[114] As with shuttlecocks, kites and swings often feature in portraits of Georgian children that are set outside in the garden.

As we have already seen, archery was one of the amusements for the Robinson boys during their summers at Wrest in the early 1790s. From the late 1770s there was a tremendous revival of interest in archery, popularised by Sir Ashton Lever. Clubs were set up around the country.[115] Fanny Burney, who had gone to visit Lever's museum at his house, Arklington Hall (Lancashire), described with wry amusement how he and two younger men dressed in green with round hats trimmed with feathers 'pranced about' and 'kept running to and fro in the garden carefully contriving to shoot at some mark, just as any of the company appeared at any of the windows'.[116] Like fishing, it was a skill and amusement for women and girls as well as men and boys. For ladies it was another excuse to get outside into the fresh air, and the necessary stance demonstrated their good posture, as well as drawing attention to a fine figure (FIGURE 50). Consequently archery clubs became opportunities for flirtations and romance. They often met in designed landscapes, for competitions and highly social dinners, usually held in tents. Against this background, the allusion to archery

FIGURE 50   *Archery shooting at Hatfield House*, by Thomas Rowlandson, 1790.
The ladies are showing off their good posture and fine figures.

as a pastime in Zoffany's group portrait of the sons of the
Earl of Bute in the park at Luton Hoo in the mid-1760s looks
remarkably ahead of its time.

Evidence of Lord Aylesford's passion for the sport was
scattered throughout the park laid out by Brown in the 1750s
at Great Packington (Warwickshire). In 1789 John Byng described how 'the Park is dotted by low stone pillars which are
the roving butts that Lord Aylesford shoots at, a sport of which
he is furiously fond, a most capital performance – perhaps the
best archer in the Kingdom.' Aylesford, who founded the club
the Woodmen of Arden (with its historicist allusions to Shakespeare and the England of Good Queen Bess), constructed an
octagonal building on the edge of the park for their meetings.
Byng continues: 'The place of archery has lately been enclosed,
turf'd, and planted by Lord A in the stile of an extended

bowling-green; and there is a rustic building erected by the club, for their meetings, dinners, &c— which are furnished by the inn.' Byng was invited to join the party. He described the food served as 'cold victuals'. After dinner, the archers returned 'to their butts' and he toured the park, which did not much impress him, returning later when a tea was served at the rustic building, with 'Lady A presiding'.[117] Here, with the serving of the main meal of the day in the late afternoon, we move on to the next phase of the day: from dinner time to dusk.

FIVE

Evening

Food — Drink — Music

July 28 – Drank tea twenty of us at the Hermitage; the
Miss Batties and the Mulso family contributed much
to our pleasure by their singing and being dressed as
shepherds and shepherdesses. It was a most elegant
evening; and all parties appeared highly satisfied. The
Hermit appeared to great advantage.

GILBERT WHITE, 'Garden Kalendar'[1]

IN THE SUMMER of 1763 three young ladies left London
for a holiday in the country. They were heading into deepest Hampshire, to the 'happy valley' in which the village of
Selborne was nestled, under the looming hill of the Hanger.
This was the home of the naturalist Gilbert White; then a
remote place, only reached down narrow lanes worn deep into
the landscape by centuries of use, so that the tangled roots of
the trees on their edge were well over head height and the
roads were barely passable in a carriage.[2] Anne, Catherine and
Philadelphia Battie, daughters of a leading London physician,
spent two months staying with their cousin, whose husband was
the vicar of Selborne. Gilbert White, along with his brother

Harry, became master of ceremonies, entertaining the young ladies regularly at his Hermitage up on the Hanger and in the garden below with many a 'sylvan repast', as well as tea, music, poetry, classical role-play and haymaking. Catherine Battie's 'Little Journal of some of the Happiest days I have had in the happy Valley in the year 1763' gives a charming account of how they passed their time and embellishes White's more prosaic record.

While they often spent the whole day together, many of the entertainments took place in the late afternoon, lasting through the evening and sometimes into the night-time. Dinner and tea were central. Through the Georgian period the time that dinner was served became progressively later, so while in the 1720s in high society circles it might be served at three, by the 1820s the hour might be as late as seven or eight. Given the fluidity of times for the serving of the main meal of the day through our period, the focus of this chapter is from dinner time to dusk. It describes how dinner was served in the pleasure ground, along with tea or coffee, and sometimes a separate dessert. It concentrates on the private parties, involving relatively small groups of friends and family, like the Whites and the Batties. While many grand fêtes and public entertainments in the Georgian park and garden started in the afternoon and lasted through the evening and into the night-time, these were so often characterised by their illuminations and so frequently culminated with fireworks, which were necessarily staged after dark, that they follow in the next chapter. Here the contrasting smaller, more intimate entertainment is described.

Beyond the basic activity of taking a walk, eating and drinking were the most common leisure activities in the Georgian
garden. This was usually focused at or around a specific garden
building. Early on in the eighteenth century these buildings
might be called banqueting houses, a hangover from Tudor
times, when the 'banquet' was a course, usually dessert, that
was served at a separate location from the main meal. With the
proliferation of garden buildings during the Georgian period,
the term became less frequently used for a building the main
function of which was dining. Food was served at a wide variety
of locations from four-square, solid structures with multiple
rooms through tents and marquees, to a rug upon the ground,
as shown in Repton's view from Heaven's Gate at Longleat
(FIGURE 15). Both the facilities for preparation and serving, and
the food itself, could be relatively sophisticated or they could
be simple, depending upon the circumstances, the company and
the location. Cold food was, unsurprisingly, most frequently
served, but many garden buildings were equipped with kitchens.
Though all meals of the day were served outside, sometimes,
especially in more extensive designs, different elements of
refreshment were staged at different locations. Often dessert was
served outside after a dinner in the house, rather in the same
way that the Elizabethans had enjoyed their 'banquet'. Being
in the country in the summer meant that it coincided with the
ripening of fruit like cherries and strawberries, which were, of
course, freshly picked and therefore at their best. It also meant
there was easy access to dairy products; if the estate had an
ice house, ice cream was another luxury served in the garden.

Dinner, tea, syllabub, music and dancing: all these were the standard ingredients of an idyllic evening's entertainment, for which the garden and its buildings became the perfect backdrop. Grandeur and scale were not prerequisites, however. The setting could be a huge garden of over a hundred acres, which had the advantage – when necessary – of accommodating hundreds or even thousands of guests. Alternatively the setting could be relatively modest. Gilbert White's designed landscape at Selborne consisted of less than 4 acres of garden, with views across fields, often called 'the park', between it and the Hanger. The 'park' was, in fact, merely meadows and pastureland cleverly drawn into the design, ornamented with occasional trees and clumps, and embellished with statues made of board painted to give the impression of stone from a distance. From the far side of these fields a zigzag path was cut up the steep slope of the Hanger and here, where there were fine panoramic views for miles across the landscape, White built his Hermitage. It was constructed, like so many others, from readily available materials: gnarled branches for the structure and thatch for the roof. The walls were probably woven hazel, with the surrounding vegetation growing through them (FIGURE 51). White used his alcove seat in the garden and his tent, either in the garden or erected at other viewpoints surrounding the village (FIGURE 12), for entertaining, but the Hermitage created the most enchanting atmosphere.

Gilbert White's account of the evening spent at the Hermitage on 28 July 1763, with tea-drinking, singing, dressing up and the appearance of the hermit, is corroborated by Catherine Battie's diary. His account was written in his garden calendar

along with accounts of the progress of his much-loved melons, the first harvest of marrowfat peas and the state of his hay crop, which seems slightly at odds with the hearty dose of fantasy injected into the parties. The guests dressed as shepherds and shepherdesses, which perhaps hints at the sort of pastoral songs they might have been singing, and there may also have been country dances, which Catherine records at other times. But the highlight was the appearance of the hermit, which added a frisson of excitement and further element of fantasy. Unlike the hapless hermit at Painshill, who was at least supposed to be the genuine article, this hermit was really Gilbert's younger brother, Harry. They must all have known this by that stage and the fact probably added to the amusement. However, after the first occasion on which he appeared Catherine confessed that his sudden arrival made her 'start'. The soirée of 28 July

was, as it transpired, the last time the Hermitage hosted the
company, as the sisters left Selborne a few days later. It must
have been a grand finale. After a ride in the morning, followed
by dinner at home, Catherine records that they 'went up to the
D[ea]r Hermitage, we drank tea, afterwards the old Hermit
came'. He told their fortunes (a nice touch as they were about
to go their separate ways), then sat with them for some time.
When he left they walked to the tent, which must have been
pitched at another strategic spot. She continued that here 'we
Shepherdesses danced; at nine the lamp was lighted, enchanting scene'. Catherine's account ends with 'oh never did I see
anything like it … 'tis Arcadia Happy, happy vale…'[3]

When the Battie sisters arrived at Selborne in early June
the weather had been fine, dry and warm for several weeks,
though it broke while they were there.[4] That good weather in
May was favourable for another entertainment in a somewhat
grander garden, just a couple of weeks before the sojourn in
Selborne. In the middle of May 1763 Horace Walpole wrote to
his friend George Montagu, 'I never passed a more agreeable
day than yesterday', describing his experience as the guest of
Miss Pelham at Esher Place (Surrey). He wrote, 'the day was
delightful, the scene transporting, the trees, lawns, concave,
all in perfection as the ghost of Kent would joy to see them',
evoking the designer of the landscape at Esher (who died in
1748). The party numbered around 20 and the entertainment
began with a tour of the landscape in carriages. The dinner,
eaten al fresco, was 'magnificent', but given a somewhat rustic

FIGURE 52 A detail from *A View of Esher in Surrey the Seat of the Rt. Hon. Henry Pelham Esq.* by Luke Sullivan, 1759. Here, in the background of the view, the Belvedere, where tea was served, and the Grotto, where the ladies circled their chairs at the opening of the cave, can be seen to the left of the house.

edge by being 'cloaked in the modesty of earthenware'. While the guests ate, they were entertained by carefully selected instruments favoured for outdoor music-making: 'French horns and hautboys on the lawn'.

After drinking tea and coffee at the Belvedere, the party moved to a different location, no doubt evoking a different atmosphere (FIGURE 52). In the wood the ladies made a circle of chairs in front of the grotto, which Walpole referred to as the 'cave'. Here, the sensual pleasures of the food and drink and the garden itself were added to by the scent of the honeysuckle, lilac and laburnum which draped themselves over the 'cave'. As the party moved off again, the French horns struck up and Walpole noticed the servants wandering by the river, where they had presumably eaten their own meals at a discreet distance from their masters and mistresses. He likened the scene to a painting by Watteau. As the evening wore on they were served a 'rural syllabub'. Some of the guests returned to London, but were replaced by new arrivals and the party entertained themselves with music; the gentlemen playing violin and bass, with Miss Pelham, Lady Rockingham and the Duchess of Grafton singing. Walpole says 'this little concert lasted past ten; then there were minuets, and as we had seven couples left, it concluded with a country dance – I blush again, for I danced, but was kept in countenance by Nivernois, who has one more wrinkle than I have.' The evening concluded with a supper and Walpole came home by moonlight.

⚬⚬⚬

Walpole's last sentence suggests he felt that such Arcadian entertainment was really the province of the young, like the sisters at Selborne, who were in their late teens and early twenties in the summer they spent there. Walpole's attitude had only deepened six years later, when he was a guest for a five-day house party at Stowe. By this time the host, Earl Temple, and most of the guests, including Princess Amelia, in whose honour the party was organised, were in their mid- to late fifties. As Walpole wrote with wry humour to his cousin, Henry Seymour Conway, 'we are all of us young giddy creatures of near three-score', and to his friend Montagu, 'we were none of us young enough for a pastoral'.

FIGURE 53 *The Grotto at Stowe*, by Thomas Medland, 1797. This was Earl Temple's favourite place for al fresco supper, with its intimate setting in a wooded, steep-sided valley. For such entertainments the trees were hung with lanterns. On grander occasions musicians were stationed on boats on the water.

The party spent their mornings touring the garden on foot or in chaises before long, mid-afternoon dinners in the mansion. They were back in the garden in the early evening, and days were further punctuated with the amusement of fishing, which Princess Amelia enjoyed with Lady Mary Coke. Walpole had thought he might get bored, but admitted that the wealth of garden buildings and their differing settings added variety. In the middle of the week 'a small Vauxhall was acted out' for them at the Grotto, as Earl Temple always enjoyed taking his supper there (FIGURE 53). Such entertainments in the private pleasure ground of the country house were often likened to the public pleasure gardens in London such as Vauxhall and Ranelagh, with their music and illuminations. However, the weather at Stowe that summer was less than ideal. To Conway, Walpole reported with a mild note of sarcasm: 'we supped in a grotto in the Elysian fields, and were refreshed with rivers of dew and gentle showers that dripped from the trees...' Montagu received a longer description of the evening's entertainment. The shrubs and trees were hung with lanterns. Two small boats on the lake in front of the grotto were also illuminated. Returning to his theme of idyllic scenes being more suitable for youth, Walpole continued:

> I did not enjoy the entertainment *al fresco* as much as I
> should have done twenty years ago. The evening was more
> than cool and the destined spot anything but dry.... I could
> not help laughing as I surveyed our troop, which instead
> of tripping lightly to such an Arcadian entertainment, were
> hobbling down, by the balustrades, wrapped up in cloaks
> and great-coats for fear of catching cold... We supped in the
> grotto, which is as proper to this climate, as a sea-coal fire
> would be in the dog-days at Tivoli.[5]

Though he conceded that the idea of the evening's entertainment was 'pretty', the reality did not live up to it. There were not quite enough lights and the music was provided by a solitary 'ancient militia-man who played cruelly on a squeaking tabor [drum] and pipe'. When they got back to the house, Walpole immediately ordered cherry brandy to warm himself up.

Although Earl Temple had a 200-acre garden, with five substantial garden buildings capable of holding a party of at least 20, not to mention myriad smaller seats and alcoves, the Grotto was his favourite place for evening entertainment. Its setting was intimate: at the head of a narrow valley, with trees and shrubs up the steep banks on either side, perfect for hanging with lanterns and water in front for reflections. It was of the garden, but discrete from it, so efforts to dress the surroundings with lights and other embellishments could be easily concentrated in that area. The interior of the building itself was described in the 1744 version of Seeley's guidebook as being 'furnished with a great Number of Looking-glasses both on the Walls and Ceiling, all in artificial Frames of Plaister-work, set with Shells and broken Flints'. At the back of the central chamber was 'a Marble Statue of Venus on a Pedestal stuck with the same'. Forty years later it had changed slightly: '[the] inside is finished with a variety of shells, spars, fossils, petrifactions, and broken glass, which reflect the rays of light.'[6] The decoration had become more sophisticated but the effect was still the same, to reflect light. In the growing darkness of the evening, in its shady setting, lit by tin lamps with flickering candles, the twinkling interior must have been enchanting, and this explains why Earl Temple was always so keen to use the building at that time of day.

The reflection and refraction of light were common themes in the use of grottoes in Georgian gardens. In a letter written in 1766, the writer and amateur garden designer, Joseph Spence, gave an account of Lord Lincoln's Grotto at Oatlands (Surrey), its construction and setting. He evoked an imaginary, though typical, occasion on which the building would be seen to its best advantage. The effect must have been what Earl Temple was aiming at, and indeed achieved on other occasions.

In a still Summer's-Night, what a charming effect must
a great number of Chrystal Lamps have, fixt properly, &
all sparkling from amidst the leaves of these Trees? All
this enliven'd with the Music of the Nightingales ... or by
Instrumental Music, & perhaps a Dance on the Green-Carpet
all over the midst of it; fill one with an Idea of pleasure not
elsewhere to be met with, and if the Evening shou'd not
continue fine throughout ... what more charming place can
there be to retire to, than the Upper Grotto?[7]

The last line acknowledges the ever-present spectre of the
weather during a British summer.

Horace Walpole's account of his visit to Esher suggests that the
servants and ladies' maids were on hand if needed, close by,
but separate from the main party. Walpole saw them drifting
by the lake, adding animation to the scene. It is possible to
imagine that it made quite a pleasant evening for them too. It
is not clear whether there were servants in attendance at Gilbert
White's Hermitage, or how the tea-making equipment and
other refreshments were transported to it. Given the distance
from the house and the steepness of the climb, the logistics
must have been a consideration. It is possible that a donkey
might have been employed to plod up the hill with the accoutrements of the entertainment: food, drink, lanterns. Elsewhere
'eatables' and 'drinkables' were transported to such locations
by wheelbarrow. A letter from the poet William Cowper gives
a glimpse at the likely logistics of many an entertainment.
In July 1781, he was a guest at a party centred on a similar

FIGURE 54 The Root House (or Moss House) at Weston Underwood, from Edward
Wedlake Brayley's *Cowper Illustrated by a Series of Views*, 1803.

building to White's Hermitage. This was a rustic root house
at Weston Underwood (Buckinghamshire) belonging to Anna
Maria Throckmorton (FIGURE 54). Cowper wrote a detailed
description of the event, which illustrates how the food was
transported and served, how the party was waited upon, and
how the meal fitted into the greater entertainment of the day:

Yesterday sev'night we all dined together in the
Spinney, a most delightfull retirement belonging to Mrs.
Throgmorton… Lady Austen's laquey and a lad that waits
on me in the garden, drove a wheelbarrow full of eatables
and drinkables to the scene of our fete champetre. A board
laid over the top of the barrow served us for a table, our
dining room was a roothouse lined with moss and Ivy. At Six
o'clock the Servants who had dined under a great Elm upon
the ground at a little distance, boiled the Kettle, and the said
Wheel:barrow served us again for a tea table. We then took a
walk from thence to the wilderness about half a mile off, and
were at home again soon after eight.[8]

At Weston Underwood it is clear that having waited during
the meal the servants retreated to a discreet distance to eat their
own food. The ability to be waited on by minimal servants was
certainly one of the attractions of the garden and the garden
building.[9] In the house, especially if it were a grand one, dinner
was often served with great ceremony. Continental visitors
remarked on the formality of dinners in England. In the 1780s
François de La Rouchfoucauld observed that there was a good
deal more 'ceremony' surrounding dinner than he was used to
in France. Outside this could be done with greater informality
and the size of buildings restricted the size of a party, making
it more intimate. At Croome, where Lord Coventry had com-
plained of his house being 'an inn', the Rotunda, in the Home
Shrubbery, a gentle amble from the house, was 'fitted up as an
evening apartment', the implication being as somewhere to sup
or retreat. Garden buildings were also used as family dining
rooms when building work was going on at the main house.
Given the extent of architectural improvement at many houses

during the period this must have been frequent. At Holkham the family retired to dine in the Temple. As had been done for William Cowper's party at Weston Underwood, their food was wheeled out there for them in a specially adapted barrow, with compartments for bread and wine. When not in use it was stored in the butler's pantry.[10]

During the eighteenth century, the taking of the main meal of the day, in the house at least, was, as Rouchfoucauld suggested, a highly formal affair continuing for several hours. There would be one or two main courses, and during a course several of the main dishes would be 'removed' and others put in their place. The first course was likely to have been somewhat heavier, with roast and boiled meats featuring prominently; the second might be lighter with more emphasis on fish and fowl, again with certain dishes removed. Both courses would include savoury and sweet dishes, like tarts, and dishes would be arranged symmetrically on the table. Guests were not expected to eat everything, but rather help themselves to a few things that they fancied. The etiquette was described by Martha Bradley in *The British Housewife* (c. 1756):

> When there are but two or three at table, and but two
> or three dishes, the Mistress of the House should help
> everybody at once... When there are a great many Dishes
> and a great deal of company, she should tell them she leaves
> them to the French Ease, the Dinner is before them, and they
> are expected to take care of themselves and of each other.[37]

The British had a rather paradoxical attitude to the French where food and dining were concerned. While the richest in the land employed French cooks to create elaborate dishes both sweet and savoury, generally there was an ambivalence, with many a patriotic Englishman feeling that it was inappropriate to employ cooks from across the Channel. There was a general distrust of their more complicated cooking of dishes with gravies and sauces made of many ingredients, and the British stuck steadfastly to their traditional roast beef.[11] In spite of the expression 'French Ease' used by Martha Bradley, there was also a feeling that the French habits of dining were rather strict.

~~⋇~~

To make it easier to serve more sophisticated meals outside, many garden buildings were equipped with kitchens. Sometimes these were within the main structure. Robin Hood's Temple at Halswell has three internal spaces, one of which was a kitchen. In 1767, while planning the building, Kemeys-Tynte wrote to his steward, 'as for the Building on the Hill in the Park, the first room wch I call the Hermit's room, must have an earthen floor, the kitchen on the left, a brick, and the little room for China, must be board'd', which neatly illustrates the function and place within a hierarchy of each of the spaces.[12] The 'little room for China' would have been the dining room and refreshments would have utilised some of the collection of ceramics that was housed here. Though the kitchen was under the same roof, it was actually entered via its own external door, so keeping functional space distinctly separate from that dedicated to pleasure, and meaning that food had to be taken outside and then in again, though its journey was a short one.

Other ways of providing food preparation space within a building were to create an anteroom, as in the Bowling Green House at Wrest, which would act as a servery and place to store equipment, though not to actually cook food, or in a basement. The kitchen space remains in the undercroft of the Ionic Temple at Rievaulx Terrace. This was particularly well equipped because, according to an inventory of 1783, it had among other implements: spits, skewers, a dripping pan, two sauce pans, a grid iron and a chafing dish, proving that roast meats as well as a variety of other dishes could have been cooked or warmed here. In a cupboard plates, cups, saucers and glasses were kept, along with '4 sauce boats, 2 fruit basins, one glass fruit basin ... one octagon cistern and one square Mahogany cistern', giving clues as to dessert and drinks.[13]

Where a basement was not possible, but there was a desire to serve more than just cold collations, a detached kitchen block was sometimes built. Few of these survive. Although his father had utilised the anteroom arrangement in his Banqueting House at Studley Royal, William Aislabie clearly favoured the detached approach. He used it at both Studley and Hackfall. At the former, William's Gothic Octagon Tower perched on the other side of the valley from the Banqueting House. The tower, which performed the same function, being used for dining, is flanked by a pair of rocky arches. One forms the entrance to the tunnel, by which visitors climbed up through the hill to reach the tower; the other was a simple kitchen. Rectangular in plan, the simple structure was topped by a barrel-vaulted roof. At the far end was a primitive range to allow food to be heated over a pair of charcoal-fuelled warmers.[14]

At Aislabie's other garden, Hackfall, at least two of his garden buildings were given similarly detached kitchens, hidden in shrubbery close to the dining place. Originally Mowbray Point had an internal kitchen in a similar arrangement to that at Robin Hood's Temple at Halswell, and likewise there was also no internal communicating door. However, a detached kitchen block was built sometime later. This survives, albeit in ruined form, around 30 metres from its parent building. In contrast, that for Fisher's Hall does not. In 1783, in his description of Fisher's Hall, William Bray reported that here 'Mr. Aislabie sometimes dined, or indulged his friends with the liberty of so doing, and for this purpose kitchens are built near'.[15] The small octagonal room of Fisher's Hall, which would not seat more than eight, at a squeeze, was decorated inside with 'petrifications', rocky grotto-work, between which shards of coloured glass and mirrors were stuck into the walls (FIGURE 55). So in the evening, by candlelight, it would have twinkled, making it a magical place to have dinner or supper.[16]

Not all garden buildings used for dining were this intimate. The Chinese House, built on an island in the middle of Drakeloe Pond at Woburn, could hold a ducal-sized party of 30 people. To serve such a number there was a kitchen 'in the adjoining woods ... for making ready the repasts his grace takes in the temple'.[17] Later, in 1808, Humphry Repton designed a rustic cottage, providing the Duke of Bedford with yet another novel place to feed his guests. The 6th Duke of Bedford was a great horticultural patron, and much expanded the botanic interest of his principal seat. Among these features was a thornery, in which 'are to be found every species of

FIGURE 55 *Fisher's Hall at Hackfall*, by John Swete, 1783. This building, with its twinkling interior, made the perfect place for a meal as daylight faded and candles were lit.

thorns which will bear the climate'. This plantation has given its name to the cottage. The interior is painted as a *trompe l'œil* trellis to continue the rustic al fresco mood. Again, as this is a vast designed landscape and the Thornery is a considerable distance from the house, it is provided with a semi-subterranean kitchen, entered from the bottom of the bank on which it sits. It was originally equipped with a simple dinner service of Wedgwood caneware, which probably served twelve people, a more modest number than the Chinese House.[18]

⁓✺⁓

The spits and skewers in the Ionic Temple at Rievaulx suggest that roast and grilled meats were served there and that further food was either warmed or cooked slowly in chaffing dishes. However, a 'cold collation' was more often what was served in the Georgian garden. Sanderson Miller served cold collations to his guests at his Castle, but this was not always preferred by his friends. In 1752 George Lyttleton acknowledged that dining outside was the elegant, preferable thing, but bowed to the frequent practicalities of the situation. He wrote to his friend and host Sanderson Miller: 'Mrs Lyttleton will like to dine at the house better than at the Castle, and my stomach prefers hott meat to cold, though not my taste; so if you please, we will dine [in the house] at the foot of the hill, and have the pleasure of looking up to your Castle...'.[19]

Clearly the advantage of cold food was its practicality. It was easily portable and needed little or no preparation. It could be simple and informal, like the sandwiches Jane Austen's brother's family ate on their walk in Chawton Park 'seated upon an old tree' or the cold partridges they took on an excursion to the New Forest.[20] In her novels Austen gives glimpses of the sort of outdoor fare that was typical of the food served in the pleasure ground. In *Sense and Sensibility* one of Sir John Middleton's congenial qualities is that he was 'in summer ... for ever forming parties to eat cold ham and chicken out of doors'.[21] In *Emma* the food anticipated for the projected outing to Box Hill was to include pigeon pies and cold lamb.[22] Simple cold chicken was an obvious picnic meal taken in the park at Saltram, and was regretted when lacking. Ann Robinson described a leisurely walk in August 1790. It was a warm summer's day so they stopped to sit down in the shade whenever they felt like it. After spending an hour at their destination, enjoying the scene, they returned, but she told her sister-in-law that they 'wanted only a Cold Chicken and Tankard, to have kept us there all day'.[23]

A few summers later, in 1798, Ann was invited by some friends to 'eat a few sandwiches' at what might today be called a 'beauty spot', south of the park at Saltram, looking across Plymouth Sound to Mount Edgcumbe. While this was not within the designed landscape, the setting and spread are illustrative. To Ann's surprise the picnic party turned out to be rather less modest than she had supposed. She arrived in the late afternoon to find dinner spread out in a large tent and 40 guests assembled. She felt as though she had been 'conveyed there by Magick'. The food served was actually rather more sophisticated than 'a few sandwiches'.[24] Her description continued: 'when we got there to the surprize of every body we found a large party and not only a very handsome cold dinner but a haunch of venison, very fine fish and the finest fruit I ever saw.' The implication in not including the venison within the 'handsome cold dinner' is that it was served hot. It could have been cooked over an open fire, or transported there in a hay box, which would have kept it warm.

It is not surprising to find venison on the menu. In the Georgian house and garden it clearly remained the high-status, prized meat it had been since the time of the Normans. It could not be bought, only given as a gift. It was eaten both as a large joint, as implied by Ann Robinson's description, and as venison pasties, one of the favourite foods eaten al fresco in the garden. Sanderson Miller's diary of 1750 records the story of a haunch of venison brought by Earl Temple (then Lord Cobham) to Radway from Stowe.[25] On 20 July Lord and

FIGURE 56   A design for a Stag Pasty from Edmund Kidder's *Receipts in Pastry and Cookery*, *c*.1720. The pastry encasing the haunch of venison would usually be highly decorative, like this oval version. The pasty made of Lord Cobham's venison that Sanderson Miller served at his Castle may have looked something like this.

Lady Cobham met Miller at Wroxton. They must have stayed either there or at nearby Radway with Miller, because they were there the following day (21 July) when the party supped in the novel surroundings of the Castle 'on Lord Cobham's venison'. The following day the party, of which the Cobhams were still members, dined 'on venison pasty at Castle'. Perhaps Cobham was generous with his venison, since it appeared again, four days later, when Miller was eating 'Lord Cobham's venison pasty' (FIGURE 56). A venison pasty was something quite different from our modern conception of a pasty, which is usually associated with Cornwall. This was much larger, sometimes as much as 3 feet long. The pastry case was not necessarily intended for eating; it was highly decorated and served to preserve the meat inside, which would be a whole boned joint. It makes sense that this was a favoured dish for eating in the garden as it was easily transportable and a good way of protecting such a prized meat. So perhaps Lord Cobham generously brought more than one haunch for his friend Miller, as it seems to have appeared both as merely 'venison' and as a pasty. This incident also illustrates that not all his guests were as fussy as the Lyttletons and some actually liked the novelty of dining at the Castle, even if the food was cold.

Venison was likewise one of the delicacies enjoyed in the summer at Wrest. In 1690 the Duchess of Kent wrote to the Duke, who was away, that the 'bowling green and venison pasties want you', tantalisingly suggesting the combination of location, activity and food.[26] Some 50 years later, Elizabeth Yorke (later Anson) listed the venison as one of the highlights of her father's recent visit in a letter to her new sister-in-law:

> Papa has said so much at dinner today of Wrest, of
> the improvements made in the house, of the beauty of
> the garden, the excellence of the pineapples, cherries,
> strawberries, venison, etc., etc., and above all the company,
> that I can form no idea how it is possible to live anywhere
> else.[27]

Elizabeth Yorke's letter highlights the joy of being at Wrest, especially in the summer: the beauty of the garden and the pleasure of the company. It also touches on an important element in the experience of dining in the pleasure ground:

the freshness of the food. The rich could afford to buy luxury provisions in London, such as the olives that Marianne is tempted with to relieve her broken heart in *Sense and Sensibility*, and they had the resources to have food transported from their country estate to their town house.[28] However, this was not the same as eating it there, where it was as fresh as possible. Part of the joy of being in the country, especially in the summer when the family were most likely to be there, was the availability of the finest fruit and vegetables from the kitchen garden, home-reared meat, fish (particularly if, like Ann Robinson at Saltram, you lived near the sea) and a variety of produce from your dairy herd, or in more modest circumstances your house cow. The cream from the house cow manifested itself most often in al fresco dining in the form of syllabub, but, if the family were rich enough for an ice house, also as ice cream.

Fruit was the most frequently eaten dessert in the Georgian garden. Today when supermarkets stock strawberries practically all year round it is hard to appreciate the luxurious quality of such foods. Not only was the eating of strawberries limited to a short season, but it was during this period that different varieties were being developed in the United Kingdom by crossing native wood strawberries with varieties from North America and Chile, thus developing the strawberry we are most familiar with today. Those eaten from the extensive kitchen garden at Wrest in 1740 would have been the small, native wood strawberry. By 1780 Parson James Woodforde was serving modern scarlets alongside wood strawberries. While Mrs Elton was gathering fruit in Mr Knightley's garden in *Emma* her amusing, contradictory stream-of-consciousness demonstrates Jane Austen's knowledge of commonly eaten varieties by 1815: 'every sort good – hautboy infinitely superior – no comparison – the others hardly eatable – hautboys very scarce – Chili preferred – white wood finest flavour of all...'[29] Thus the monologue continues, uninterrupted until she is so exhausted she has to go and sit in the shade. For visitors to the picturesque ruins of Roslin Castle (south of Edinburgh), where Paul Sandby portrayed Lady Scott sketching with the camera obscura (FIGURE 36), picking strawberries in the surroundings of the castle was an additional layer of pleasure to the experience of a jaunt there. Lady Louisa Stuart, daughter of the Earl of Bute, described a trip there, including a dinner 'spread out in a very neat garden looking upon the castle'. She continued, 'I never enjoyed anything more as we had the most delightful strawberries and cream that ever was ... it's the custom here for people to make parties to come and eat them here.'[30] Thomas Robins's painting of an unknown garden of the 1740s (see the cover of this book) shows some of the company enjoying a game of bowls, while the figures in the foreground are brought a basket of fruit by the gardener, straight from the kitchen garden to the right. Given the date of the painting, the size of the basket and the accompanying plate, these would be small wood strawberries; the fruits on the platter being proffered by the hostess are probably white cherries.

Gilbert White grew a surprising variety of strawberries at Selborne in the late 1750s, including what must have been new introductions. He also grew cherries, gooseberries, currants and raspberries, as well as more tender fruits such as figs and grapes, but it was the cultivation of melons that he poured his energies and ingenuity into and that were woven into the experience of using his garden and its buildings. Like the pineapples grown in hothouses at Wrest, melons required specific conditions and were equally prized as exotic fruit. But White proved that melons could be cultivated with more humble resources. The hard-won pleasure of this fruit suggested that it be savoured in suitable surroundings. To add further novelty to the full pleasure of eating the melon, he would hold 'a Cantaleupe-feast' at the Hermitage up on the Hanger. So while the refreshment was simple, it was spiced with exoticism and, moreover, was something to share with friends. On a fine, warm day in September 1759 fourteen people were invited to partake in eating two and a half melons while gazing out across the early autumn landscape.

Gilbert White was not grand enough to have an ice house. However, they were increasingly common in parks and gardens of country houses through the Georgian period.[31] Having one gave an owner the ability to make ice cream and sorbet, with which he could treat and impress his guests. Precedents for serving a sweet course after a meal outside in the garden date back to the sixteenth century, and indeed this was the origin of the banqueting house. The first ice cream recipes in English were published by Mary Eales, confectioner to Queen Anne, in 1718.[32] Ice cream soon became very popular, with specially designed vessels becoming available, and was served in confectioners' shops, at grand dinners and al fresco parties in the pleasure ground.[33] In July 1749, Lord North wrote to his friend Sanderson Miller: 'If you think we shall escape a wet day tomorrow, I hope we shall have the pleasure of your company to cold meat and Iced cream at the Chinese House… My Chinese House is so warm she [Mrs Miller] will not get cold.'³⁴

Miller, in turn, served his guests with syllabub at his Castle. Syllabub was made with whipped cream, sugar and wine, and during the eighteenth century evolved from a liquid to a semi-solid dessert (FIGURE 57). In one of his many references to it, Miller says he 'drank' a syllabub, so in the early 1750s, at least, Miller was still serving the liquid form.³⁵ The word 'drank' was still being used in relation to syllabub in the 1770s.

FIGURE 57   *A Sense of Taste*, by Philippe Mercier, 1744–47. Here syllabub, in its earlier eighteenth-century liquid form, is being served, along with peaches and plums.

Mary Rebow of Wivenhoe Park in Essex reported a trip to nearby Alresford Park, where two of her companions were 'in high spirits and drank syllabub at such a rate' that one of them was 'quite lillyvated'.[36] Like ice cream, syllabub was a popular luxury, for which fresh cream was a prerequisite. It was, therefore, symbolic of the pleasures of the country life, the cream being far harder to procure in town than in the country. Earl Temple served syllabub in the appropriately fantastical surroundings of the grotto at Stowe, including to Miller. Perhaps significantly, the only specific foodstuff Horace Walpole mentioned in his letter describing the Arcadian entertainment at Esher in May 1763 was a 'rural syllabub'.

✦

Tea was without doubt the most commonly served refreshment in the garden, especially in the early evening, after dinner. Walpole enjoyed it at the Belvedere at Esher, Gilbert White served it to his guests at the Hermitage, William Cowper drank it from a wheelbarrow tea-table at Weston Underwood. Today, especially in Britain, where it is something of a national institution, tea is actually a rather mundane, everyday drink, but it is important to understand its status during the Georgian era. At the beginning of the period it was the most costly of household commodities, kept under lock and key along with expensive culinary and medicinal spices, and distributed by the mistress of the house, who therefore usually presided over the making of the drink. A century and a quarter on, by the 1830s it was available to practically all levels of society, though this did not reduce its being served in the gardens of the affluent classes.[37]

The use of the garden as a pleasant place to serve tea was a phenomenon that pervaded all strata of society, from the grandest duchess down to the country clergyman, the prosperous merchant and the tenant farmer. In *Emma* (published in 1816), the Martins (the family of tenant farmers who Emma considers too inferior for her friend Harriet to marry into) have a garden building. This can seat as many as twelve guests for refreshments. Harriet, at least, was impressed, talking 'of their having a very handsome summer-house in their garden, where some day next year they were all to drink tea:– a very handsome summer-house, large enough to hold a dozen people'.[38] Though, by implication, the summerhouse is used on red-letter days, it is not a mere portico, alcove seat or recess; this is a building substantial enough to hold a sizeable party.

The food historian Ivan Day has linked the rise in tea drinking with the fashion for chinoiserie from the 1730s onwards. The ritual of drinking of tea was part of a wider fashion that encompassed gardening, architecture, interior decoration and applied arts, including ceramics; and its consumption was closely linked with the use of oriental porcelain. In the garden this vogue led to the building of Chinese houses, pavilions and temples. While there is evidence for tea being served in many of these Chinese buildings, its prevalence in the pleasure ground meant that it was served in myriad other types of buildings as well, as we have seen. Where no direct accounts exist of a guest or host describing the use of a building, inventory evidence gives a strong suggestion of tea drinking in the items listed in a place. One of the most influential Chinese garden buildings was that at Shugborough (Staffordshire), famed because its designer, Piercy Brett, had actually seen Chinese architecture first-hand in Canton, while on the famous round-the-world voyage of Admiral Anson.[39] Here the building contained chairs and oriental porcelain; it would have been unusual if tea had not been served there. Lord North at Wroxton (Oxfordshire) was so fond of the chinoiserie style that he had four garden structures built in that taste: the Chinese House, a Chinese Seat, a bridge and the Keeper's Lodge, all of which were built around 1740, meaning that they were at the forefront of fashion. As well as serving cold collations and ice cream at his Chinese House, he also served tea. In July 1750 Sanderson Miller wrote an account of his day at Wroxton in his diary: 'to Lord North's to breakfast. Drawing floor for the building and Mr. Child's plan. Music. Lord and Lady Cobham and Miss Banks came there to dinner. Walked etc. Drank tea at Chinese House.'[40]

Oriental porcelain was kept in many garden buildings. At Robin Hood's Temple, Halswell, the finest room of the three spaces in the building, the one that was used for entertaining, was referred to as the 'little room for China'.[41] This suggests, as elsewhere, oriental ceramics were displayed there as well as used. An owner did not have to have a garden covering hundreds of acres to have a garden building in which to store, display and use oriental ceramics for drinking tea. In *Emma*, it will be remembered, the Martins have a summerhouse that is used for taking tea in, and can hold up to a dozen people. The sort of structure that Jane Austen was imagining was probably somewhat like a lost but well-documented middle-class

FIGURE 58   A detail from *Wallbridge*, *c*.1790, unknown artist. Mr Cole's summerhouse and detached garden can be seen on the far left of the painting. Here he entertained his friends with evening tea parties.

summerhouse in Stroud (Gloucestershire). In the eighteenth century Stroud was prosperous because of its cloth industry. A number of gardens, fashionable in their detail but relatively small in scale, were built by the men who had made money from all aspects of this industry, from sheep farming to cloth dying. One such garden was at Wallbridge, sadly lost to road widening in the nineteenth century. Here Mr Cole, a wealthy shear-grinder, erected a summer house in his garden. A few years later it was separated from the house by the newly built Stroudwater canal, but continued to be used and connected to the main residence by an ornamental Chinese bridge tacked to the side of the canal bridge. The locally typical view of mills, canal and cloth drying was painted in around 1790 (FIGURE 58); it also shows the garden. The summerhouse was lavish enough to stand out in the memory of Paul Hawkins Fisher, who had known it as a boy and described it in his *Notes and Recollections of Stroud*, published in 1871, making it a remarkably well-documented middle-class garden of the time:

> At the upper angle of the garden, pointing towards the town,
> he erected a small, elegant, summer-house, in exquisite
> taste as to its proportions, and the architectural disposition
> and enrichment of its parts. It was embellished with eagles
> and other figures carved of stone, and was surmounted
> by a handsome weather-cock. Its interior was adorned
> with pictures of the four seasons... It was fitted up rather
> sumptuously; being furnished with oriental china ornaments,
> together with a tea service for the rural entertainment of
> friends, – all arranged in elegant open buffets, and closed
> cupboards with the painted and gilded panels.

There is a suggestion that it may also have been used for music
by the next generation.[42]

The number and scale of the garden buildings that Marchioness Grey inherited from her grandfather, the Duke of Kent,
were rather different from the small but beautifully formed
Wallbridge summerhouse. They afforded her several different
possible locations for taking tea, but the most favoured were
the vast, domed Pavilion, designed by Thomas Archer and set
on axis with the house, and the Bowling Green House. This
is a building of two facades, each with an open loggia: one
looking east across the bowling green and the other facing west
with views across the park, giving users the option of sun or
shade, morning or evening use. So the west loggia might have
been favoured for tea in the evening. Internally there is a finely
decorated 'banqueting room', with a small anteroom off it, and at
the far end a privy. At the time Jemima Grey inherited the estate
in 1740, the room was furnished with 16 walnut chairs, a card
table, a tea table and a round mahogany table with a claw foot.
There was a pair of corner cupboards, presumably at one end,

decorated with 'Indian pictures'.[43] These housed all the necessary utensils for making and serving tea, including a coloured Chinese teapot and stand, cups and saucers, sugar dish, milk porringer and silver tea spoons. After a visit to Wrest, following the marriage of her brother to Jemima in 1740, Elizabeth Yorke, who had received a warm welcome and friendly hospitality, wrote to the marchioness lamenting her departure from Wrest and giving a vivid impression of how her time there had been spent, including where they had taken tea in the garden:

> Your ladyship will easily believe I do not as yet know very well where I am, for I expect to go to billiards after dinner, to hear some tunes on the harpsichord, doubt whether we shall drink tea at the pavilion or the bowling green, do not know what object to look for in the prospect, can't guess what book you and I shall read next, miss the terrestrial maps extremely, the agreeable companion of my walks much more, and was vastly disappointed last night on asking about 9 o'clock what star shone so bright on the lefthand of the north window in the library, to find the person I addressed knew neither the star nor the place.[44]

These two buildings were still the preferred locations for taking tea five years later, when Jemima's childhood friend Catherine Talbot made a journal of her summer holiday at Wrest and recorded taking tea in both the Pavilion and the Bowling Green House, along with carriage tours, walking in the garden and playing billiards.[45]

Almost no images of people enjoying refreshments inside garden buildings exist, though clearly it was a common occurrence. Sometimes, however, an artist seems to have transposed

FIGURE 59   *Mr Richard Edgcumbe (afterwards 1st Lord Edgcumbe) entertaining his friends in front of the Garden House at Mount Edgcumbe,* after a drawing by Thomas Badeslade, 1735. The guest sit around an oval or circular table and on shell-back chairs, one of which still survives in the house. The servant on the right is bringing baskets of fruit, while a band of musicians plays.

a scene to the exterior of the building, which must have been an easier way to depict such happenings. This is probably true of Thomas Badeslade's view of the al fresco dinner at the Garden House at Mount Edgcumbe in 1735. Here 12 diners sit and stand around a table on the gravel apron in front of the building, which is set in a clearing in the wilderness (FIGURE 59). One servant is heading away from the table with a plate or tray, perhaps clearing an earlier course, while another enters the clearing carrying two laden baskets, presumably of freshly picked fruit. On the left of the clearing a band of six musicians play. Given the rarity of the view, it is unfortunate that it is too small to see the detail of the food they are eating. This event may in fact have taken place inside the building, but it was easier to depict outside. Johan Zoffany could have been employing the same technique in his pair of canvases of the actor David Garrick's garden by the Thames at Hampton (Middlesex) of 1762.[46] In the first painting the domed Temple to Shakespeare dominates the scene, with Garrick and his wife standing on the steps and his nephew peeping round a column. The butler is bringing the tea tray to the right of the scene. In the other painting the viewpoint is reversed and we are looking out from the Temple (FIGURE 60). Here the tea is served at a table on the lawn by the river. While Garrick's brother fishes on the bank, he and his wife entertain a guest. The furniture they are sitting on is unusual for the garden. It appears to be finer than the usual green or grey Windsor chairs and circular table, perhaps suggesting that it was brought out of the Temple for use on the lawn. Although the butler holds a cup and saucer, it is Mrs Garrick whose hand is on the teapot ready to pour it herself. The different outfits worn by the three figures common to both scenes suggest the intention to portray different moments in the garden. The fact that the tea tray appears in both is telling of its constant currency in the life of the pleasure ground.

Accounts for the drinking of coffee in the garden are much less frequent than those of tea drinking. Although it was served along with tea to Horace Walpole at the Belvedere at Esher, it was also served for Princess Amelia at the Doric Arch erected in her honour when she visited Stowe in 1770. Alcoholic drinks were sometimes served too and some inventories of garden buildings record wine coolers stored there. In June 1780 Parson James Woodforde took his turn to entertain his neighbours at a 'rotation dinner'. The party dined in the house on the best

FIGURE 60 *The Garden at Hampton House with Mr and Mrs David Garrick taking tea*, by Johan Zoffany, 1762.

that Norfolk could offer in June: a spread of pike, eels, mutton, carrots, veal, goose, peas and gooseberry tarts, with three large dishes of 'scarlet' and 'wood' strawberries for dessert.[47] The gentlemen then retired to the garden to walk and smoke their pipes in Woodforde's Temple, which had just been built. Like his fellow clergyman Gilbert White, Woodforde was hands-on, planning the Temple himself and painting the interior a pea green colour. Later he would sit there and shoot seagulls. In this novel setting the gentlemen must have drunk both wine and beer, for while they then took tea, presumably meeting up with the ladies again at some other part of the garden, perhaps in a tent, the younger members of the group took it upon themselves to likewise indulge in some alcoholic drinks. Woodforde wrote: 'After Dinner the Gentlemen walked about and smoked a Pipe in the Temple – And while we were at Tea the 2 Boys got into the Temple where was left some Wine & some strong Beer, and Little Nunn got himself Very drunk &

vomited a great Deal – the other was very well – Nunn is a sad unruly Lad indeed.'[48]

~જૂ~

All these meals and refreshments were frequently combined with music, both as an accompaniment and as the primary entertainment, with food a secondary pleasure. While a small party dined, they might be entertained by a solo musician, often a humble estate worker. At the other end of the scale the music could be provided by one of the stars of the Italian opera, brought from London into the country ostensibly as a guest for the summer, but in the hope of also providing entertainment for friends and family. In this period, long before television and cinema, the importance of music as mainstream entertainment cannot be overstated. Many owners of designed landscapes and their families were keen and proficient amateur musicians; some were more than proficient and played alongside professionals during private parties. Instruments were kept in garden buildings, which provided locations both for practice and simply to play for pleasure. Portable instruments such as a flute might be carried into and around the garden and singing which, at its simplest, requires no equipment or props, might break out almost spontaneously in the shrubbery or the temple.

When, in *Evelina* (1778), Fanny Burney's naive young heroine visits the London pleasure garden at Vauxhall, she reports, in spite of her dissatisfaction with her party, that 'there was a concert, in the course of which, a hautbois concerto was so charmingly played, that I could have thought myself upon enchanted ground... The hautboy in the open air is heavenly.'[49]

It will be remembered that Miss Pelham's party at Esher in May 1763 was entertained by French horns as well as 'hautboys on the lawn'.[50] The 'hautboy' was an early form of the oboe. It had the reputation of working well in the open air, like the French horn, which was also frequently used in parks and gardens because its sound travelled well outdoors. At least one of the musicians in the scene at Mount Edgcumbe (FIGURE 59) is playing a French horn, while the other identifiable instruments are two violins and a trumpet. The horn also had connotations with hunting; another reason for its popularity. When, as a young bride, Theresa Parker arrived with great celebrations at Saltram in 1769, she was hailed by music in the pleasure ground, with French horns playing while the guests dined and then later in the evening in the wood. Hiding musicians in shrubberies and undergrowth was an accepted ploy to give a more magical air to the music. It happened at Vauxhall, and is implied in a letter from Mrs Montagu describing how William Pitt, while staying in Kent, had found an enchanting scene on his morning's ride and later in the day had taken a party back to the spot, where he 'ordered a tent to be pitched, tea to be prepared and his French horn to breathe music like the unseen genius of the wood'.[51]

Pitt's friend Sanderson Miller was a keen and proficient musician. He owned a harpsichord, which was housed at Radway, but he kept his spinet at the Castle and sometimes went there alone to practise.[52] In the early evening, after dinner, he and his family would often stroll up the hill to the Thatched House and the Castle. His diary records concerts at both locations, sometimes with the added delight of a syllabub. On 2 July 1750 he noted: 'Spent the evening at the Castle. Music at the

Castle. Seventeen there; ten supped. Fine day.' In September 1750 Miller and Colonel Conway played duets at the Castle. He played with Conway on other occasions too, along with Mrs Lyttleton when at Hagley. He gives no detail about what kind of duets they played at the Castle, though presumably one instrument played was the spinet. The only specific references to composers in his diaries are to playing pieces by Corelli and the 'King of Prussia'. This was Frederick the Great, who was a celebrated flautist and composed many pieces for that instrument. Miller certainly played the flute. The pieces by Corelli may have been sonatas, as these were highly popular at the time.[53] The tone of the music was somewhat different for the ball at the Castle, which he organised to celebrate the completion of the building. For this event Miller hired 'Richardson the Piper', 'Howel the Harper' and a fiddler, who probably played music for country dances.

Though his two surviving diaries do not record him doing it at home, Miller also sang. In Oxford he sang at the Catch Club. Singing clubs were popular at the time and members would get together to sing both catches and glees. Catches were sung as rounds. In the late seventeenth and early eighteenth centuries they could be quite bawdy; alone one part might sound innocuous, but when several were sung together they took on another dimension. Glees were more sophisticated part-songs for two or more solo voices. The garden was an appropriate setting for the pastoral nature of some glees.[54] In turn, singing was a convenient way of making music in the pleasure ground. No cumbersome instruments had to be carted up to Gilbert White's Hermitage, because the music made there in the summer of

1763 was vocal. In July 1756, during an evening walk around the garden at Stowe, Sanderson Miller and the party sang at the Grecian Temple (later called the Temple of Concord and Victory). To this day the main chamber of the building still has fine acoustics. If not inside, the party may have sat in the portico, with the arcadian Grecian Valley spread out before them, the statues in the fringes of trees picked out by the setting sun.[55] The concert may have been impromptu, as is suggested elsewhere, the pieces pastoral folk songs, catches or glees. When Henry Bates toured the grounds of the Earl of Exeter's Burghley in July 1778, he noted that the company 'stopped at every new opening to a fine prospect and the company sang catches and were in the highest spirits', suggesting spontaneity rather than planning or staging. The earl, who was one of Lancelot Brown's longest standing clients, was a keen musician and an enthusiastic patron of music.

When away from home visiting the houses of his friends, Miller also took his flute. He played it at Stowe, possibly in the garden, and he performed for Mrs Nugent at Gosfield (Essex) too. One contemporary engraving gives the impression of the frequent informality of music-making in the pleasure ground and some of the instruments favoured for this. In the right of the view of Foots Cray are a couple who appear to be walking back to the house. In one hand the man is holding a flute, along with what appears to be a mandolin (FIGURE 61). In his other hand he holds sheet music. Clearly both instruments were easily portable and would be convenient for playing in the garden. Like Miller, John Hervey, 1st Earl of Bristol, was also a proficient flautist and played his instrument in the

FIGURE 61   A detail from *A View of Foots-Cray Place in Kent, the Seat of Bourchier Cleeve, Esq.* 1760. The man on the right holds a mandolin and a flute in one hand and sheet music in the other.

pleasure ground at Ickworth in Suffolk.[56] In July 1719 his wife, who was with the court of the Prince and Princess of Wales (later George II and Queen Caroline), wrote to her husband describing a concert that had just been performed for them at Richmond: 'we were last night with a very great Court to hear the fine musick the Prince has taken for the summer … but I would willingly have exchangd it all to have heard you pipeing in the summerhouse.'

While many owners of country houses and their friends and family were talented musicians and able to entertain the gathered company, the richest and most powerful lords vied with each other to host the leading professional performers and composers of the day at their country estates for the summer. It was in the summer of 1772, while he was a guest of his patron, the Duke of Ancaster at Grimsthorpe Castle, that the young composer Thomas Linley died in the boating accident. More happily, George Frideric Handel was one of the most sought-after and consequently well-travelled country house guests. Lord Burlington was an early patron and Handel

FIGURE 62   A detail from *A View of such parts [of Stowe] as are seen from the building at the head of the lake*, by Jacques Rigaud, 1733. The figure singing is said to be the great Italian castrato Senesino and the man on the right is Alexander Pope.

lived at Burlington House for many years. Another patron was the Duke of Chandos. Handel stayed at his palatial Cannons (Middlesex), where the opera *Acis and Galatea* was first performed. Handel stayed, too, with the Earl of Gainsborough at Exton (Rutland) in June 1745, with the intention of finding some 'quiet and retirement'.[57] The Earl's brother, John Noel, reported that, though the family intended to respect this desire, eventually 'selfishness however prevail'd' and the composer was persuaded to write a piece to be performed while he was there. Noel's letter continued to report that

> The whole scheme was concerted and executed in five
> Days... It was intended to have been performed in the
> Garden, but the weather would not favour that design.
> We contrived however to entertain the Company there
> afterwards with an imitation of Vaux Hall: and, in the style
> of a newspaper, the whole concluded with what variety of
> fireworks we could possibly get.

The piece performed at Exton was probably adapted, in part at least, from one of Handel's works for a larger group of players. Many such pieces were adapted for small chamber groups and it might be assumed that at Exton the most proficient members of the family and friends played alongside professional musicians.[58]

Rivalries were also exercised over who would attract the stars of Italian opera for the summer as well as composers, up and coming or well-established. In his scene of an al fresco music party at Stowe, Jacques Rigaud depicts the castrato Francesco Bernardi, known as Senesino, performing with a trio of musicians, possibly friends rather than professionals – a flautist, a cellist and a violinst – while other guests enjoy the performance.[59] In a letter to his wife Elizabeth, written in 1753, Mr Montagu describes a musical evening staged in the Banqueting House at Gibside (County Durham):

I ought not to omit telling you that he has already erected
upon rising ground a gothick building which he calls a
Banquetting room, in which the night before there was a
concert of Musick, at which Jordain and an Italian woman
performed, whom Mrs. Lane brought with her from
Bramham.[60]

This was sophisticated, fashionable music, of the sort generally
enjoyed in London. But in the garden, especially for smaller-
scale entertainments, music was likely to be more rustic. At
Stowe, during evening suppers in the Grotto, guests tended
to be entertained by solitary musicians playing fiddles and
bagpipes. Those musicians playing the fiddles and bagpipes
were likely to be estate workers earning a bit of extra cash in
the evening after a day at work, while the 'ancient-militia man'
who played the tabor and pipe might have had a long-standing
military connection with one of the family.

Worker-musicians entertained Sir Samuel Hellier, High Sher-
iff of Staffordshire. At The Wodehouse he laid out a modest-
sized landscape garden in an 8-acre wood in the 1760s. Though
almost unknown now, it was then on the circuit of popularly
visited gardens in the Midlands, along with neighbouring
Hagley, Enville and The Leasowes.[61] Hellier never married,
saying he could not afford to do so, though his domineering
grandmother, who lived until her ninety-ninth year, probably
also had something to do with it. Instead his passion was
directed towards gardening and music and he owned many
musical treasures, including a Stradivarius, which still bears
his family name. Around 1760 he built a Music Room in his
pleasure ground; indeed it was the first garden building he

erected. He later also added a Temple dedicated to Handel. In the Music Room an organ was housed; it seems that, when the garden was open to the public, visitors were able to hear it played, or possibly play it themselves. When he was at the Wodehouse, which was infrequently, he expected to be entertained in the evening by music. In 1769 he wrote to his steward saying he planned to pay for local people to learn music: 'I shall call them my Band... I intend they shall play when I'm in the Country ... every evening when they've left work for an hour to divert me.' Then, afterwards, he would 'go sailing upon the water'. This reinforces evidence elsewhere that suggests that the upper classes were often entertained by bands of musicians formed by their estate staff. Henry Hoare alluded to 'his choir' in one of his letters, and it is likely that the fiddler, harpist and piper who played for Miller's ball at the Castle at Radway, and the band shown by Badeslade at Mount Edgcumbe, were all part-time musicians who earned extra money by playing for the local landowner.

To record his gardening achievements Sir Samuel Hellier commissioned J. Hughes to draw a series of eight pictures of his landscape at The Wodehouse. Within the set of views he was very specific that one should be a moonlight scene, a view of his grotto at night, which is something of a rarity among illustrations of Georgian gardens. It is possible that this was inspired by his enjoyment of his garden, and possibly that building, by the light of the moon. So, now, as the darkness grows and evening turns to night-time, we come to the final phase of the day in the garden.

SIX

The Night-time

Moonlight —— *Fêtes* ——
Illuminations —— *Fireworks*

The garden was illuminated, and was quite a fairy
scene. Arches and pyramids of lights alternately
surrounded the enclosure; a diamond necklace of lamps
edged the rails and descent with a spiral obelisk of
candles on each hand; and dispersed over the lawn were
little bands of kettledrums, clarinets, fifes etc., and the
lovely moon, who came without a card...

HORACE WALPOLE, on the Duchess of
Northumberland's 'Festino', June 1762[1]

I T WAS AT NIGHT-TIME that the pleasure ground was at
its most magical. As darkness fell this time of day lent itself
to private, sometimes solitary, moonlit walks or, in contrast,
to fantastical 'fêtes champêtre nocturne', as Earl Temple called
them.[2] Then the garden became a stage set, with lanterns
strung among the trees and other illuminations. Hundreds, even
thousands, of guests would enjoy food and music, accompanied
by an extravaganza of fireworks. Such festivities might start in
daylight, but would go on well past midnight until the small
hours of the morning. This was the climax of the day in the

life of the Georgian pleasure ground. Although we begin with quieter experiences of the garden at night, most of this chapter is dedicated to describing grand public entertainments, which were characterised by illuminations and fireworks, so necessarily took place after dark.

Today, when gardens that are open to the public close their doors at five o'clock in the afternoon, very few people are able to enjoy these great creations in a quiet manner at night.[3] One of the least appreciated aspects of the Georgian designed landscape is how it was experienced at night, especially when nothing in particular was happening. But Georgian letters and diaries illustrate how the garden was appreciated by moonlight. For those planning social engagements, considering the phase of the moon was important. In an age long before electric or even gas light, when candles for the table and general household lighting were expensive, and travelling on unpredictable roads in the dark could be hazardous, social gatherings were usually timed to coincide as closely as possible with a full moon. This allowed guests to return home safely afterwards. Horace Walpole noted that the entertainment staged at Esher in May 1763 was blessed by a full moon and no doubt had been arranged to coincide with it.

The design elements and visual qualities of the Landscape Style meant that it lent itself to being seen and experienced at night-time, when the moon was reflected in the lake, its silvery light danced off the shiny leaves of the laurels (which formed the structural planting of so many shrubberies), and light-coloured, gravel paths snaked off into the darkness. Night-time, especially when there was a full or near full moon, was a good time to appreciate the garden alone, for solitary walks. Elizabeth Talbot wrote to her sister Harriot in 1798, saying that her neighbours at Lacock (Wiltshire) thought her 'deranged for liking moonlight walks and drives'. Horace Walpole reported that during a visit to Stowe in June 1744 George Hervey shut himself away during the day and only went out into the gardens at night to walk by moonlight.[4]

Elsewhere a night-time stroll in the park or the garden was an acknowledged pleasure. Marchioness Grey and her husband, Philip Yorke, certainly thought so. In August 1740, on their first visit to Wrest after their wedding, the young couple arrived at the house in the evening. Jemima, who was keen to show her new husband the beauties of her beloved garden, reported that 'the sun was but just set, and it was perfectly calm and fine. It was exactly the time I think the most pleasant of the whole day. The sereneness of the evening light spread a peculiar beauty over the whole place. We had a short but very pretty walk by owl-light and moonlight together.' It was so enchanting that Philip slipped out for another walk while she was getting ready for bed. Jemima was disappointed, continuing: 'for I wanted to have been with him every time he was to see anything in the garden'.[5] Occasionally guests and visitors were lucky enough to experience it at that time of day too. Elizabeth Anson, Philip's sister, wrote in 1748 to report that 'the Duchess of Bedford with a party have been at Wrest since you left it, in order to shew it to Lady Louisa Trentham. They were at the Hill House by Day-light, they say, but walked over the Garden by Moon-shine', so experiencing the best of both worlds.[6] Jemima enjoyed such walks at Philip's family house, Wimpole (Cambridgeshire), too. In August 1749, when staying there without him, she wrote to her husband: 'I found the family very well.' Her father-in-law, Lord Hardwicke, was in good spirits and 'very much pleased with the yearly improvements' there. She continued: 'this summer has finished the gallery, which is really a charming room, and the gravel paths about the park are very pretty and lead us into walking out these fine moonlight nights later than the [hours] of this place used to allow.'[7]

Today most people who experience the landscape park or garden at night do so at a concert or similar event, often ending with fireworks. What they are seeing is not so far from the grand entertainments of 200 years ago, which was the way most Georgians who were lucky enough to be entertained in the garden enjoyed it. This was a complete change of tempo for the pleasure ground from the *adagio* solitary time, with the bats flitting over the lake and the hoot of the owl in the trees above, to the *allegro* of crowds, noise and lights and the *crescendo* of fireworks as a finale.

Sometimes large-scale entertainments also involved the mansion, perhaps starting with dinner there in the afternoon or early evening for the guests who were in residence, but often, given the numbers of people expected, the only practical way of coping with the scale of the event was to stage the entertainment in the garden. This was even true of the grandest houses, which had been designed specifically with suites of impressively decorated, interconnecting rooms for balls and other hospitality expected of a great landowner.[8] Occasionally, however, hosts solved the problem of lack of inside space by constructing a temporary ballroom. The most notable example was that designed by Robert Adam for the Earl of Derby's sumptuous pre-nuptial fête at The Oaks (Surrey) in 1774 – although for this event much use was also made of the garden.[9] Elsewhere, when entertainments were staged outside it was not uncommon to find that one of the garden buildings was the epicentre of the celebration, the most prestigious location, where the grandest guests would be expected to dine or sup, listen to the music and watch the fireworks. Significantly, on such occasions the garden building had a higher status than that of the house. This was particularly true when the guest of honour was a member of the royal family. A visit from such an impressive personage was often an excuse for the staging of a fête. Other reasons for these events were coronations, royal birthdays, military victories and to celebrate the coming of age of the heir to the estate. The subtext to these costly entertainments is often supposed to be political, as a tactic to keep favour with the voters, but when the number of guests recorded is five times greater than the population of the nearest town, it is certain that only a small percentage of those enjoying the hospitality of the landlord would have been eligible to vote.[10] Less concrete motives of prestige and a reinforcing of a family's status may partly account for the effort and expense outlaid, but it is possible that there was also an element of paternalism on the part of the owner, as landlord and employer, in providing food and entertainment for large numbers of the local population.

The 'fête champêtre nocturne' (characterised by the combination of food, drink, music, illuminations and a multitude
catered for in marquees that typified the night-time entertainment in the pleasure ground) had its origin in a number of
disparate sources. First, there are some similarities with Elizabethan entertainments, staged for the Queen on her progresses
around the country, with their theatrical performances and
tableaux vivants set in and around gardens, and their associated temporary architecture. There were also influences from
France, in the form of the *divertissements* staged for Louis XIV
at Versailles, when the garden became a stage for lavish, semi-
theatrical, illuminated entertainments. Italian *feste* were also
important because they had a direct influence on public events
staged in London, which in turn influenced those in the pleasure ground. Those that happened in Rome were particularly
important, namely the Festa della Chinea and the Girandola,
which involved the construction of temporary architecture,
illuminations and fireworks. These spectacular festivals were
witnessed by the English *milordi* on their Grand Tours, as well
as many aspiring young architects, including William Kent and
specifically Robert Adam, who went on to design temporary
architecture and illuminations for royal celebrations. In London
it was often Italians who were commissioned to mastermind
state-sponsored celebrations, like the stage designer Giovanni
Niccolò Servandoni, who created the ill-fated *macchina* in Green
Park for the celebration of the Peace of Aix-la-Chapelle in
1749 (FIGURE 63).[11] This was a massive temple built of wood
and canvas in which the orchestra was hidden, as well as the
apparatus to launch the fireworks. An hour into the display, one

FIGURE 63   A detail from the *Perspective View of the Building for the Fireworks in the Green Park*, by Paul Angier after P. Brookes, 1749. As well as Servandoni's *macchina*, in all its glory, the view shows the free-standing illuminations on their spiral and pyramidal frames.

of the pavilions in which the fireworks were stored caught light, setting off some of the stored fireworks and ruining the whole effect. Thanks to the brave efforts of one of the carpenters the rest of the building was saved.

After the fiasco of the display in Green Park the Duke of Richmond opportunistically bought the remaining fireworks. Two weeks later, Horace Walpole reported that 'under the pretence of the Duke of Modena' being in London the Duke staged his own display in the garden of Richmond House and on the adjoining Thames.[12] The border of a contemporary engraving (FIGURE 64) details 14 different types of pyrotechnic devices that were set off, along with some of the illuminations. The evocatively named fireworks included: 'vertical suns' and 'fixed suns', 'flights of sky rockets', 'water rockets' and 'water ballons with three stages of lights'. This illustrates the wide variety available at the time. Accounts of entertainments in the gardens of country houses are often also specific in their names for them. A bill from a firework artist in Holborn among the Croome papers lists the purchase of 'Chinese Trees of Silver Flowers, Italian Suns, Roman Candles to throw up blazing Stars, Gold Flower-pots' as well as 'Water Rockets'.[13] This bill may relate to the visit of King George III to Croome in 1788. With such an array to let off, these displays could last a considerable time. At the ill-fated celebration in Green Park in 1749, the fireworks had already lasted an hour before things went wrong and were due to go on longer. In happier circumstances, when King Christian VII of Denmark was fêted by Princess Amelia at Gunnersbury (Middlesex) in 1768, the firework display lasted for 45 minutes (FIGURE 65).[14]

As well as state-sponsored celebrations, there were a number of entertainments set in parks and gardens staged personally by the royal family. In July 1763, Queen Charlotte held a fête in the garden of Buckingham House, as a surprise celebration for George III's birthday. The centrepiece of the garden decoration was a structure designed by Robert Adam that was part temporary architecture, part lighting effect. Like

FIGURE 64   (overleaf) *A View of the Fireworks and Illuminations at his grace the Duke of Richmond's at Whitehall and on the River Thames, on Monday 15th May 1749*. The borders show some of the wide range of illuminations and fireworks.

Regulated Piece of 5 Mutations.

Brutoni.

Vertical Wheel.

Spirali with Horisontal Wheel

Vertical Sun.

Battery of Marons.

Pots d'Aigretts with Fountains

N°1. Pavillon beautifully illuminated.
2. The Duke of Richmonds House.
3. The Boats and Barges, for the
Aquatic Fire-workes.
His Majesty's Barge

Vùe des FEUX d'ARTIFICE et des ILLUMINATION
sur la TAMISE et vis a vis de son l

Corded Mortars with Air Ballon

Do. with Saucissons.

Flights of Sky Rocket

Pots de Brin.

Water Rocketts.

Jatte d'eau.

Water Ballons with 3 Stages of Lights

Vertical Illumination

N° 1. Le Pavillion magnifiquement Illuminé.
2. L'Hotel de Monsig.r Le Duc de Richmond.
3. Les Bateaux employés aux Feux d'artifices Aquatique

par Monseigneur le Duc de RICHMOND de LENOX et d'AUBIGNY,
...undi le 15.ieme de Mai 1749. Sous la direction de Mons. Frederick.
a Londre.

FIGURE 65 *Windsor on a Rejoicing Night*, by Paul Sandby, 1768. Note the effect of the bonfire back-lighting the tower, the fireworks and the full moon peeping through the tree.

Servandoni's *macchina* in Green Park, but on a smaller scale, it was made of wood and canvas and was lit at night with 4,000 glass lamps.[15] The central sections included transparencies. These were among the most sophisticated forms of eighteenth-century illuminations and owed much to effects developed for the theatre. They were pictures painted on translucent fabric, usually linen. After dark they were back-lit, highlighting and often transforming the image.[16] Five years later, when the King staged an entertainment in the park at Richmond for his brother-in-law, King Christian VII of Denmark (who had already been feted at Gunnersbury), William Chambers created a vast pavilion, which was again part temporary architecture, part lighting effect and contained illuminated transparencies.[17] Both of these entertainments and their props were of a suitably regal scale.

It might be expected that these entertainments, staged by the King and Queen, such as those at Buckingham House and Richmond, influenced those in the pleasure ground of the country house. In fact, the comparison made was most often to the experience of the famous London pleasure gardens of Vauxhall. The pleasure gardens at Vauxhall had been a resort for Londoners since the mid-seventeenth century. In the 1730s they were relaunched by Jonathan Tyers and became the pre-eminent pleasure garden in the city. The site was laid out with tree-flanked walks, some broad and open, others dark and narrow. The Dark Walks were infamous for 'liaisons of all sorts', one of the many attractions of the garden.[18] Tyers also introduced exquisitely decorated supper boxes and employed the most fashionable musicians. The admission charge was modest, so that another attraction of Vauxhall was that a broad cross-section of society could rub shoulders there. All these elements contributed to the draw of the gardens but, arguably, what gave them their greatest enchantment was the lighting.

In the 1740s there were a thousand lamps in the garden at Vauxhall, and this number steadily increased during the eighteenth century.[19] Across several acres of ground these could all be lit in under two minutes, making the transition from growing darkness seem almost instant and utterly magical.[20] This was achieved by the lights being connected to long lengths of fuse, which could illuminate whole sections at a time. Two types of light were employed: large globe lamps, mounted on buildings and trees, gave the ambient light, whilst smaller strings of lights provided atmosphere. Tyers cunningly made use of illuminations both to add enchantment to the scene and to extend the hours of opening, and therefore potential profits. It was the charm and magical quality of the lights that seem to have so characterised the experience of Vauxhall, and it was this that was most emulated in the pleasure ground of the country house. So, when the coming-of-age celebration for Edward Coke at Holkham was described, it was in these terms: 'the splendour of the birthday was wonderfully great ... the ball began at 8', as elsewhere festivities did not finish until four o'clock in the morning after 'an admirable fire layed off upon the lake ... and the orangery was illuminated far beyond Vauxhall'.[21]

In the park or garden, illuminations might be achieved in a number of ways. Wax candles are recorded being used to add enchantment to the Grotto at Wentworth Woodhouse.[22] Tin lamps were used in the Grotto at Stowe; presumably they had a reflective quality.[23] These may have been fuelled by spermaceti whale oil, which is also recorded. In front of the Grotto floating lights dotted the water, in which they would have been reflected, doubling their effect, and strings of lanterns were hung in the surrounding trees. Sometimes specific sculptural or architectural features were illuminated. In 1805 the urns by the south portico of the house were specially lit for a fête for the Prince of Wales. Elsewhere lights were mounted on frames in the shape of stars, spirals or pyramids, as Walpole described for the Duchess of Northumberland's 'festino' (FIGURE 63).

Bonfires were also used at night in the Georgian garden, both as beacons and as part of the lighting effects, often to highlight a feature or backlight a building, as at Bretton Hall (Yorkshire). In July 1771, Sir Thomas Wentworth gave a fête here. The reason for it is unknown, but Sir Thomas was a well-known bon viveur and probably needed little excuse for a party. Like many others it started in the afternoon with more leisurely entertainments, but as darkness fell the excitements increased. Guests were fed 'a genteel cold collation', accompanied by 'French horns, and other field music'. Then, according to the *General Evening Post*,

> The front of the temple, and the woods, on both sides, were illuminated by a great number of lamps interspersed among the trees, which together with a large bonfire at the lower end of the lake and two other very splendid ones at a considerable distance upon the top of Woolley-edge, exhibited (after it was dark) a night-scene of a most grand appearance. To complete the whole, a great variety of fireworks were played off.[24]

The night finished with guests being rowed down the lake away from the scene of the entertainment, with cannon fired and to the 'cheers of the populace'.

Military and naval victories were often marked by the lighting of fires and beacons, as they had been for centuries, and were often a reason for staging a celebration. The earliest detailed description of a victory celebration in the gardens at Stowe recounts the events staged in 1758 to celebrate the victory of Louisbourg during the Seven Years War. In a letter to his sister Hester Pitt, George Grenville described how a bonfire was lit on the high ground in front of the Ladies Building, the Grotto was illuminated and fireworks set off, all accompanied by the ringing of bells (from the nearby church). Further music was provided by a 'chearfull Tabor & pipe accompany'd by the violin & voices'.[25] A small family party of 13 people was present, but 'multitudes in the Garden passed numbering'. The small number in the family party and the nature of the event celebrated, which would have been news-dependent, might suggest that this festivity was staged at short notice. This account also hints at the role of the garden at Stowe within the local community, as a place at which to gather at times of national celebration, which would not have been unique.

Later in the century such events were marked at Godmersham, then the estate of the adoptive father of Jane Austen's brother Edward. Just over two weeks after a significant naval battle in the Atlantic, on 18 June 1794, the inhabitants of the village and estate gathered to celebrate. The occasion was 'the important victory obtained by Lord Howe, and the Brave British Tars, over the French Fleet' and for those invited 'to testify their loyalty and attachment to their King and Country'. There were parades in front of the house and the singing of patriotic songs. Guests, both 'respectable visitors' and workers, were then entertained in the park with music and dancing. The night finished with 'a brilliant display of fireworks ... to the joy and satisfaction of every person in the neighbourhood'.[26]

Perhaps the most common reason for staging an entertainment in the park or pleasure ground was to celebrate the coming of age of the heir to the estate. This was a rite of passage, but in an age when infant mortality was so high, even among the wealthy and well-fed, it was a genuine cause of celebration for a young man to reach his majority. If he had made it through all the dangers of childhood to the age of 21 there was a strong chance he would outlive his father and the inheritance and security of the estate would be guaranteed.[27] William Beckford was one of those long-desired male heirs.[28] His father had several older sons, but they were illegitimate. William was therefore an only son born to an older father. With his legendary wealth and influential connections, young William's coming of age celebrations might be expected to have been lavish. They were staged at Fonthill over three days in early October 1781 and included in Beckford's own words 'a tumult of balls, concerts and illuminations'. The gardens and park were used as the stage and backdrop for much of the entertainment, for both aesthetic and practical reasons, as the guest list ran into such a number as could only be accommodated outside. Beckford himself reported that there were above 10,000 people spread out across the lawn and hill in sight of the house. The farmers and 'substantial tradesmen' were treated to feasting in tents erected below the terrace. As darkness fell, both the marquees and a specially constructed arch were illuminated. A series of bonfires were lit, as was the temple, which 'presented a continued glow of saffron-coloured flame and the throng that assembled before it looked devilish by contrast'. Watching the scene Beckford caught snatches of music from wind instruments, probably oboes and French horns, which were so popular outside, and 'at intervals mortars were discharged and a girandola of rockets burst into clear bluish stars that cast a bright light for miles'.[29]

FIGURE 66   A detail from *The Dinner in Mote Park, Maidstone, after the Royal Review of the Kentish Volunteers*, by William Alexander, *c.*1799. When King George III came to review the Kentish volunteers, hundreds of people dined at long tables in the park, each with a large barrel at the end. The royal standard flies outside the grandest of the tents on the right.

Ten thousand people may seem a large number, but an account of a similar celebration at Castle Howard (Yorkshire) in 1794 for Lord Morpeth, the heir to the estate, estimated that 14,000 people were entertained in the park (FIGURE 66). At Chatsworth (Derbyshire), for the coming of age of Lord Hartington in May 1811, an estimated 40,000 people, mainly the middle and working classes, were entertained to food, drink and music in the park, with the polite guests hosted by the estate steward in the courtyard of the house, which had been given a temporary roof for the occasion. The event was also celebrated at the family's other estate, Hardwick Hall (Derbyshire), where the proceedings turned into something of a riot. Neither the Marquess of Hartington nor his father, the Duke of Devonshire, was actually in attendance for either of these events and a ball had already been held at Devonshire House in London. The Duke died just a few weeks later. [30]

The Duke and his Duchess, the famous Georgiana, had preferred using Chiswick House, their villa near London, for such events.[31] This must have been more convenient for the city, perhaps allowing a greater ease of acquiring more sophisticated musicians and other elements of the entertainments. The garden at Chiswick would also have provided a more intimate setting. In 1800 the Duchess hosted a fête there to celebrate the entrance into society of her eldest daughter Georgiana, known as Little G. The guest of honour was the Prince of Wales. The garden, again, played a central role, with bands of musicians carefully situated in strategic places. The focal point, where the most important guests were to dine, was one of the garden buildings, probably the Ionic Temple in the Orange Tree Garden as it was the only building substantial enough at that time. The amphitheatrical setting would have lent itself to an enclosed, exclusive gathering. One guest, Lady Jerningham, wrote an account in a letter to her daughter, Lady Bedingfield, saying that she 'found it extremely pleasant and was very much amused'. She was particularly taken by the music, observing: 'several Bands of Musick were very well placed in the garden, so that as soon as you were out of the hearing of one Band, you began to catch the notes of another; thus Harmony always met your

FIGURE 67   *View from the North Portico of Stowe House, Feb. 1818, showing the celebrations for the coming of age of the heir of the Duke of Buckingham & Chandos at Stowe, including Morris dancers*, by an unknown artist, 1818. Even in the winter, with snow on the ground, the local population was entertained at Stowe by morris men and music provided by what might have been 'militia men with tabor and pipe'. Dinner was provided in thatched, tent-like structures.

ears. This sort of continued concert had always a pleasant effect upon my nerves.' She continued to explain that the Duchess, the Prince and eighteen others dined in the Temple, saying that 'when we understood that the Duchess and these fine People were in the Temple, we Goths took possession of the House, where we found in every room a table spread, with cold meat, fruit, ice, and all sorts of Wine... After the eating and quaffing was over, the young ladies danced on the Green.'[32]

The aristocracy had a clear interest in celebrating the coming of age of the heir to the estate. There is evidence, however, that again the middle classes emulated the upper classes by staging similar celebrations. In 1768, Joanna Melliar, wife of the vicar of Castle Cary (Somerset), hosted a celebration for the coming of age of the son of the Earl of Ilchester in her modest garden. She had long been friendly with the family as her father had been their steward at Redlynch, so she had a personal interest in the event too. She gave a 'public breakfast' in the garden of the vicarage. The food and drink were suitable to her standing as the wife of a clergyman: no 'wine of all sorts here'; instead 'there was coffee, tea, chocolate and all kinds of cake etc. proper for the above'; and the guests were entertained by a 'very good band of musick' and the ringing of bells, and '80 loaves' were 'given to the poor of Cary'.[33]

The presence of the Prince of Wales at the entertainment at Chiswick in 1800 was not the catalyst for the event, though he was the guest of honour. Elsewhere royal visits might occasion a fête in the garden with the diversions of food and drink, music, illuminations and fireworks. Although the Stowe estate did not host a reigning monarch until the visit of Queen

Victoria in 1845, other members of both the British and foreign royal families were entertained. When Princess Amelia made her first visit in 1764, Earl Temple planned a 'fête champêtre nocturne', for which the Grotto was, as usual, the centrepiece. For two days the weather was too wet, but on the third it became more favourable and preparations went on all day, so that as it became dark enough the Princess and other guests could enjoy the garden in a completely different guise from their morning and afternoon experiences. An account was written by Lady Temple's maid. She reported:

> At ten the gardens were illuminated with above a thousand lights and the water before the Grotto was covered with floating lights. At the farther end of the canal on the ship, which was curiously figured with lights, was a place for the music, which performed all supper time.[34]

The repetition of the word 'lights' gives some idea of her impression of the scale of the illuminations. She estimated that there were over a thousand people in the gardens to see them, many presumably also hoping to catch a glimpse of a member of the royal family. Princess Amelia walked down to the Grotto at half past ten and took in the scene, walked a little in the gardens, then returned to the Grotto to 'an elegant cold supper'. 'Nothing was seen but lights and people, nothing was heard but music and fireworks, and nothing was felt but joy and happiness' continued Lady Temple's maid, who was herself among the crowds and did not return home until just before midnight.

A generation later an even grander entertainment was given to mark the visit of the Prince of Wales, later George IV, in 1805. The Grotto was once again the centrepiece of the entertainment, and the surrounding Elysian Fields were further ornamented by three temporary structures erected for the event. One was an obelisk, probably constructed of wood and painted to look like stone. The second was a bridge, which would have provided another means of crossing the water for the many people in the gardens, so helping circulation. And the third was a canopied seat that faced down the water towards the Grotto.[35] Two complementary descriptions of the evening were written by sisters Betsey Fremantle and Harriet Wynne.[36] The entertainment for the Prince's party started when they left the house and walked down into the gardens at nine o'clock at night. Huge crowds of local people were present to see the Prince and enjoy the music, illuminations and fireworks; Betsey Fremantle suggested perhaps as many as 10,000. To control such a number certain areas were roped off. Although the sisters were close friends of the family, and spent some of the evening in the Grotto, they were not grand enough to sup there, and Betsey ate in one of the large number of marquees, which her sister referred to as 'Villas Marques', where supper was served to most guests. The Prince and his immediate party ate in the Grotto. Both sisters were impressed by all the elements of the entertainment. Harriet wrote that 'the Scene was something most magnificent – The Grotto, bridge [and] Villas Marques formed a most enchanting coup d'oeil' and Betsey reported that the gardens had 'the appearance of enchantment, the Grotto & surrounding scene being illuminated most brilliantly'.

The Prince, his party and the crowds were also entertained by 'maskers' and several groups of morris men; these were always popular at Stowe, appearing in earlier accounts too. They are seen in one of the three pictures of the coming-of-age celebrations for the son of the Marquess of Buckingham in 1818 (FIGURE 67). The crowds gathered for the entertainment for the Prince of Wales also enjoyed the music of the 'Pandeans', panpipes intended to evoke pastoral or even bacchanalian associations and 'Savoyards', itinerant musicians playing the hurdy-gurdy. In the Grotto during supper the Prince's party listened to the fashionable singing group the Knyvetts performing catches and glees; Charles Knyvett was regarded as one of the finest proponents of these part-songs of the time. The Prince and other guests walked around the Elysian Fields viewing the temporary architecture, which was probably lit, as well as the illumination of the Grotto and the surrounding trees. Before supper the fireworks were set off; Betsey Fremantle recorded that they 'succeeded wonderfully well, the water rockets had a particularly good effect & the whole went off with great éclat'.

Today we might expect the fireworks to be the climax of an event, but at Stowe they were let off before supper, which may have been served as late as midnight, as it was when Walpole was entertained at Esher in 1763. Betsey Fremantle did not go home until one o'clock and her sister Harriet reported that the gardens were still full of people until four in the morning. As the night wore on through the small hours, bonfires would have burnt down to embers and the oil run out in the lanterns. If they were estate workers, the musicians would walk back to their cottages or, if they had been hired from London, to their inns. All the revellers, from the grandest duchess to the lowly lady's maid, the tenant farmer to the tradesman, would wend their way home to bed. Soon the sounds of French horns or panpipes would give way to the dawn chorus. Elsewhere, in another garden, the owner was about to get up and enjoy an early morning walk accompanied by the singing of the birds before breakfast. He might, perhaps, meet the gardener's boy sweeping the gravel path, or the lad leading the nag pulling the garden roller across the grass, which was still slightly wet with dew, and another day in the life of the Georgian garden would begin.

Afterword

A S THE NINETEENTH century progressed and the Georgian age became the Victorian, fashions in garden design naturally changed. Long vistas and parkland sweeping up to the house went out of favour, although on many estates parkland remained the setting for gardens that were, once again, more formal and structured. The buildings that Thomas Whately had described as 'beautiful objects' and 'agreeable retreats' were not so fundamental to the aesthetic as they had been in the Georgian garden; they did not proliferate and they tended not to be created as distant eye-catchers. For much of the twentieth century the landscape garden was deeply unfashionable; its foremost proponent, 'Capability' Brown, was regarded as a vandal, accused (with a liberal use of cliché) of 'sweeping away' so many formal gardens of the earlier generation.[1] But in the last decades of the twentieth century his reputation, and that of the Landscape Style in general, experienced a renaissance, so that these parks and gardens were, once again, celebrated as masterpieces of art.

Against this background the tradition of the eye-catcher has experienced something of a quiet revival. In the late twentieth and early twenty-first centuries, owners of gardens and parks across Britain have continued the tradition, building structures in the spirit of their Georgian predecessors, which have both a functional and a visual *raison d'être*, and there are more examples than you might expect. I have often visited gardens where I have been surprised by a garden building that so clearly evokes the Georgian eye-catcher. These structures offer a place of retreat and solitude or contemplation; they may be created in a elegaic vein, or more sociably used for dining and music; and they all relate to their landscape setting in the Georgian manner.

One of the most striking is the Pavilion at Oare House (Wiltshire).[2] Built of glass and steel, and unashamedly modern, it does not pretend to be Georgian, or historic in any way.[3] It is the only work in Britain of the architect I.M. Pei, who is probably best known for his pyramids at the Louvre in Paris. In its scale and siting it is, for me, reminiscent of the Pavilion by Thomas Archer at Wrest Park. Just as at Wrest, the Pavilion at Oare is set at the end of an avenue, on alignment with the house. The pagoda-like structure references oriental architecture and might be seen as a modern take on eighteenth-century chinoiserie buildings, like the Pagoda at Kew, for example. It is used as 'a comfortable living space-cum-function room providing areas for dining, sitting and studying'. In Georgian nomenclature it might be described as a banqueting house, a retreat and a belvedere.

The Hurlstone Tower (Northumberland) is also both a banqueting house and a belvedere. Sited on the top of a hill looking across to the Cheviots, it was created to mark the millennium. The tower was built by Duncan Davidson as an eye-catcher for his house, Lilburn Tower, just over a kilometre away. It is circular in plan and Gothic in detail. In complete contrast to the Pavilion at Oare, it overtly references the Georgian eye-catcher. It was based on a design by William Kent. Like many of its Georgian counterparts the tower has a kitchen on the lower floor, with a dining room above; its eight Gothic windows giving panoramic views across this stunning landscape.

The Folly at Doddington Place (Kent) (FIGURES 68 and 69) was built by Richard Oldfield as a memorial to his first wife, Alexandra, so follows in the elegiac tradition of Georgian garden creators like William Shenstone. It was also constructed to form a visual punctuation mark at the end of a walk from the house, which previously went nowhere in particular. In plan it is a flattened octagon, of two storeys in height and Gothic in character. The staircase inside is decorated with *trompe l'œil* campanulas and jasmine that appears to be sprouting from cracks in the wall, and a realistic-seeming cock pheasant which peeps round the doorway. From the panelled upper room there are good views across the park and out to the wider landscape; in the reverse vista it works as an ensemble with the house. In the same way that eighteenth-century owners such as Coplestone Warre Bampfylde designed their own buildings, the Folly was constructed from sketches made by Richard Oldfield himself; his drawings are reminiscent of Bampylde's hastily scribbled ideas on the back of an apothecary's business card. Sir Roy Strong has called it 'a piece of Hampton Court', but equally it fits in the Georgian tradition and has a feeling of

FIGURE 68   The eye-catcher known as The Folly at Doddington, built as a
memorial to Richard Oldfield's wife, Alexandra. On a bright winter's day, the bricks
reflect the orangey-pink trunks of the Scots pines behind.

the alternative sketches by Bampfylde and the painter Richard
Phelps for a garden building at Dunster Castle (Somerset).[4]
The upper chamber is a quiet room, a good place to escape
with a book.

Bignor Park (West Sussex) is very much a family house,
rooted in the community; the garden is used to stage plays,
concerts and village fêtes. As with the other examples, here
the history of the designed landscape is respected, but it is
not fossilised. It is vibrant and looking to the future, while

FIGURE 69   The upper room inside The Folly at Doddington; from the Gothic windows there are wide vistas across the park and out to the remarkably unspoilt Kent countryside. As well as being a quiet place to read, it is used for occasional meals.

nodding to the past. This attitude is embodied by the Temple (FIGURE 70), a new building in an older tradition. Following the storm of 1987 the shrubbery close to the house was left tattered and bare, and a scheme was conceived to both give a new visual focus and mark the eightieth birthday, in 1992, of the 4th Viscount Mersey's mother, Kitty. Set on a lawn fringed with rhododendrons laid out in the 1820s, it is an open octagon. The inside of the dome bears an inscription from a Jacobite ballard by Kitty's ancestor, Maud Lansdowne, Lady Nairne. It is used now for theatrical performances and concerts, and by the present Viscount Mersey's daughters for teddy-bear picnics.

Each of these modern eye-catchers stands out as the one notable building in their respective park or garden. As I was writing this book and had started to reflect on this continuing tradition, I was invited to a garden nestled under the South Downs, ostensibly to see the Belvedere, a modern building in the eighteenth-century tradition. When I arrived, however, I found not just one fine eye-catcher in the Georgian spirit, but four. The house and garden are modest in relation to Bignor, Doddington, Lilburn and Oare, and this discovery has most strongly illustrated the continuing prevalence of the eye-catcher. The interest and significance of this garden increased

FIGURE 70   The Temple at Bignor Park, used for theatricals and teddy bear picnics.

FIGURE 71   The interior of Professor Middlemas's Gazebo, with its Piranesi prints,
but no longer with the chaise longue where he used to nap after lunch.

with the discovery that it has a connection that brings me back
to where this book began.

The setting of the garden and small area of parkland at the
foot of the hills and the scale of the design are reminiscent
of Gilbert White's landscape at Selborne. There is even a
turning seat, though not in the form of a barrel like White's,
and its creator was similarly hands-on. The Belvedere, a small
classical temple, is set on rising ground looking eastwards
along the north scarp of the Downs. It is simply a place to sit
and take in the fine view. The Gazebo, which is closer to the

house, has an enclosed room and offers greater possibilities for goings-on in the garden, including dining, music and sleep. It is built of brick and flint and the simple design is similar to the lost Wallbridge summerhouse in Stroud (FIGURE 58). Topped with a pyramidal tiled roof, the main room is a cube decorated with eighteenth-century Italian topographical prints (FIGURE 71). The buildings were all created by the late Keith Middlemas, a professor of history at the University of Sussex, who largely built them single-handedly. All were created out of recycled materials and happy discoveries in reclamation yards. The Belvedere was nominally yet another millennium project; however, it was inspired not by the date but by a load of fine, dressed stone in need of a purpose.

It seems entirely natural that a history professor with a strong sense of aesthetics and a grasp of the practicalities of building might create such eye-catchers, but it became even more understandable when I discovered that he had been educated at Stowe School, whose Georgian gardens were probably the most densely populated with such structures. Here, as a schoolboy, Professor Middlemas must have wandered through the gardens, at a time when many of the buildings were shrouded in shrubbery, giving a magical air of potential discovery. It is easy to imagine it being a formative experience for him. It was at Stowe that I started my journey investigating how Georgian gardens and their buildings were lived in and used, so finding a connection in this modest-sized private garden feels like a journey coming full circle.

Notes

CHAPTER I

1. It was the influential art historian Kenneth Clark who first pointed out the importance of the Landscape Style in his pioneering television series and book of 1969 *Civilisation*.

2. For much of the Georgian period the majority of landowners favoured the classical style for their houses; Horace Walpole's Gothic fantasy Strawberry Hill being a notable exception. Eye-catchers on the other hand were often, as Giles Worsely observes, far more stylistically adventurous than their parent house. Building on a smaller scale and smaller budget allowed patrons to experiment with style. Garden buildings in the oriental taste, for example, were created from the late 1730s onwards, but this style was not used for a large-scale parent building until the Royal Pavilion at Brighton in the early nineteenth century. G. Worsley, *Classical Architecture: The Heroic Age* (New Haven CT, 1995), p. 212.

3. Thomas Whately, *Observations on Modern Gardening* (Dublin, 1770), p. 117. Although Whately spelled his 'agreable retreats' with only one 'e', I have taken the liberty of using the standard modern spelling 'agreeable' for the rest of the book.

4. There are precedents for distant garden buildings in the earlier period, for example the Elizabethan retreats of the New Beild at Lyveden (Northamptonshire) and Wothorpe at Burghley (Lincolnshire), but there is a difference in scale between these sorts of retreat and most Georgian garden buildings; moreover they were not part of a proliferation of structures within the design.

5. This compares with the wealth of pictorial sources for activities in the garden in pre-revolutionary France. One particularly charming and informative series derives from the transparencies of Carmontelle (1717–1803), who experimented with long scrolls of translucent paper, rolled across a beam of light, while accompanied by a commentary. Intended to evoke a stroll through a garden, they have been described as the 'cinema of the Enlightenment'.

6. Although a wide range of jolly goings-on and more sedate pastimes are included here, there are some necessary omissions. Blood sports particularly are not discussed. Hunting, which was perhaps the most dominant form of sport, was not exclusively carried out within parks and not deliberately within gardens, but rather ranged across the wider countryside. Shooting did take place within landscape parks and

help to shape their form. Kennels were used as eye-catchers, but tended to be noisy and rather un-fragrant, so not places where the general company would want to take a picnic, or sit and read a book. The relationship between these activities and the designed landscape warrants a book in itself.

CHAPTER 2

1. Jane Austen, *Pride and Prejudice* (London, 1973 [1813]), pp. 266, 382, chs 42 and 59.
2. John Phibbs has calculated that the acreage of landscape on which Brown had influence adds up to around half a million acres, the equivalent of an average English county.
3. The nickname 'Capability' was barely used in his lifetime and, as Jane Brown has pointed out, never to his face.
4. Jane Austen, *Mansfield Park* (London, 1985 [1814]), p. 87, ch. 6.
5. For a detailed discussion of the development of the Landscape Style during the Georgian period, see Tom Williamson, *Polite Landscapes* (Stroud, 1998); Timothy Mowl, *Gentlemen and Players* (Stroud, 2000).
6. Mark Girouard, *Life in the English Country House* (London, 1980), charts the evolution of the architecture of the country house away from the medieval tradition of the household as a family to one where, by the eighteenth century, servants were kept at arm's length, which manifested itself with the development of back stairs and garrets.
7. For the management of water by Brown, see Steffie Shields, '"Mr Brown Engineer": Lancelot Brown's Early Work at Grimsthorpe Castle and Stowe', *Garden History*, 34:2 (2006). See also Judith Roberts, '"Well Temper'd Clay": Constructing Water Features in the Landscape Park', *Garden History*, 29:1 (2001).
8. Oliver Rackham, *The History of the Countryside* (London, 2000), pp. 122–9.
9. Quoted in Williamson, *Polite Landscapes*, p. 122.
10. The agricultural revolution is intrinsically linked to the phenomenon of 'enclosure', by which private owners took control of land that had for centuries been cultivated or grazed communally. The extent to which the Enclosure Acts affected the designed landscape has been hotly debated by economic and landscape historians. For a summary, see Williamson, *Polite Landscapes*, pp. 9–15.
11. John Phibbs, *The Art of Capability Brown: Place-making 1716–1783* (London, 2016).
12. A term used by Catherine Battie in the journal of her stay in Selborne in 1763; see Rashleigh Holt-White, *The Life and Letters of Gilbert White of Selborne*, vol. 1 (London, 1901), pp. 139–40.
13. See Stella Tillyard, *Aristocrats: Caroline, Emily, Louisa and Sarah Lennox 1740–1832* (London, 1995), p. 131.
14. Nicola Shulman, *Fashion and Gardens* (London, 2014), pp. 27–31.
15. The number of views of each seat should not be taken as a fair representation of their degree of influence; much was due to the ease of finding views with which to illustrate such an extensive service. Thus, while Stowe justifiably takes up 48 views, some fairly obscure Staffordshire seats are also represented, being close to Wedgwood's factory at Etruria. Peter Hayden, *Russian Parks and Gardens* (London, 2005).
16. Thomas Weiss, *Infinitely Beautiful: The Dessau–Worlitz Garden Realm* (Berlin, 2005), pp. 130–42.

17. Hayden, *Russian Parks and Gardens*, pp. 82, 96.
18. Amanda Vickery, *Behind Closed Doors: At Home in Georgian England* (New Haven CT, 2010), p. 6.
19. In the Georgian period the term 'polite' would denote a knowledge of taste and a sense of decorum. This was not limited to the upper classes but, increasingly as the period progressed, filtered down to the middle echelons of society too.
20. Vickery, *Behind Closed Doors*, pp. 26–7.
21. Girouard, *Life in the English Country House*, p. 189.
22. Lord Coventry, then Lord Deerhurst, to Sanderson Miller, February 1750, in Lilian Dickens and Mary Stanton (eds), *An Eighteenth Century Correspondence* (London, 1910), p. 162.
23. For example, see Joanna Martin, *Wives and Daughters: Women and Children in the Georgian Country House* (London and New York, 2004), p. 305.
24. Girouard, *Life in the English Country House*, p. 161.
25. Earl Temple to Hester Pitt, Lady Chatham, summer 1770, Public Record Office 30/8/62 Folio 199.
26. Beckford to Sir Isaac Heard, Fonthill, 24 July 1799, in Lewis Melville, *The Life and Letters of William Beckford of Fonthill* (London, 1910), p. 256. Sir Isaac Heard was officer of arms at the College of Arms in London.
27. Vickery, *Behind Closed Doors*, p. 147.
28. Girouard, *Life in the English Country House*, p. 210.
29. John Summerson, 'The Classical Country House in the Eighteenth-Century', in *The Unromantic Castle* (London, 1990). See also Giles Worsely, *Classical Architecture in Britain: The Heroic Age* (New Haven CT, 1995). Vickery, however, states in *Behind Closed Doors* that an appetite for new buildings was 'far from universal among the peerage' (p. 129).
30. '"A Bullock a Week": Provisioning the Georgian Household', lecture by Mary-Anne Garry at Georgian Group symposium 'Georgian Food and Drink', London, June 2001. The barrow was listed in an inventory of 1760; see Tessa Murdoch, *Noble Households: Eighteenth Century Inventories of Great Houses* (Cambridge, 2006), p. 217.
31. Vere Birdwood (ed.), *So Dearly Loved, So Much Admired: Letters to Hester Pitt, Lady Chatham from Her Relations and Friends 1744–1801* (London, 1994), p. 17.
32. Martin, *Wives and Daughters*, pp. 97–8.
33. For a simple summary of dining in Tudor England, see Peter Brears, *Food and Cooking in 16th Century Britain: History and Recipes* (London, 1985), p. 18.
34. Peter Brears, *Food and Cooking in 17th Century Britain: History and Recipes* (London, 1985), p. 23.
35. Martin, *Wives and Daughters*, p. 118.
36. Luncheon was originally a meal eaten away from home by workers. It evolved during the nineteenth century as the gap between breakfast and dinner increased.
37. Horace Walpole to Montagu in W.S. Lewis (ed.), *The Yale Edition of Horace Walpole's Correspondence*, vol. 10 (New Haven CT, 1937–83), p. 73.

CHAPTER 3
1. Joanna Martin, *Wives and Daughters* (London, 2004), p. 112.
2. For the Duchess's landscaping, see Laura Mayer, 'Landscape as Legacy: 1st

Duchess of Northumberland, and the Gothick Garden Buildings of Alnwick, Northumberland', *Garden History*, 39:1 (2011).

3. Martin, *Wives and Daughters*, p. 301.

4. Ibid., p. 288.

5. As at Maddingley, Cambridgeshire; see Jane Brown, *Lancelot 'Capability' Brown: The Omnipotent Magician, 1716–1783* (London, 2012), p. 111.

6. Jane Austen, *Pride and Prejudice* (London, 1973 [1813]), ch. 10, p. 97. Mavis Batey has observed that in this little incident Jane Austen was demonstrating her knowledge of William Gilpin's picturesque theories, which said that if one painted cows they should be grouped as three, with one detached. Mrs Batey suggested that there was a subtext giving Eliza's opinion of the other ladies.

7. Letter from Frances Irwin, Public Record Office 30/29/4/2 f.20, quoted in Brown, *Lancelot 'Capability' Brown*, pp. 191–2.

8. Martin, *Wives and Daughters*, p. 274.

9. Edmund Burke, *A Philosophical Enquiry into the Sublime and Beautiful* (Harmondsworth, 1998 [1757]), p. 182. I am grateful to John Phibbs for this reference.

10. Note of 15 July 1784, taken from Norman Scarfe's translation. I am grateful to John Phibbs for this reference.

11. 1817 edition of the guide to Blenheim. I am grateful to Laura Mayer for this quotation.

12. William Felton, *A Treatise on Carriages*, vol. 2 (London, 1795), pp. 9, 49, quoted in Martin, *Wives and Daughters*, p. 297.

13. Martin, *Wives and Daughters*, pp. 296–7.

14. William Hawkes (ed.), *The Diaries of Sanderson Miller of Radway* (Stratford-upon-Avon, 2005) p. 65.

15. At the time Miller was designing the finials for the Gothic building – see entry for 6 November 1749 – another strong indication that improvements were being discussed.

16. Elizabeth Anson to Marchioness Grey, Admiralty, 19 May 1752, Lucas Papers, Bedfordshire and Luton Archive Service (BLAS) L 30/9/3/33.

17. Martin, *Wives and Daughters*, p. 280.

18. The 1758 Rievaulx Terrace complemented the earlier (1730s) terrace at Duncombe Park. They are now, however, in separate ownership. Duncombe's terrace is also ornamented with fine buildings.

19. Mark Girouard, *Old Wardour Castle: Guidebook* (London, 2012).

20. John Henry Michell, *The Tour of the Duke of Somerset, and the Rev. J.H. Michell, through parts of England, Wales and Scotland, in the year 1795* (London, 1845), p. 206.

21. There is such an example in Brown's design at Ampthill Park (Bedfordshire). Elsewhere evidence of tents survives in names in the landscape, like Tent Hill at Studley Royal.

22. R.L. Winstanley (ed.), *The Ansforde Diary Of James Woodforde 1761–2* (Castle Cary, 1977), pp. 22–6.

23. For example, at Ingress in Kent; towards the end of October 1772, a time of year when one might expect outdoor furniture to be in store, there were chairs in the Temple, the Cave, the Tunnel Under the Road and the Mausoleum, including green-painted Windsor chairs, and in the Cave 'chairs imitating nature', so probably in a rustic style, fashioned out of gnarled branches of trees. I am grateful to Hugh Vaux for passing on details of the inventory for Ingress. National Archives, C104/242.

24. Georgina Battiscombe, *English Picnics* (London, 1951), pp. 3–8.
25. Jane Austen, *Emma* (Harmondsworth, 1988 [1815]), p. 348, ch. 42.
26. Deidre Le Faye, *A Chronology of Jane Austen* (Cambridge, 2006), p. 345, 21 September 1807. This is an early reference to a sandwich as part of a picnic.
27. Ibid., p. 312.
28. Mavis Batey suggested that the redesign of the garden at St John's College, Oxford, and the innovation of the shrubberies there coincided with the outlawing of chamber pots, and therefore it is possible that the new shrubberies were developed primarily to conceal privies.
29. For example, as seen in paintings by Thomas Robins of Painswick and the detached pleasure ground of Pan's Lodge.
30. Just under half a mile from the mansion at Goodwood is a detached pleasure ground, skirted by a wall on one side and a ha-ha on the other, which allowed views back towards the house and beyond, across the landscape towards Chichester Cathedral and out towards the Solent. Within it are two further interesting garden buildings: Carné's Seat and the Shell House (notably decorated with shells from around the world by the 2nd Duchess of Richmond and her daughters, the famous Lennox sisters). Carne's Seat was used as a dining room.
31. Jane Austen, *Sense and Sensibility* (London, 1986 [1811]), pp. 91–2, ch. 12.
32. All the City livery companies and guilds had their own ceremonial barges; see Kenneth Nicholls Palmer, *Ceremonial Barges on the River Thames* (London, 1997). For an example of the ceremonial use of the Thames, see also the description of George I's trip from Whitehall to Chelsea, accompanied by members of the court in other boats and musicians in a City company's barge playing music composed for the occasion by Handel, in Donald Burrows, *Handel* (Oxford, 1996), p. 78.
33. For example, on the greensand at Ampthill Park, Bedfordshire.
34. F.A. Blaydes (ed.), *Bedfordshire Notes & Queries*, vol. 1 (Bedford, 1886), p. 47.
35. Humphry Repton, *Sketches and Hints on Landscape Gardening* (London, 1794), p. 41.
36. Prince Frederick was the eldest son of George II and father of George III. He had a bad relationship with both his parents. He died in 1751, nine years before his father.
37. More detail about the boats at Stowe and the argument for Lord Cobham's galley being designed by William Kent can be found in my article 'Boats and Boating in the Designed Landscape 1720–1820', *Garden History*, 34:1 (2006).
38. Earl Temple's ship can be seen in the view looking across the lake to the Temple of Venus, by Chatelain, engraved by Bickham in 1753. It is the only known view.
39. Philippa Kielmansegge (ed.), *Diary of Journey to England, 1761–62* (London, 1902), p. 233.
40. The earliest known example was performed for Julius Caesar in the flooded Campus Martius in Rome. But possibly the most epic of these naumachias was played out for the Emperor Claudius on Lake Fucino in AD 52; it included 100 ships and 19,000 combatants. The phenomenon was resurrected in Italy during the Renaissance, though on a smaller scale.
41. See Alistair Roach, 'Miniature Ships in Designed Landscapes', *The Mariner's Mirror*, 98:1 (2012), pp. 44–8.
42. A 'snow' was a modification of a brig. Ibid., p. 46.

43. For records for the ship at Wotton, see for example Henry E. Huntington Library, Stowe MS, STG Accounts box 123 (Wotton repairs), National Trust database ID number 4195. The battery at Wotton can be seen on the 1847 estate plan by Henry Howard, Buckinghamshire Record Office, Ma/298. George Moutard Woodward, *Eccentric Excursions in England and South Wales...* (London 1796), p. 94. See also my article 'Using the Pleasure Grounds: Their Social History' in Patrick Eyres (ed.), *The Grenville Landscape of Wotton House, New Arcadian Journal*, 65/66 (2009).

44. Byron was tried for murder, found guilty of manslaughter, but got off with a fine. He also apparently shot his coachman.

45. Alan G. Jamieson, 'Byron, John (1723–1786)', *Oxford Dictionary of National Biography* (Oxford, 2004); online edn, October 2009, www.oxforddnb.com/view/article/4282, accessed 20 December 2015.

46. Michael Cousins and Patrick Eyres, 'Naumachia: The Parkland Phenomenon of the Mock Naval Battle', *New Arcadian Journal*, 39/40 (1995).

47. John Anthony, *The Gardens of Britain*, no. 6 (London, 1979), pp. 129–30.

48. I am grateful to Professor Timothy Mowl for the information about Batchacre and to Dr Clare Hickman for photographs.

49. Chatham Papers, Public Record Office, fols 278–278v.

50. Humphry Repton, Red Book for Holkham, Norfolk, 30 October 1789.

51. BLAS, Lucas Papers, L30/9/3/16.

52. Amabel Polwarth to Catherine Talbot, 29 July 1766, BLAS, Lucas Papers, L 30/21/2.

53. Jane Roberts, *Royal Landscape: The Gardens and Parks of Windsor* (New Haven CT, 1997), p. 429.

54. Florence Ambrose Rathbone (ed.), *Letters of Lady Jane Coke* (London, 1899), p. 129.

55. Martin, *Wives and Daughters*, p. 286.

56. Thomas Linley Junior: www.oxfordmusiconline.com/subscriber/article/grove/music/16713pg3, accessed 3 October 2015.

57. Godfrey Clark (ed.), *Gleanings from an Old Portfolio, Containing Some Correspondence between Lady Louisa Stuart and her Sister Caroline, Countess of Portarlington*, vol. 1 (London, 1895), p. 40.

58. Catherine Symonds, 'Parson Woodforde as Gardener', *Parson Woodforde Society Quarterly Journal*, XXXII:3 (1999), p. 26.

59. The context of the building has changed since Earl de Grey, Jemima's grandson, rebuilt the house on a different site, and much of the shrubbery in which the building was set is gone, although some of the associated ponds remain.

60. The earliest edition in the British Library is a 2nd edition of 1706. There were subsequent editions in 1715 and 1722. He had already published *An Enquiry into the Right Use and Abuses of the hot, cold and temperate Baths in England*, in 1697.

61. Floyer quoted in Susan Kellerman, 'Bath Houses: An Introduction', *Follies Journal*, 1 (2001), p. 24.

62. George Cheyne, *An Essay on Health and Long Life* (London, 1724), p. 102.

63. To Sanderson Miller from T. Lennard Barrett, May 1745, in Lilian Dickens and Mary Stanton (eds), *An Eighteenth Century Correspondence: Being the Letters to Sanderson Miller, Esq., of Radway* (London, 1910), p. 111.

64. A wilderness was usually a small, discrete area of dense woodland or shrubbery within a garden, often with winding paths, offering seclusion and sometimes surprise features like seats or statuary.

65. The original layout around the cold bath can be seen in the bird's-eye view of the gardens by Thomas Robins.

66. It is not known where Copley built his pool, though it seems most likely that it was in the garden – due to its size it was probably not in the house as this would have occasioned major adaptation of space. Moreover, the examples of other pools in gardens prove that this would have been seen as a sensible place to site it. The location is discussed in Michael Klemperer, *Style and Social Competition between the Landed Classes, Articulated through the Large Scale Ornamental Landscapes of the Doncaster District of South Yorkshire*, Ph.D. thesis, University of Sheffield, 2003, pp. 232–4.

67. British Library, Sloane MSS, 4041, fol. 12, quoted in Alice Dugdale, 'The First Heated Swimming Pool in Modern Times?', *The Georgian Group Journal*, XII (2002), p. 6. Dugdale has also suggested that there was a pool at Brockenhurst Park in Hampshire which was situated near the brewhouse to provide a source of warm water.

68. Alice Dugdale, 'John Hallam: "A Poor Mean Country Joiner"?', *The Georgian Group Journal*, VII (1997), pp. 37–42.

69. For the reinterpretation of Stourhead, see particularly Timothy Mowl, *Historic Gardens of Wiltshire* (Stroud, 2004); Oliver Cox, 'A Mistaken Iconography? Eighteenth-century Visitor Accounts of Stourhead', *Garden History*, 40:1 (2012), pp. 98–116.

70. Jonas Hanway, *A Journal of Eight Days Journey from Portsmouth to Kingston upon Thames, with miscellaneous thoughts, moral and religious, in a series of letters* (London, 1757) p. 137.

71. Henry Hoare II to Lord Bruce, Wiltshire and Swindon Record Office, Box file 2, T32 family correspondence 1760–81.

72. Ibid.

CHAPTER 4

1. The lines originally come from Alexander Pope's translation of Horace's *Epodes* II. Its significance to the poet is described in Mavis Batey, *Alexander Pope: The Poet and the Landscape* (London, 1999), p. 46. The nomenclature of the Mausoleum at Hestercombe is confusing: it has very little in common with other contemporary mausoleums and was not just a place to inter remains, yet the name was first used by Edward Knight, Coplestone Warre Bampfylde's brother-in-law, in the 1760s.

2. Walton was born in Stafford in 1593, and died in 1683, in his ninety-first year, his long life having spanned the reign of five monarchs and seen the Civil War and the Interregnum. In 1653, he published the first edition of *The Compleat Angler*. Over the next quarter of a century he both supplemented and enriched the book. It became the seminal work on angling and many further additions were published after his death. Around 1655, he met Charles Cotton, also a native of Staffordshire, who was 40 years his junior. Cotton contributed to the enlarging and widening of the scope of *The Compleat Angler* and the book became a bible for fishermen, a work of reference the influence of which was akin to that of Evelyn's *Sylva*.

3. Izaak Walton, *The Experienced Angler, Or Angling Improved*, 3rd edn (London, 1668). As well as the first edition of 1653 and this one, other editions within Walton's lifetime date from 1655, 1661 and 1676. There are numerous nineteenth- and twentieth-century editions. The British Library Catalogue includes four editions from the eighteenth century: 1750, 1759, 1760 and 1772, showing how popular it remained.

4. Ibid., vol. 3, p. 136.

5. J.A. Home (ed.), *The Letters and Journals of Lady Mary Coke*, vol. 2 (Edinburgh, 1889), pp. 310, 316.

6. July 1768, ibid., vol. 3, p. 252.

7. Roger North, *A Discourse of Fish and Fishponds* (London, 1713), p. 72.

8. Thomas Robinson, Lord Grantham to Frederick Robinson, 1 September 1790, Morley Papers, West Devon Record Office, 1259/1/219.

9. Theresa Parker was Ann's niece. After her sister's death she moved to Saltram to bring up Theresa and her brother.

10. Anne Robinson to Mrs Frederick Robinson, 17 August 1790, Morley Papers, West Devon Record Office, 1259/2/104.

11. Christopher Currie, 'Fishponds as Garden Features, c. 1550–1750', *Garden History*, 18:1 (1990), p. 23.

12. Roger North's *Discourse on Fish and Fish-ponds* bears this out, though his terminology for the sorts of pond is not the same. At Stowe there are many surviving accounts for the management of the stew ponds in the late seventeenth and early eighteenth centuries (1699 and 1712): Huntington Library, Stowe MS, STTM box 6, bundle 54; STT box 66, bundle 10; STTF box 64, bundle 3c.

13. Such large lakes were sometimes created out of millponds too, e.g. Eleven Acre Lake, Stowe.

14. For more on the construction of lakes in the eighteenth century, see Judith Roberts, 'Well Temper'd Clay', *Garden History*, 29:1 (2001).

15. It may be that these two views show the garden as it was planned to be, but not yet at the time complete; see Roy Strong, *The Artist and the Garden* (New Haven CT, 2000), pp. 79–80.

16. Vere Birdwood (ed.), *So Dearly Loved, So Much Admired: Letters to Hester Pitt, Lady Chatham from Her Relations and Friends 1744–1801* (London, 1994), p. 38. In 1786 Thomas Jefferson reported that the Lake at Wotton yielded '2000 brace of carp every year'; see Edwin Morris Betts, 'Thomas Jefferson's Garden Book 1766–1824', *Memoirs of the American Philosophical Society*, vol. 22 (Philadelphia, 1944), p. 112.

17. Joanna Martin, *Wives and Daughters: Women and Children in the Georgian Country House* (London, 2004) p. 155.

18. The Boathouse, probably a late work of Sanderson Miller, dates from 1769; see Jennifer Meir, *Sanderson Miller and His Landscapes* (Chichester, 2006), pp. 151–2. The Boathouse was destroyed by a falling tree in the 1970s, but its brick foundations survive by the lake edge. See also Michael Cousins, 'The Garden Buildings at Enville Hall', *The Follies Journal*, 2 (2002), p. 84; Sandy Haynes and Michael Symes, *Enville, Hagley, The Leasowes: Three Great Eighteenth Century Gardens* (Bristol, 2010).

19. Joseph Heely, *A Description of Envil* (London, 1777), p. 32.

20. The Fishing Pavilion was built 1770–72. The original Adam drawings are among the Kedleston archives held in the house. There is also a design for the lakeside

elevation in Sir John Soane's Museum, London.

21. See David Coffin, *The English Garden: Meditation and Memorial* (Princeton NJ, 1994), p. 60.

22. Quoted in Timothy Mowl, *Gentlemen and Players* (Stroud, 2000), p. 36.

23. Brian Earnshaw and Timothy Mowl, *Architecture without Kings* (Manchester, 1995), p. 214.

24. Beckford to Alexander Cozens, Fonthill, 10 May 1780, in Lewis Melville, *The Life and Letters of William Beckford* (London, 1910), pp. 85–6.

25. Jane Brown, *My Darling Herriot: Henrietta Luxborough, Poetic Gardener and Irrepressible Exile* (London, 2006), p. 160.

26. Ibid., pp. 152–4, 177.

27. Robert Morris, *Lectures in Architecture* (London, 1734), p. 175.

28. In 1908 a note was discovered inside an urn at Radway, Sanderson Miller's house, commemorating the fact that Pitt had planted three trees on the spot in 1754. For Pitt as gardener, see Michael Symes, 'William Pitt the Elder: The Gran Mago of Landscape Gardening', *Garden History*, 24:1 (1996).

29. Home, *Lady Mary Coke*, vol. 2. p. 303, Wednesday 6 July 1768.

30. Martin, *Wives and Daughters*, p. 277.

31. Ibid.

32. Ibid., p. 287.

33. Ibid., p. 280.

34. Stella Tillyard, *Aristocrats* (London, 1995), p. 201.

35. Joyce Godber, *The Marchioness Grey of Wrest Park* (Bedford, 1968), p. 27.

36. Elizabeth Anson to Jemima Grey, 6 June 1750, Bedfordshire and Luton Archive Service (BLAS), Lucas MSS, L30/9/3/16.

37. Timothy Mowl and Dianne Barre, *The Historic Gardens of England: Staffordshire* (Bristol, 2009), p. 130.

38. Philippa Kielmansegge (ed.), *Diary of a Journey to England, 1761–62* (London, 1902), p. 73.

39. The only surviving illustrations of the Hermitage show a barn-like structure that seems to be constructed of rough-hewn stone; yet letters from the time of its construction describe it as constructed of roots and wood. The illustrations, a pair of watercolours, both date from the early nineteenth century and it is conceivable that they depict a second incarnation, since the original rustic wooden structure may well not have lasted the intervening 60 plus years. See Twigs Way, *Review of LUC Master Plan for Wrest Park*, unpublished report for English Heritage, 2005, p. 192.

40. Elizabeth Anson to Jemima Grey, 6 June 1750, BLAS, Lucas MSS, L30/9/3/16.

41. Admiral George Anson leased Carshalton House 1749–52 before buying Moor Park in Hertfordshire; see A.E. Jones, *The Story of Carshalton House* (Sutton, 1980).

42. Jemima, Marchioness Grey to Philip Yorke, August 1749, Hardwicke MSS, British Library, Add MSS 35, 376.

43. For a general description of the development of the landscape at the Leasowes, see Christopher Gallagher, 'The Leasowes: A History of the Landscape', *Garden History*, 24:2 (1996).

44. Gordon Campbell, *The Hermit in the Garden: From Imperial Rome to Ornamental Gnome* (Oxford, 2013).

45. Sally Semple Aall and George Mott, *Follies and Pleasure Pavilions* (London, 1989), p. 52. The Temple was built in 1785.

46. Edgehill itself gave another historicist reference, being the site of the first battle of the English Civil War. The Thatched House is now more commonly called Egge Cottage.

47. William Hawkes (ed.), *The Diaries of Sanderson Miller of Radway* (Stratford-upon-Avon, 2005), p. 8.

48. Ibid., p. 156.

49. Elizabeth Knight, *The History of William Cowper's Summer House*, unpublished report for the Cowper and Newton Museum, 1995. I am grateful to Elizabeth Knight, Honorary Archivist at the Museum, for this information.

50. John Britton and Edward Wedlake Brayley, *The Beauties of England and Wales*, vol. 5 (Durham, 1810), pp. 98–9.

51. *A Walk Through Hardwicke Gardens, near Sedgefield, in the County of Durham* (Stockton upon Tees, 1800). I am grateful to Michael Rudd for this reference. The building also contained tea-making equipment.

52. Britton and Brayley, *The Beauties of England and Wales*, pp. 98–9.

53. For more information on both artists, see John Bonehill and Stephen Daniels (eds), *Paul Sandby: Picturing Britain* (London, 2009); Philip White, *A Gentleman of Fine Taste: The Watercolours of Coplestone Warre Bampfylde* (Taunton, 1995).

54. For an excellent history of the Ordnance Survey, see Rachel Hewitt, *Map of a Nation: A Biography of the Ordnance Survey* (London, 2011).

55. Hawkes, *Sanderson Miller*, pp. 127, 136, 161.

56. Brown, *My Darling Herriot*, p. 169.

57. James Joel Cartwright (ed.), *The Travels through England of Dr. Richard Pococke*, vol. 1 (London, 1889), p. 107. The artist Sir Joshua Reynolds, who was supported in his early career by Lord Edgcumbe, also had a camera obscura which folded into the binding of a book. It is now in the Science Museum in London.

58. 'Telescope', *Encyclopædia Britannica*, 2009, online library edition, http://library.eb.co.uk/eb/article-9111077.

59. Telescopes were certainly affordable for the upper classes by the end of the seventeenth century. In 1698 Maynard Colchester, at the relatively modest estate of Westbury Court in Gloucestershire, possessed a telescope; it has been suggested that the lantern of the Tall Pavilion was used for this purpose. Colchester accounts, Gloucestershire County Record Office, D36/A4, quoted in K. Feluś, *Westbury Court Conservation Plan*, unpublished report for the National Trust, 2004.

60. Hawkes, *Sanderson Miller*, p. 162.

61. James Collett-White, *Inventories of Bedfordshire Country Houses 1714–1830*, vol. 74 (Bedfordshire Historical Records Society, 1995), p. 270.

62. William Marshall, *On Planting and Rural Ornament* (London, 1803), p. 33.

63. For an overview of Wright's career, see Eileen Harris (ed.), *Arbours and Grottoes* (London, 1979).

64. A letter from Elizabeth Anson to Marchioness Grey mentions studying 'the terrestrial maps', perhaps implying that there were also celestial maps to scrutinise. Moreover, in the same letter Elizabeth wrote to Jemima that she 'was vastly disappointed last night on asking about 9 o'clock what star that was which shone so bright on the

lefthand [of] the north window of the library, to find the person I addressed knew neither the star nor the place', implying that Jemima would have known. Godber, *The Marchioness Grey*, p. 25.

65. Unlike Wright, he was a man of independent means, having inherited the estates of his brother.

66. The plan by William Thomas is undated. Thomas was working in the 1780s and 1790s; he died in 1800. He also drew proposals for a pair of garden temples for Bowood, Wiltshire. See Howard Colvin, *A Biographical Dictionary of British Architects* (London, 1995), p. 973.

67. See Shirley Family MSS, Leicestershire Record Office, ref. 26 D53/2138. Information on the temple at Chartley has been kindly provided by Dianne Barre. Elsewhere garden buildings were also used for billiards. The building at Enville now known as the Museum, but originally called the Gothic Greenhouse when it was first built in the late 1740s, was by the 1770s used as a billiard room. Joseph Heely described the interior in 1777 as 'richly and curiously adorned with stucco; the ceiling remarkably so. At one end in a niche is a bust of Homer: at the other end a Cicero. A billiard table and a small organ, are the furniture of this superb room.'

68. In the end it seems that Ferrers may have used one of the towers of the medieval ruined Chartley Castle as a location for his astronomical observations, perhaps a parallel with the medieval Shepherd's Lodge at Enville.

69. David Watkin, *The Architect King: George III and the Culture of the Enlightenment* (London, 2004), pp. 108–9.

70. Examples from an account of the Tradescant collection written by Georg Christoph Stirn in 1638, cited at: www.ashmolean.org/ash/amulets/tradescant.

71. Mike Sutherill, 'The Garden Buildings at Audley End', *Georgian Group Journal*, VI (1996), pp. 110–12.

72. Mark Catesby's *Natural History of Carolina, Florida and the Bahama Islands* was financed by Peter Collinson, who, through his connection with the plant collector John Bartram, was responsible for a number of significant American plants being introduced to England. It is notable for its beautiful illustrations of plants and animals. The first volume was published in 1731 and the second in 1743.

73. Sally Festing, 'Menageries and the Landscape Garden', *Journal of Garden History*, 8:4 (1988), pp. 104–17.

74. The Diary of Lady Sophie Newdigate's Tour of the South of England in July 1747, Warwickshire County Record Office, CR1841/7.

75. See Timothy McCann, '"Much Troubled with Rude Company": The 2nd Duke of Richmond's Menagerie at Goodwood', *Sussex Archaeological Collections*, 132 (1994), pp. 143–9. Although the menagerie was dispersed after the 2nd Duke's death, the 3rd Duke did keep lions.

76. The Duke's interests were reflected in his collection of books, still at Goodwood. These were the latest texts, exquisitely illustrated and full of observations on discoveries in the natural world, such as Mark Catesby's *Natural History of Carolina, Florida and the Bahama Islands* and George Edward's *Natural History of Birds*. I am grateful to James Peill, curator at Goodwood, for additional information, including about the Duke's books.

77. Kielmansegge (ed.), *Diary of a Journey*, p. 77.

78. Ray Desmond, *The History of the Royal Botanic Gardens Kew* (London, 2007). The Ting, a sort of Chinese temple, was designed by Sir William Chambers.

79. Festing, 'Menageries and the Landscape Garden', p. 115.

80. The building was designed by the architect and astronomer Thomas Wright for Lord Halifax in the mid- to late 1750s. The Menagerie was saved from dereliction and vandalism by architectural historian Gervase Jackson-Stops in the late 1970s and early 1980s. Though the main house is lost, other buildings from the circuit do survive – the triumphal arch and a small temple – but neither is, or arguably was, as impressive as the Menagerie.

81. W.S. Lewis (ed.), *The Yale Edition of Horace Walpole's Correspondence*, vol. 10 (New Haven CT, 1937–83), p. 335.

82. Gervase Jackson-Stops, *The Menagerie, Horton*, privately published guidebook, 1989. In the guidebook Jackson-Stops speculates that the end pavilions may have been used for storing food for the animals or tools (p. 3).

83. The collection and cultivation of plants at Woburn was carried out with more of a spirit of scientific enquiry than the collection of birds. For a discussion of the intellectual interests of the 6th Duke and how they evidenced themselves in the landscape at Woburn, see Stephen Daniels, *Humphry Repton: Landscape Gardening and the Geography of the Georgian Landscape* (New Haven CT, 2000), pp. 170–72.

84. James Forbes, *Hortus Woburnensis* (London, 1833), p. 285.

85. The catalogue was the Hortus Kewensis by John Hill. See Desmond, *The History of the Royal Botanic Gardens*, pp. 39–42.

86. Fiona Cowell, *Richard Woods (1715–1793): Master of the Pleasure Garden* (Woodbridge, 2009), p. 134.

87. I am grateful to Bruce Bailey and Timothy Mowl for the 1779 inventory. Drayton and the Banqueting Houses are discussed in Timothy Mowl and Clare Hickman, *The Historic Gardens of England: Northamptonshire* (Stroud, 2008), p. 61.

88. Collett-White, *Inventories of Bedfordshire Country Houses*, p. 230.

89. For plans and discussion of both these buildings, see Anthony Beckles Wilson, 'Alexander Pope's Grotto in Twickenham', *Garden History*, 26:1 (1998), pp. 31–59; John Harris, *The Palladian Revival: Lord Burlington, His Villa and the Garden at Chiswick* (London, 1984), pp. 56–8.

90. Benton Seeley, *Description of the Gardens of Lord Viscount Cobham* (Buckingham, 1744), p. 11, quoted in George Clarke (ed.), *Descriptions of Lord Cobham's Gardens at Stowe (1700–1750)* (Aylesbury, 1990), p. 131.

91. Henry E. Huntington Library, Stowe Estate Accounts, National Trust database ID number, 1834.

92. Lord and Lady Cobham had no children, which was apparently due to the sexually transmitted disease given to Lady Cobham by her promiscuous husband (though this would hardly have been unusual at the time). See Jane Brown, *Lancelot 'Capability' Brown: The Omnipotent Magician, 1716–1783* (London, 2012), p. 44.

93. Horace Walpole, *Memoirs of the Last Ten Years of the Reign of George II*, vol. 2 (London, 1822), p. 48.

94. *The Political Register*, 1, May 1767.

95. For the gardens of West Wycombe and the rivalry with Stowe, see Richard Wheeler, '"Pro Magna Charta" or "Fay que voudras": Political and Moral Precedents for

the Gardens of Sir Francis Dashwood at West Wycombe', in Patrick Eyres (ed.), 'Gardens of Desire', *New Arcadian Journal*, 49/50 (2000).

96. Gilbert West, *Stowe, The Gardens of the Right Honourable Richard Lord Viscount Cobham*, 1732, reproduced in Clarke (ed.) *Descriptions of Lord Cobham's Gardens*, pp. 37–51.

97. In the 1742 edition of *Pamela*, vol. 1, this image appears after p. 358. I am grateful to Michael Liversidge for bringing this edition to my attention.

98. William Gilpin, *A Dialogue upon the Gardens of the Rt. Honourable the Lord Viscount Cobham at Stow in Buckinghamshire* (London, 1748).

99. See Timothy Mowl, *The Historic Gardens of Gloucestershire* (Stroud, 2002), p. 136. Caroline Holmes, in *Follies of Europe* (Woodbridge, 2008), p. 143, says that the garden was built by the Reverend David Edwards, who married an heiress called Miss Purnell.

100. Paul Stamper, *The Historic Parks and Gardens of Shropshire* (Shrewsbury, 1996), p. 54.

101. *The Trial of Lady Ann Foley... Containing the Whole of the Evidence* (London, 1786). See also Sarah Lloyd, 'Amour in the Shrubbery: Reading the Detail of English Adultery Trial Publications of the 1780s', *Eighteenth Century Studies*, 39:4 (2006).

102. The case is outlined in great detail by Lawrence Stone in *Broken Lives: Separation and Divorce in England 1660–1857* (Oxford 1993), pp. 162–247. Although many cold baths had beds adjoining or nearby, it is unlikely that the room adjoining the Stockeld Bathing Well contained a bed or this would have been mentioned in the evidence presented in the case.

103. Stella Tillyard, *Aristocrats* (London, 1995), pp. 244–8.

104. Martin, *Wives and Daughters*, p. 282.

105. From Mary Grantham (Mouse) to 'Fritz' Robinson, Wrest, 18 August 1790, West Devon Record Office (WDRO), Morley papers,1259/1/218.

106. From Thomas Robinson to Uncle Fritz, Wrest, 1 September 1790, WDRO, Morley papers, 1259/1/219 and Putney Heath, 21 September 1790, WDRO, Morley papers, 1259/1/220.

107. From Thomas Robinson to Uncle Fritz, Wrest, 26 August 1791, WDRO, Morley papers, 1259/1/231.

108. Bedfordshire and Luton Archives Service, Lucas Papers, L 31/106, Journal of Catherine Talbot at Wrest, summer 1745.

109. J.A. Home (ed.), *The Letters and Journals of Lady Mary Coke*, vol. 2 (Edinburgh, 1889), p. 310. Lady Mary Coke was 42 in 1768; the pursuit of bowls by herself and her hosts may be indicative of a game more popular in their youth in the 1730s and 1740s.

110. See John Phibbs, 'The Englishness of Lancelot 'Capability' Brown, *Garden History*, 31:2 (2003), pp. 128–9.

111. Jane Roberts, *Royal Landscape: The Gardens and Parks of Windsor* (New Haven CT, 1997), p. 229.

112. Humphry Repton, Red Book for Ashridge, 20 March 1813. I am grateful to John Phibbs for this reference.

113. Brian Fitzgerald (ed.), *Correspondence of Emily, Duchess of Leinster*, vol. 1 (Dublin, 1949), p. 239.

114. Deirdre Le Faye, *A Chronology of Jane Austen* (Cambridge, 2006), p. 316.

115. Martin Johnes, 'Archery, Romance and Elite Culture in England and Wales, *c.* 1780–1840', *History*, 89:294 (2004).

116. Quoted in ibid., p. 196.

117. From Tour of the Midlands, 1789, in C. Bruyn Andrews (ed.), *The Torrington Diaries*, vol. 2 (London, 1934–38), pp. 106-10.

CHAPTER 5

1. Rashleigh Holt-White, *The Life and Letters of Gilbert White of Selborne*, vol. 1 (London, 1901), pp. 139–40.

2. Richard Mabey, *Gilbert White: A Biography of the Author of the Natural History of Selborne* (London, 1986), pp. 17–18.

3. Holt-White, *The Life and Letters*, vol. 1, pp. 131, 135.

4. Francesca Greenoak and Richard Mabey (eds), *The Journals of Gilbert White*, vol. 1 (London, 1986), pp. 128–31.

5. Presumably Earl Temple had been insistent on the entertainment going ahead in the evening though the weather was not ideal. W.S. Lewis (ed.), *The Yale Edition of Horace Walpole's Correspondence*, vol. 10 (New Haven CT, 1937–83), p. 314.

6. Benton Seeley, *A Description of the Gardens at Stowe* (Buckingham, 1783), p. 25.

7. Joseph Spence to Richard Hoare, March 1766; see Michael Symes, 'Oatlands Grotto Revisited', *The Follies Journal*, 6 (2006).

8. William Cowper to William Unwin, quoted in David Coffin, *The English Garden: Meditation and Memorial* (Princeton NJ, 1994), p. 106.

9. In Britain one of the attractions of the garden building was the more intimate space for entertaining and the consequent need for a minimum number of servants. This idea was taken further in Europe, especially in France and Russia. Peter the Great had a garden pavilion at Peterhof, where he could dine with an intimate group without the need for any servants to be present. The dining room was on the first floor of the pavilion; the table laden with food would magically appear from the kitchen on the lower floor by means of a mechanical 'elevating table'. Such devices were seemingly never known in Britain.

10. Tessa Murdoch, *Noble Households: Eighteenth Century Inventories of Great Houses* (Cambridge, 2006), p. 217.

11. Simon Varey, 'The Pleasures of the Table', in R. Porter and M. Mulvey Roberts (eds), *Pleasure in the Eighteenth Century* (London, 1996, pp. 43–4), points out that though English cuisine has always been a bit of a joke, there was in fact a culinary two-way traffic between England and France, illustrating just how complex the cross-currents between English and French dining really were during the eighteenth century.

12. Journal of the estate steward, Richard Escott, Somerset County Record Office, DD/S/WH/269.

13. I am grateful to Mark Newman of the National Trust for this information. North Yorkshire Record Office, Feversham Papers, ZEW MIC 1418/1528.

14. I am grateful to Mark Newman, National Trust Archaeologist, for information about the structure of the kitchen at of the Octagon Tower.

15. For a full description, see William Bray, *Sketch of a Tour into Derbyshire and Yorkshire* (London, 1783), pp. 280–83.

16. An octagon was a popular plan for places used for dining, a remnant of the Tudor tradition. Other examples include the Octagon Summerhouse at Hestercombe. The Octagon Tower at Studley contained six chairs in an inventory of 1768; Vyner MSS, Leeds Record Office, 5570 c.29/F/7.

17. Daniel Defoe and Samuel Richardson, *A Tour through the Island of Great Britain*, vol. 3 (London, 1778), p. 50.

18. Stephen Daniels, *Humphry Repton: Landscape Gardening and the Geography of the Georgian Landscape* (New Haven CT, 2000), p. 178. See also David M. Pendergast, 'The Wedgwood Caneware Service at Woburn Abbey', *Ars Ceramica*, 27 (2015), pp. 12–23.

19. George Lyttleton to Sanderson Miller, 6 August 1751, in Lilian Dickens and Mary Stanton (eds), *An Eighteenth Century Correspondence: Being the Letters to Sanderson Miller, Esq., of Radway* (London, 1910), p. 182.

20. Fanny Austen Knight on holiday in Hampshire, 17 September 1807, in Deirdre Le Faye, *A Chronology of Jane Austen* (Cambridge, 2006), p. 344.

21. Jane Austen, *Sense and Sensibility* (Harmondsworth, 1986 [1811]), p. 65, ch. 7.

22. Jane Austen, *Emma* (Harmondsworth, 1988 [1815]), p. 349, ch. 42. A recipe for pigeon pie, which as well as pigeon breast included chopped ham and steak, was included in Maria Rundell's *A New System of Domestic Cookery* (London, 1806). The recipe is reproduced in a modern form in Maggie Black and Deirdre Le Faye, *The Jane Austen Cookbook* (London, 1995), p. 97.

23. Anne Robinson to Mrs Frederick Robinson, Saltram, 17 August 1790, West Devon Record Office, Morley MSS, 1259/2/104.

24. *Oxford English Dictionary* cites 1762 as the first use of the word to mean a light meal consisting of a filling between two slices of bread, named after the 4th Earl of Sandwich (1718–1792); it was first used by Edward Gibbon in his journal entry of 24 November 1762 (*Journal*, London, 1929, p. 185). Ann Robinson's use of the word in the 1790s illustrates that both the word and the food were in common usage a generation after they were first recorded.

25. William Hawkes (ed.), *The Diaries of Sanderson Miller of Radway* (Warwick, 2005), pp. 150–53.

26. Bedfordshire and Luton Archives Service (BLAS), Lucas Papers, 30/8/31/7.

27. Elizabeth Yorke (later Anson) to Marchioness Grey, in Joyce Godber, *The Marchioness Grey of Wrest Park* (Bedford, 1968), p. 25. Elizabeth Anson later noted the fine food, especially 'Venison, Cheese and Fruit, &c, &c…', in a letter to Marchioness Grey in July 1748; BLAS L30/9/3/5.

28. Austen, *Sense and Sensibility*, p. 204.

29. Austen, *Emma*, p. 354, ch. 42.

30. 18 July 1781, in Godfrey Clark (ed.), *Gleanings from an old portfolio, containing some correspondence between Lady Louisa Stuart and her sister Caroline, Countess of Portarlington, and other friends and relations*, vol. 1 (London, 1895), p. 134.

31. Ice houses were semi-subterranean structures built near lakes. Inside they generally had an inverted cone-shaped chamber dug down into the earth, with a drain at the bottom. In winter this was packed with ice from the lake, in layers, with straw in between for extra insulation. The ice was not meant to be consumed, but was used to chill desserts such as ice cream.

32. Mary Eales, *Mrs. Eales Receipts for Confectionary* (London, 1718).
33. See Phillipa Glanville and Hilary Young (eds), *Elegant Eating* (London, 2002), pp. 86–8; Ivan Day, *Ice Cream* (Oxford, 2011).
34. Dickens and Stanton, *An Eighteenth Century Correspondence*, p. 160.
35. Hawkes (ed.), *The Diaries of Sanderson Miller*, pp. 122, 136, 146, 247.
36. Mary Rebow from Wivenhoe, 17 July 1778, in A.F.J. Brown, *Essex People* (Chelmsford, 1972), p. 65. I am grateful to Fiona Cowell for bringing this to my attention.
37. See Ivan Day, 'Teatime', in Ivan Day (ed.) *Eat, Drink and Be Merry* (London, 2000), pp. 112–19.
38. Austen, *Emma*, p. 57, ch. 4.
39. Shugborough was the estate of Anson's older brother, Thomas.
40. Hawkes (ed.), *The Diaries of Sanderson Miller*, p. 150.
41. Journal of the estate steward, Richard Escott, Somerset County Record Office, DD/S/WH/269.
42. Paul Hawkins Fisher, *Notes and Recollections of Stroud* (Stroud, 1986 [1871]), p. 128.
43. Inventory of 1740, from James Collett White, *Inventories of Bedfordshire Country Houses 1714–1830* (Bedford, 1995), p. 266.
44. Quoted in Godber, *The Marchioness Grey of Wrest Park*, p. 25.
45. Journal of Catherine Talbot at Wrest, summer 1745, Bedfordshire and Luton Archives Service, L31/106.
46. An excellent essay on the pair of canvases appeared when they were sold at Sotheby's in 2011: www.sothebys.com/en/auctions/ecatalogue/2011/old-master-and-british-paintings-evening-sale/lot.38.html, accessed October 2015.
47. R.L. Winstanley (ed.), *The Diary of James Woodforde*, Volume 9: *1780–1781* (Castle Cary, 2000).
48. Woodforde had a tent earlier in his life, in his parents' garden near Castle Cary, Somerset.
49. Fanny Burney, *Evelina* (London, 1990 [1778]), p. 193.
50. Lewis (ed.), *The Yale Edition of Horace Walpole's Correspondence*, vol. 10, p. 73.
51. Stanley Ayling, *The Elder Pitt* (London, 1976), p. 106.
52. Hawkes (ed.), *The Diaries of Sanderson Miller*, p. 122.
53. Jane Clark asserts that the popularity of Corelli was second only to that of Handel, even though Corelli never came to England – his music being brought home by Grand Tourists. Corelli's sonata in F was a very popular teaching piece. See Jane Clark, accompanying notes to the CD *The Country House: Domestic Music of the Eighteenth Century*, Janiculum Recordings, London, 1999, p. 2.
54. Thomas Arne, best known as the composer of 'Rule Britannia', set at least one of William Shenstone's poems to music. He also composed a glee, 'An elegy to Mr. Shenstone'.
55. Thomas Whately wrote at length about the effect of the setting sun on the Temple of Concord in his *Observations on Modern Gardening* (Dublin, 1770).
56. S.H. Hervey (ed.), *The Letterbooks of John Hervey, 1st Earl of Bristol*, vol. 2 (Wells, 1894), pp. 77–8.
57. David Burrows, *Handel* (Oxford, 1996), p 285.
58. Clark, *The Country House* (CD), accompanying notes, p. 1.

59. Richard Quaintance, 'Who's Making the Scene? Real People in Eighteenth Century Topographical Prints', in Gerald Maclean, Donna Landry and Joseph P. Ward (eds), *The Country and City Revisited: England and the Politics of Culture 1550–1850* (Cambridge, 1999).

60. Emily Climenson (ed.), *Elizabeth Montagu, The Queen of the Blue Stockings* (London, 1906), pp. 36–7.

61. Dianne Barre, 'Sir Samuel Hellier and His Garden Buildings: Part of the Midlands "Garden Circuit" in the 1760s–70s?', *Garden History*, 36:2 (2008), pp. 310–27.

CHAPTER 6

1. The excuse for the 'festino' was the visit of Prince Ernst of Mecklenburg-Strelitz, brother of Queen Charlotte. Walpole to Montagu, 8 June 1762, in W.S. Lewis (ed.), *The Yale Edition of Horace Walpole's Correspondence*, vol. 10 (New Haven CT, 1937–83), pp. 34–5. In 1764 the Countess gave another celebration, this time to mark the King's birthday, at which 10,000 lamps were used, of which 4,000 were arranged on the balustrade of Northumberland House; see ibid., vol. 38, p. 401.

2. Earl Temple to William Pitt, Stowe, 28 August 1774, Public Record Office, 30/8/61 fols 132–5.

3. Although in 2002 the contemporary artist Andy Goldsworthy created an artwork to be experienced at night, for three successive full moons. The 'Moonlit Path' installation was set in Petworth Park, making it a high-profile combination of eighteenth-century experience and modern art. It was a 3-kilometre-long path of crushed chalk from the South Downs, which snaked through the parkland and woodland on the Petworth estate in West Sussex. Walkers were allocated time slots and had to set off individually to experience the night and the moonlight on their own.

4. Joanna Martin, *Wives and Daughters* (London, 2004), p. 116; Lewis (ed.), *The Yale Edition of Horace Walpole's Correspondence*, vol. 30, p. 51.

5. Joyce Godber, *The Marchioness Grey of Wrest Park* (Bedford, 1968), p. 19.

6. Eliabeth Anson to Marchioness Grey, 13 August 1748, Admiralty, Bedfordshire and Luton Archives Service (BLAS), Lucas Papers 30/9/3/7.

7. Jemima Yorke, Marchioness Grey to Philip Yorke, from Wimpole, 20 August 1749, BLAS, CRT 100/27 (fo. 22).

8. Mark Girouard, *Life in the English Country House* (London, 1980), pp. 193–4.

9. This was one of the most famous fêtes of the eighteenth century. Although his principal seat was Knowsley Hall (Merseyside), the Earl of Derby staged a lavish pre-nuptial entertainment to celebrate his marriage in 1774 at his villa The Oaks (Surrey). The reason may have been because it was much closer to London, making it easier to source actors and musicians, among other things necessary to the entertainment. The event combined a variety of entertainments staged in the garden and a lavish, specially constructed, temporary ballroom designed by Robert Adam. The whole night was theatrical in its staging and all the elements highly choreographed. Groups of actors were strategically placed around the garden indulging in 'country pursuits' while guests moved among and around them – effectively what today might be called immersive theatre. There were also music and illuminations, followed by a ball. The event may have been atypical in its detail, but it was not unique in its staging

and use of the garden. For a detailed description, see Melanie Doderer-Winkler, *Magnificent Entertainments: Temporary Architecture for Georgian Festivals* (New Haven CT, 2013), pp. 59—74.

10. For example, in 1801 the population of Buckingham, 2 miles from Stowe, was 2,605 people. In 1805, when the Prince of Wales was entertained in the gardens, there were an estimated 10,000 people in attendance. Figures from Muriel T. Vernon and Desmond C. Bonner, *Buckingham: A History of a Country Market Town* (Buckingham, 1969).

11. Doderer-Winkler, *Magnificent Entertainments*, pp. 7—19.

12. Alan Brock, *A History of Fireworks* (London, 1949), p. 51.

13. Catherine Gordon, *The Coventrys of Croome* (Chichester, 2000), p. 99.

14. J.A. Home (ed.), *The Letters and Journals of Lady Mary Coke*, vol. 2 (Edinburgh, 1889), p. 341.

15. David Watkin, *The Architect King: George III and the Culture of the Enlightenment* (London, 2004), p. 100.

16. Though used in London and at the royal estate of Richmond, transparencies were rarely if ever used in entertainments staged in gardens of country houses, perhaps because those with the skills to create them were often associated with the theatre and therefore based in London.

17. Watkin, *The Architect King*, p. 106.

18. On the subject of sexual encounters at Vauxhall, Coke and Borg say: 'It was as if Vauxhall were entirely disconnected from the world outside, and, in an unspoken conspiracy between Tyers and his visitors, quite different standards of morality and social intercourse applied there.' David Coke and Alan Borg, *Vauxhall Gardens: A History* (New Haven CT, 2012), p. 76.

19. Ibid., pp. 202—5.

20. Such was their proficiency that the lamp-lighters of Vauxhall were offered to the organisers of the Green Park celebrations of 1749. See Doderer-Winkler, *Magnificent Entertainments*, p. 11.

21. Rosamond Bayne Powell, *Housekeeping in the Eighteenth Century* (London, 1956), p. 109.

22. William Tyler, R.A. (sculptor and architect), *Account of Tour with Theodosius Forrest 1773*, British Library Add. 42232 fols 22—56, f. 41v. I am grateful to Karen Lynch for this account.

23. Accounts of June 1778, Henry E. Huntington Library, Stowe Papers, STG A/C Estate Box 8 bundle 1, NT ID number 1440.

24. Newspaper report in *General Evening Post*, 16 July 1771 (Issue 5891).

25. George Grenville to Hester Pitt, undated letter, probably summer 1758, Public Record Office 30/8/34 folio 17.

26. Deirdre Le Faye, *A Chronology of Jane Austen* (Cambridge, 2006), p. 167.

27. History is littered with the tragedies of solitary male heirs pre-deceasing their fathers, like the son of Henry Hoare of Stourhead. Despite their affluence, the upper classes were no strangers to child mortality. Much has been said here of the famous Lennox sisters, Caroline, Emily, Louisa and Sarah; they had one surviving brother, who became the 3rd Duke of Richmond, but five other siblings died in infancy. Cecilia, the last of the 2nd Duke's offspring, died aged 19.

28. Timothy Mowl, *William Beckford: Composing for Mozart* (London, 1998), pp. 29–30.
29. Lewis Melville, *The Life and Letters of William Beckford of Fonthill* (London, 1910), pp. 121–2.
30. James Lees-Milne, *The Bachelor Duke: The Life of William Spencer-Cavendish, 6th Duke of Devonshire 1790–1858* (London, 1991), p. 14; *Derby Times*, 28 May 1811. I am grateful to Oliver Jessop and Aiden Haley for information on Chatsworth.
31. The Duchess of Devonshire died in 1806.
32. Letter from Lady Jerningham to Charlotte Bedingfeld, July 1800, in Egerton Castle (ed.), *Jerningham Letters 1780–1843*, vol. 1 (London, 1896), pp. 192–3.
33. Martin, *Wives and Daughters*, pp. 142–3.
34. W.J. Smith, who had been librarian at Stowe and who edited the Grenville Papers, believed the anonymous account to have been written by Lady Temple's maid. W.J. Smith (ed.), *The Grenville Papers*, vol. 2 (London, 1852), p. 408.
35. These can be seen in three watercolours by Jean Claude Nattes, now in the Buckinghamshire Museum.
36. Betsey Wynne had married into the Fremantle family, whose seat was at Swanbourne Manor, about 10 miles south-east of Stowe. See Anne Fremantle (ed.), *The Wynne Diaries: The Adventures of Two Sisters in Napoleonic Europe* (Oxford, 1982), pp. 398–401.

AFTERWORD
1. Brown's involvement at Wrest, where he both admired and retained the formal layout of the 1690s–1710s, demonstrates what a gross generalisation this was.
2. Colin Amery, *I.M. Pei: Oare Pavilion* (privately published, 2010).
3. In 2005 the Georgian Group gave the Pavilion at Oare their 'Best New Building in a Georgian Context' award, saying 'this building is light, airy and ethereal; bravely contemporary in its design but also entirely harmonious in its setting.'
4. Somerset County Record Office, Luttrell Papers, DD/L 1/22/7.

Select Bibliography

CONTEMPORARY MANUSCRIPTS

Three principal collections of manuscript sources have provided me with a good source of information about how life was lived in the Georgian garden: the Lucas papers (the collection pertaining to the Grey-Yorke family); the connected Morley papers (especially correspondence of the Parker and Robinson families); and the Temple-Grenville papers.

Lucas Papers, Bedfordshire and Luton Archives Service: an extensive collection of papers pertaining to Wrest Park and Wimpole, but also other estates connected to the family by marriage, such as Shugborough. It includes correspondence between Jemima Grey, Philip Yorke and Elizabeth Anson, plus various drawings and plans.

Morley Papers, West Devon Record Office, Plymouth: an extensive collection of correspondence of the Parker and Robinson families, much from the 1780s and 1790s, pertaining to Saltram, Wrest, Newby (Yorkshire) and other estates.

Temple-Grenville Papers, Henry E. Huntington Library, San Marino, California: an extensive collection of varied material, including estate accounts, pertaining to several Temple-Grenville estates, including Stowe and Wotton Underwood. The National Trust, which now owns the gardens at Stowe, has been systematically transcribing these, so the identification numbers from its archival database are also referenced in the endnotes to the text.

There is additional material pertaining to Wrest in the Hardwicke papers in the British Library, and pertaining to Stowe and the other Grenville estate of Wotton in the Chatham papers in the Public Record Office, along with correspondence discussing Pitt's own properties.

CONTEMPORARY PRINTED SOURCES

Birdwood, Vere (ed.), *So Dearly Loved, So Much Admired: Letters to Hester Pitt, Lady Chatham from Her Relations and Friends 1744–1801* (London, 1994).

Bray, William, *Sketch of a Tour into Derbyshire and Yorkshire* (London, 1783).

Bruyn Andrews, C. (ed.), *The Torrington Diaries: Containing the Tours through England and Wales of the Hon. John Byng (later Fifth Viscount Torrington) between the Years 1781 and 1794*, 4 vols (London, 1934–38).

Castle, Egerton (ed.), *The Jerningham Letters, 1780–1843* (London, 1896).

Cheyne, George, *Essay on Health and Long Life* (London, 1724).

Clarke, George (ed.), *Descriptions of Lord Cobham's Gardens at Stowe (1700–1750)* (Aylesbury, 1990).

Clarke, George, and Christopher Gowing (eds), *Drawings by Jean Claude Nattes in the Buckinghamshire County Museum* (Aylesbury, 1983).

Climenson, Emily (ed.), *Passages from the Diaries of Mrs. Philip Lybbe Powys* (London, 1899).

——, *Elizabeth Montagu, The Queen of the Blue Stockings* (London, 1906).

Decker, Paul, *Chinese Architecture* (London, 1759).

Defoe, Daniel, and Samuel Richardson, *A Tour Through the Island of Great Britain* (London, 1778).

Dickens, Lilian, and Mary Stanton (eds), *An Eighteenth Century Correspondence: Being the Letters to Sanderson Miller, Esq., of Radway* (London, 1910).

Fitzgerald, Brian (ed.), *Correspondence of Emily, Duchess of Leinster* (Dublin, 1949).

Floyer, John, *An Enquiry into the Right Use and Abuse of the Hot, Cold and Temperate Baths in England* (London, 1697).

——, *Psychrolousia: or, The History of Cold Bathing both Ancient and Modern* (London, 1715).

Forbes, James, *Hortus Woburnensis* (London, 1833).

Fremantle, Anne (ed.), *The Wynne Diaries: The Adventures of Two Sisters in Napoleonic Europe* (Oxford, 1982).

Gilpin, William, *Dialogue upon the Gardens of the Right Honourable the Lord Cobham at Stow in Buckinghamshire* (London, 1748).

Hassell, John, *Picturesque Rides and Walks, with Excursions by Water, Thirty Miles Round the British Metropolis* (London, 1818).

Hawkes, William (ed.), *The Diaries of Sanderson Miller of Radway* (Stratford-upon-Avon, 2005).

Heely, Joseph, *A Description of Envil* (London, 1777).

Hervey, S.H. (ed.), *The Letterbooks of John Hervey, 1st Earl of Bristol* (Wells, 1894).

Home, J.A. (ed.), *The Letters and Journals of Lady Mary Coke* (Edinburgh, 1889).

Kielmansegge, Philippa (ed.), *Diary of Journey to England, 1761–62* (London, 1902).

Lewis, W.S. (ed.), *The Yale Edition of Horace Walpole's Correspondence*, 48 vols (New Haven CT, 1937–83).

Llandover, Lady (ed.), *The Autobiography and Correspondence of Mary Granville, Mrs. Delany*, 3 vols (London, 1861).

Macky, John, *A Journey Through England: In Familiar Letters from a Gentleman Here, to His Friend Abroad* (London, 1723).

Mavor, William, *New Description of Blenheim* (London, 1789).

Melville, Lewis, *The Life and Letters of William Beckford of Fonthill* (London, 1910).

Montagu, M. (ed.), *The Letters of Mrs. Elizabeth Montagu with Some of the Letters of her Correspondents* (London, 1809).

North, Roger, *A Discourse of Fish and Fish-ponds... Done by a Person of Honour* (London, 1713).

Rathbone, Florence (ed.), *Letters from Lady Jane Coke to Her Friend Mrs. Eyre at Derby, 1747–1758* (London, 1899).

Repton, Humphry, *Sketches and Hints on Landscape Gardening* (London, 1794).

————, *Observations on the Theory and Practice of Landscape Gardening* (London, 1803).

————, *Fragments on the Theory and Practice of Landscape Gardening* (London, 1816).

Seeley, Benton, *A Description of the Gardens of Lord Viscount Cobham at Stow in Buckinghamshire* (Buckingham, 1744).

Shaw, Reverend Stebbing, *Tour to the West of England* (London, 1788).

Smith, W.J. (ed.), *The Grenville Papers*, 4 vols (London, 1852).

Switzer, Stephen, *Ichnographia Rustica; or, The Nobleman, Gentleman, and Gardener's Recreation*, 3 vols (London, 1718).

Walpole, Horace, *The History of the Modern Taste in Gardening*, ed. John Dixon Hunt (New York, 1995).

Walton, Izaak, *The Compleat Angler. Being Instructions how to angle for Trout or Grayling in a Clear Stream* (London: 1676).

Warner, Richard, *A Tour through the Northern Counties of England and the Borders of Scotland* (Bath, 1802).

Whately, Thomas, *Observations on Modern Gardening* (Dublin, 1770).

Winstanley, R.L. (ed.), *The Ansforde Diary of James Woodford* (Castle Cary, 1977).

———— (ed.), *The Diary of James Woodforde*, 11 vols (Castle Cary, 1987–2000).

Wright, Thomas, *Arbours and Grottoes* (London, 1979).

MODERN BOOKS

Arnold, Dana (ed.), *The Georgian Country House: Architecture, Landscape and Society* (Stroud, 1998).

Baird, Rosemary, *Mistress of the House* (London, 2004).

Batey, Mavis, *Jane Austen and the English Landscape* (London, 1996).

————, *Alexander Pope: The Poet and the Landscape* (London, 1999).

Batey, Mavis, and David Lambert, *The English Garden Tour* (London, 1990).

Battiscombe, Georgina, *English Picnics* (London, 1949).

Bayne Powell, Rosamond, *Housekeeping in the Eighteenth Century* (London, 1956).

Bennett, Sue, *Five Centuries of Women and Gardens* (London, 2000).

Black, Maggie, *A Heritage of British Cooking* (London, 1977).

Black, Maggie, and Deirdre Le Faye, *The Jane Austen Cookbook* (London, 1995).

Blaydes, F.A., *Bedfordshire Notes & Queries* (Bedford, 1886).

Bond, James, and Kate Tiller (eds), *Blenheim: Landscape for a Palace* (Stroud, 1997).

Bonehill, John, and Stephen Daniels (eds), *Paul Sandby: Picturing Britain* (London, 2009).

Borg, Alan, and David Coke, *Vauxhall Gardens: A History* (New Haven CT, 2010).

Bowden-Smith, Rosemary, *The Chinese Pavilion, Boughton House, Northamptonshire* (Woodbridge, 1988).

Brears, Peter, *Food and Cooking in 17th Century Britain* (London, 1985).

Brown, Jane, *The Pursuit of Paradise* (London, 1999).

————, *My Darling Heriot: Henrietta Luxborough, Poetic Gardener and Irrepressible Exile* (London, 2006).

————, *Lancelot 'Capability' Brown: The Omnipotent Magician, 1716–1783* (London, 2012).

Burnett, John, *Liquid Pleasures: A Social History of Drinks in Modern Britain* (London, 1999).

Burrows, Donald, *Handel* (Oxford, 1996).

Buxbaum, Tim, *Scottish Garden Buildings: From Food to Folly* (Edinburgh, 1989).

Campbell, Susan, *A History of Kitchen Gardening* (London, 2006).

Carter, George, Patrick Goode and Kedrun Laurie (eds), *Humphry Repton Landscape Gardener 1752–1818* (Norwich, 1982).

Chatel de Brancion, Laurence, *Carmontelle's Landscape Transparencies: Cinema of the Enlightenment* (Los Angeles, 2008).

Clark, Kenneth, *Civilisation: A Personal View* (London, 1969).

Coffin, David, *The English Garden: Meditation and Memorial* (Princeton NJ, 1994).

Collett-White, James, *Inventories of Bedfordshire Country Houses* (Bedford, 1995).

Conner, Patrick, *Oriental Architecture in the West* (London, 1975).

Cowell, Fiona, *Richard Woods (1715–1793): Master of the Pleasure Garden* (Woodbridge, 2010).

Daniels, Stephen, *Humphry Repton: Landscape Gardening and the Geography of Georgian England* (New Haven CT, 2000).

Dashwood, Francis, *The Dashwoods of West Wycombe* (London, 1987).

Day, Ivan, *Eat, Drink and Be Merry* (London, 2000).

——, *Ice Cream: A History* (Oxford, 2011).

DeLorme, Eleanor P., *Garden Pavilions and the 18th Century French Court* (Woodbridge, 1996).

Desmond, Ray, *The History of the Royal Botanic Gardens Kew* (London, 2007).

Dillon, Maureen, *Artificial Sunshine: A Social History of Domestic Lighting* (London, 2002).

Doderer-Winkler, Melanie, *Magnificent Entertainments: Temporary Architecture for Georgian Festivals* (New Haven CT, 2013).

Fletcher, Ronald, *The Parkers at Saltram* (London, 1970).

Foreman, Amanda, *Georgiana, Duchess of Devonshire* (London, 1998).

Girouard, Mark, *Life in the English Country House* (London, 1980).

Glanville, Philippa, and Hilary Young (eds), *Elegant Eating* (London, 2002).

Godber, Joyce (ed.), *The Marchioness Grey of Wrest Park* (Bedford, 1968).

Gordon, Catherine, *The Coventrys of Croome* (Chichester, 2000).

Greenoak, Francesca, and Richard Mabey (eds), *The Journals of Gilbert White* (London, 1986).

Harris, Eileen, *British Architectural Books and Writers 1556–1785* (Cambridge, 1990).

Harris, John, *The Palladian Revival: Lord Burlington, His Villa and the Garden at Chiswick* (London, 1984).

——, *The Artist and the Country House* (London, 1995).

Harris, John, and Martin Rix, *Gardens of Delight: The Rococo English Landscape of Thomas Robins the Elder* (London, 1977).

Harris, Leslie, *Robert Adam and Kedleston: The Making of a Neo-Classical Masterpiece* (London, 1987).

Hayden, Peter, *Russian Parks and Gardens* (London, 2005).

Haynes, Sandy, and Michael Symes, *Enville, Hagley and The Leasowes: Three Great 18th-century Gardens* (Bristol, 2010).

Headley, Gwyn, and Wim Meulemkamp, *Follies* (London, 1990).

Henderson, Paula, *The Tudor House and Garden* (New Haven CT, 2005).

Hewitt, Rachel, *Map of a Nation: A Biography of the Ordnance Survey* (London, 2011).

Holmes, Caroline, *Follies of Europe* (Woodbridge, 2008).

Holt-White, Rashleigh, *The Life and Letters of Gilbert White of Selborne* (London, 1901).

Hunt, John Dixon, *William Kent: Landscape Garden Designer* (London, 1987).

————, *The Picturesque Garden in Europe* (London, 2004).

Hunt, John Dixon, and Peter Willis (eds), *The Genius of the Place* (Cambridge, 1997).

Jones, A.E., *The Story of Carshalton House* (Sutton, 1980).

Jones, Barbara, *Follies and Grottoes* (London, 1989).

Kellerman, Susan (ed.), *With Abundance and Variety: Yorkshire Gardens and Gardeners across Five Centuries* (Wetherby, 2009).

Laird, Mark, *The Flowering of the Landscape Garden* (Philadelphia, 1999).

Lambton, Lucinda, *Beastly Buildings* (London, 1986).

Lane, Maggie, *Jane Austen and Food* (London, 1995).

Lummis, Trevor, and Jan Marsh, *The Woman's Domain: Women and the English Country House* (London, 1990).

Mabey, Richard, *Gilbert White* (London, 1993).

Martin, Joanna, *Wives and Daughters* (London, 2004).

Meir, Jennifer, *Sanderson Miller and his Landscapes* (Chichester, 2006).

Mott, George, and Sally Semple Aall, *Follies and Pleasure Pavilions* (London, 1989).

Mowl, Timothy, *Gentlemen and Players* (Stroud, 2000).

————, *The Historic Gardens of Gloucestershire* (Stroud, 2002).

————, *The Historic Gardens of Dorset* (Stroud, 2003).

————, *The Historic Gardens of Wiltshire* (Stroud, 2004).

Mowl, Timothy, and Clare Hickman, *The Historic Gardens of England: Northamptonshire* (Stroud, 2008).

Mowl, Timothy, and Dianne Barre, *The Historic Gardens of England: Staffordshire* (Bristol, 2009).

Murdoch, Tessa, *Noble Households: Eighteenth Century Inventories of Great Houses* (Cambridge, 2006).

Murray, Venetia, *An Elegant Madness: High Society in Regency England* (London, 1998).

Nicholls Palmer, Kenneth, *Ceremonial Barges on the River Thames* (London, 1997).

Phibbs, John, *Place-making: The Art of 'Capability' Brown 1716–1783* (London, 2016).

Porter, Roy, and Marie Mulvey Roberts (eds), *Pleasure in the Eighteenth Century* (London, 1996).

Postle, Martin (ed.), *Johan Zoffany: Society Observed* (New Haven CT, 2011).

Quest-Ritson, Charles, *The English Garden: A Social History* (London, 2001).

Ribero, Aileen, *A Visual History of Costume: The Eighteenth Century* (London, 1983).

Ridgway, Christopher, and Robert Williams (eds), *Sir John Vanbrugh and Landscape Architecture in Baroque England, 1690–1730* (Stroud, 2000).

Roberts, Jane, *Royal Landscape: The Gardens and Parks of Windsor* (New Haven CT, 1997).

Rowan, Alistair, *Garden Buildings* (London, 1968).

Saumarez-Smith, Charles, *The Building of Castle Howard* (London, 1997)

Schulman, Nicola, *Fashion and Gardens* (London, 2014).

Stamper, Paul, *The Historic Parks and Gardens of Shropshire* (Shrewsbury, 1996).

Stead, Jennifer, *Food and Cooking in 18th Century Britain* (London, 1985).

Stone, Lawrence, *Broken Lives: Separation and Divorce in England 1660–1857* (Oxford, 1993).

Strong, Roy, *The Renaissance Garden in England* (London, 1979).

——, *The Artist and the Garden* (New Haven CT, 2000).

——, *Feast: A History of Grand Eating* (London, 2003).

Stroud, Dorothy, *Capability Brown* (London, 1984).

Summerson, John, *The Unromantic Castle* (London, 1990).

——, *Architecture in Britain 1530–1830* (London, 1991).

Tillyard, Stella, *Aristocrats: Caroline, Emily, Louisa and Sarah Lennox 1740–1832* (London, 1995).

Tinniswood, Adrian, *The Polite Tourist* (London, 1998).

Vickery, Amanda, *The Gentleman's Daughter: Women's Lives in Georgian England* (New Haven CT, 2003).

——, *Behind Closed Doors: At Home in Georgian England* (New Haven CT, 2010).

Watkin, David, *The Architect King: George III and the Culture of the Enlightenment* (London, 2004).

Webster, Mary, *Johan Zoffany: 1733–1810* (London, 1976).

Weiss, Thomas, *Infinitely Beautiful: The Dessau-Wörlitz Garden Realm* (Berlin, 2005).

White, Philip, *A Gentleman of Fine Taste: The Watercolours of Coplestone Warre Bampfylde* (Taunton, 1995).

Williamson, Tom, *Polite Landscapes: Gardens and Society in Eighteenth-Century England* (Stroud, 1998).

Worsley, Giles, *Classical Architecture in Britain: The Heroic Age* (New Haven CT, 1995).

MODERN ARTICLES AND CHAPTERS

Aslet, Clive, 'The Park and Garden Buildings at Woburn', *Country Life*, 31 March 1983.

Barre, Dianne, 'Sir Samuel Hellier and His Garden Buildings: Part of the Midlands "Garden Circuit" in the 1760s–70s?', *Garden History*, 36:2 (2008).

Beckles Wilson, Anthony, 'Alexander Pope's Grotto in Twickenham', *Garden History*, 26:1 (1998).

Campbell Culver, Maggie, 'Mount Edgcumbe', *Garden History*, 24:1 (1996).

Colton, Judith, 'Merlin's Cave and Queen Caroline: Garden Art as Political Propaganda', *Eighteenth-Century Studies*, 10:1 (1976).

Cousins, Michael, 'Wroxton Abbey, Oxfordshire: An Eighteenth-Century Estate', *The Follies Journal*, 5 (2005).

——, 'Hagley Park, Worcestershire', *Garden History*, 35 suppl. 1 (2007).

Cox, Oliver, 'A Mistaken Iconography? Eighteenth Century Visitor Accounts of Stourhead', *Garden History*, 40:1 (2012).

Currie, Christopher, 'Fishponds as Garden Features, *c.* 1550–1750', *Garden History*, 18:1 (1990)

Drury, Martin, 'Architecture of Fishing', *Country Life*, 27 July 1972.

Dugdale, Alice, 'John Hallam: "A Poor Mean Country Joiner"?' *Georgian Group Journal*, VII (1997).

——, 'The First Heated Swimming Pool in Modern Times?' *Georgian Group Journal*, XII (2002).

Eyres, Patrick (ed.), 'Naumachia', *New Arcadian Journal*, 39/40 (1995).

—————— (ed.), 'The Political Temples of Stowe', *New Arcadian Journal*, 43/44 (1997).

Festing, Sally, 'Menageries and the Landscape Garden', *Journal of Garden History*, 8:4 (1988).

Frith, Wendy, 'When Frankie Met Johnny: Sexuality and Politics in the Gardens at West Wycombe and Medmenham Abbey', *New Arcadian Journal*, 49/50 (2000), ed. P. Eyres.

Gallagher, Christopher, 'The Leasowes: A History of the Landscape', *Garden History*, 24:2 (1996).

Jackson-Stops, Gervase, 'Arcadia under the Plough: The Garden at Halswell, Somerset', *Country Life*, 9 February 1989.

Johnes, Martin, 'Archery, Romance and Elite Culture in England and Wales, c. 1780–1840', *History* 89:294 (2004).

Kellerman, Susan, 'Bath Houses: An Introduction', *The Follies Journal*, 1 (2001).

Lloyd, Sarah, 'Amour in the Shrubbery', *Eighteenth Century Studies*, 39:4 (2006).

McCann, Timothy, 'Much Troubled with Very Rude Company: The Duke of Richmond's Menagerie at Goodwood', *Sussex Archaeological Collections*, 132 (1994).

Mowl, Timothy, 'In the Realm of the Great God Pan', *Country Life*, 17 October 1996.

Mowl, Timothy, and Roger White, 'Thomas Robins at Painswick', *Journal of Garden History*, 4:2 (1984).

Musson, Jeremy, 'Her Grace's Grotto Comes Out of its Shell', *Country Life*, 25 September 1997.

Quaintance, Richard, 'Who's Making the Scene? Real People in Eighteenth Century Topographical Prints', in Gerald Maclean, Donna Landry and Joseph P. Ward (eds), *The Country and City Revisited: England and the Politics of Culture 1550–1850* (Cambridge, 1999).

Roach, Alistair, 'Miniature Ships in Designed Landscapes', *The Mariner's Mirror*, 98:1 (2012).

Sutherill, Michael, 'The Garden Buildings at Audley End', *Georgian Group Journal*, VI (1996).

——————, 'The Buildings of the Elysium Garden at Audley End', *Georgian Group Journal*, VII, 1997.

Symes, Michael, 'New Light on Oatlands Park in the Eighteenth Century', *Garden History*, 9:2 (1981).

——————, 'The Landscaping of Esher Place', *Journal of Garden History*, 8:4 (1988).

——————, 'William Pitt the Elder: The Gran Mago of Landscape Gardening', *Garden History*, 24:1 (1996).

——————, 'The Landscape at West Wycombe Park, Buckinghamshire', *Garden History*, 33:1 (2005).

Varey, Simon, 'The Pleasures of the Table', in Roy Porter and Marie Mulvey Roberts (eds), *Pleasure in the Eighteenth Century* (London, 1996).

Wheeler, Richard, 'The Gardens of Stowe and West Wycombe: Paradise and Parody?' *Apollo*, CXLV:422 (April 1997).

——————, '"Pro Magna Charta" or "Fay ce que Voudras": Political and Moral Precedents for the Gardens of Sir Francis Dashwood at West Wycombe', *New Arcadian Journal*, 49/50 (2000).

List of Figures

Too many people were involved in tracking down and supplying images to be individually thanked in the acknowledgements, but that does not mean I am less grateful for all the help I have received from individuals, archives, libraries, museums and galleries (all credited here). Moreover I would like in particular to acknowledge the Royal Collection and the Yale Center for British Art for their online collections, which have been such a rich resource for research and images.

FIG. 1   The Queen's Temple at Stowe, after Thomas Medland, 1797. Royal Collection Trust/© HM Queen Elizabeth II.

FIG. 2   A detail from *Haymaking at Sandleford Priory*, by Edward Haytley, 1744. Private Collection, c/o Lowell Libson Ltd.

FIG. 3   *An engraving of Palemon and Lavinia*, by John Raphael Smith after William Lawranson, 1780. © The Trustees of the British Museum.

FIG. 4   *The Wedgwood Family*, by George Stubbs, 1780. Wedgwood Museum Collection (Victoria & Albert Museum) © WWRD.

FIG. 5   *The Palladian Bridge at Stowe*, by Seeley after Medland, 1797. Royal Collection Trust/© HM Queen Elizabeth II.

FIG. 6   *The Garden of the Deputy Ranger's Lodge, Windsor Great Park*, by Paul Sandby, c.1790s. Royal Collection Trust/© HM Queen Elizabeth II.

FIG. 7   *Riders on an Avenue in the Park at Luton*, by Paul Sandby, c.1765. Private Collection/Bridgeman Images.

FIG. 8   *Heveningham Hall, in Suffolk, the Seat of Sir Gerard William Vanneck Bartholomew*, by William Watts after Thomas Hearne, 1782. Yale Center for British Art, Paul Mellon Collection.

FIG. 9   A detail from *North-west View of Wakefield Lodge in Whittlebury Forest, Northamptonshire*, by Paul Sandby, 1767. Yale Center for British Art, Paul Mellon Collection.

FIG. 10 A design for a Gothic Lodge from William Halfpenny's *Country Builder...*, 1756. University of Bristol, Special Collections.

FIG. 11 *Hackfall*, by J.M.W. Turner, c.1816. © Lady Lever Art Gallery, National Museums Liverpool/Bridgeman Images.

FIG. 12 *The north-east view of Selborne from the Short Lythe*, by Samuel Hieronymus

Grimm, 1776. Natural History and Antiquities of Selborne: drawings, 1776. MS Eng 731.11 (seq5), Houghton Library, Harvard University.

FIG. 13 *Sir John Shaw and his Family in the Park at Eltham Lodge, Kent*, by Arthur Devis, 1761. Chicago Art Institute.

FIG. 14 *William Berry Introduced as the Heir to Raith*, by Johan Zoffany, 1769. Private Collection.

FIG. 15 *The View from Heaven's Gate at Longleat*, by Humphry Repton, from his book *Fragments on the Theory and Practice of Landscape Gardening*, 1816. University of Bristol Special Collections.

FIG. 16 A Moss House from the architectural pattern book *Decorations for Parks and Gardens*, by Charles Middleton, 1790. RIBA Collections.

FIG. 17 The interior of the privy adjoining the Banqueting House at Wardour. Photo: author.

FIG. 18 *The View from the Head of the Lake at Stowe*, by Bernard Baron after Jacques Rigaud, 1739. Royal Collection Trust/© HM Queen Elizabeth II.

FIG. 19 A detail from *A View of the Walton Bridge, Venus's Temple, etc. in the Garden of Sir Francis Dashwood Bart at West Wycomb*, William Woollett after William Hannan, *c*.1757. Royal Collection Trust/© HM Queen Elizabeth II.

FIG. 20 *A Perspective View of Newstead Abby* [sic] *and Park...* from *The Complete English Traveller* (London, 1771). Nottingham City Council/Picture the Past.

FIG. 21 The landscape at Batchacre Hall from Stebbing Shaw's *History and Antiquities of Staffordshire*, published in 1801. University of Bristol.

FIG. 22 A detail from one of the painted panels surviving in the house at Batchacre (undated, though probably late 1750s or early 1760s; artist unknown). Photo: Clare Hickman, reproduced courtesy of John Wilcox.

FIG. 23 A detail from the design for the boat at Wrest, 1765. Bedfordshire Archives Service.

FIG. 24 *The Chinese Junk afloat on Virginia Water*, by Paul Sandby, undated, *c*.1753. Royal Collection Trust/© HM Queen Elizabeth II.

FIG. 25 The Boathouse at Fonthill, today. Photo: author.

FIG. 26 *The central chamber of the Grotto at Stourhead*, by Francis Nicholson, undated. © The Trustees of the British Museum.

FIG. 27 *A View from the Island Seat of the Lake* [to] *the Temple of Venus and the Hermitage, Stowe*, J. Course, *c*. mid-1750s. © Victoria & Albert Museum, London.

FIG. 28 *A Family of Anglers: the Swaine Family of Laverington* [sic] *Hall in the Isle of Ely*, by Arthur Devis, 1749. Yale Center for British Art, Paul Mellon Collection.

FIG. 29 *The Temple Pond, Beachborough, Kent*, by Edward Haytley, *c*.1744. National Gallery of Victoria, Melbourne, Australia, Everard Studley Miller Bequest/Bridgeman Images.

FIG. 30 A detail from *The Temple Pond, Beachborough, Kent*, by Edward Haytley, *c*.1744. National Gallery of Victoria, Melbourne, Australia, Everard Studley Miller Bequest/Bridgeman Images.

FIG. 31   A detail from *The Cascade and Water House at Calwich, Staffordshire*, by
Mary Granville Delany, 1767. National Gallery of Ireland Collection/
© National Gallery of Ireland.

FIG. 32   *The Temple Pool at Enville c.*1800. Courtesy of Mrs Diana Williams.

FIG. 33   *The Misses Van*, by Lady Salisbury, 1791 (formerly attributed to Paul
Sandby). Yale Center for British Art, Paul Mellon Collection.

FIG. 34   *A View of the Hermitage in the Royal Garden at Richmond*, after J. Gravelot,
*c.*1730s. Royal Collection Trust/© HM Queen Elizabeth II.

FIG. 35   William Cowper's Summerhouse at Olney, from *Cowper Illustrated*, by
Storer and Greig, 1803. Reproduced courtesy of the Trustees of the Cowper
and Newton Museum.

FIG. 36   A detail from *Roslin Castle, Midlothian* by Paul Sandby, *c.*1780. Yale Center
for British Art, Paul Mellon Collection.

FIG. 37   *A View of Foots-Cray Place in Kent, the Seat of Bourchier Cleeve Esq.r*, by
Woollett, *c.*1760. Royal Collection Trust/© HM Queen Elizabeth II.

FIG. 38   Sanderson Miller's Castle at Edgehill, from *Edge-Hill or the Rural Prospect
Delineated and Moralized*, by Richard Jago, 1767. Courtesy of Stephen
Rench Books.

FIG. 39   A design for a temple at Chartley, Staffordshire, by William Thomas,
*c.*1760s. Reproduced by permission of the Record Office for Leicestershire,
Leicester and Rutland.

FIG. 40   *Perspective View of the Menagerie and its Pavilion*, after Thomas Sandby,
*c.*1760s. Royal Collection Trust/© HM Queen Elizabeth II.

FIG. 41   *The Menagerie at Woburn* from Humphry Repton's Red Book. From the
Woburn Abbey Collection.

FIG. 42   *Feeding the Ducklings* by Thomas Rowlandson, undated. Yale Center for
British Art, Paul Mellon Collection.

FIG. 43   *The Vinery*, by Thomas Rowlandson, undated. Yale Center for British Art,
Paul Mellon Collection.

FIG. 44   *The Forcing Garden at Woburn* as proposed by Humphry Repton in his Red
Book, 1805. From the Woburn Abbey Collection.

FIG. 45   A detail from *The Seat near the Terrace, with a View of the Adjacent Country
to the North-east*, by Paul Sandby, *c.*1765. Royal Collection Trust/© HM
Queen Elizabeth II.

FIG. 46   Pamela and Mr. B at the Summerhouse from *Pamela* by Samuel Richardson,
illustrated by Hubert Gravelot, 1742. © The British Library Board.

FIG. 47   Stancombe Park, Gloucestershire. Photo: author.

FIG. 48   *The Blunt Children*, by Johan Zoffany, *c.*1768–70. Birmingham Museums
and Art Gallery/Bridgeman Images.

FIG. 49   *Three Sons of John, 3rd Earl of Bute*, by Johan Zoffany, *c.*1763–4. © Tate,
London 2016.

FIG. 50   *Archery shooting at Hatfield House*, by Thomas Rowlandson, 1790. Royal
Collection Trust/© HM Queen Elizabeth II.

FIG. 51   *The Hermitage at Selborne*, Samuel Hieronymus Grimm, 1776. Natural
History and Antiquities of Selborne: drawings, 1776. MS Eng 731.11 (seq
4), Houghton Library, Harvard University.

FIG. 52 A detail from *A View of Esher in Surrey the Seat of the Rt. Hon. Henry Pelham Esq.* by Luke Sullivan, 1759. Yale Center for British Art, Paul Mellon Collection.

FIG. 53 *The Grotto at Stowe,* by Thomas Medland, 1797. Royal Collection Trust/© Her Majesty Queen Elizabeth II.

FIG. 54 The Root House (or Moss House) at Weston Underwood, from Edward Wedlake Brayley's *Cowper Illustrated by a Series of Views,* 1803. Reproduced courtesy of the Trustees of the Cowper and Newton Museum.

FIG. 55 *Fisher's Hall at Hackfall,* by John Swete, 1783. Reproduced with permission of Special Collections, Leeds University Library, BC MS Trv q 4 SWE.

FIG. 56 A design for a Stag Pasty from Edmund Kidder's *Receipts in Pastry and Cookery,* c.1720. Courtesy of Ivan Day.

FIG. 57 *A Sense of Taste,* by Philippe Mercier, 1744–47. Yale Center for British Art, Paul Mellon Collection.

FIG. 58 A detail from *Wallbridge,* c.1790, unknown artist. © The Museum in the Park, Stroud.

FIG. 59 *Mr Richard Edgcumbe (afterwards 1st Lord Edgcumbe) entertaining his friends in front of the Garden House at Mount Edgcumbe,* after a drawing by Thomas Badeslade, 1735. Plymouth City Museum.

FIG. 60 *The Garden at Hampton House with Mr and Mrs David Garrick taking tea,* by Johan Zoffany, 1762. Photograph courtesy of Sotheby's.

FIG. 61 A detail from *A View of Foots-Cray Place in Kent, the Seat of Bourchier Cleeve, Esq.* 1760. Royal Collection Trust/© Her Majesty Queen Elizabeth II.

FIG. 62 A detail from *A View of such parts [of Stowe] as are seen from the building at the head of the lake,* by Jacques Rigaud, 1733. Royal Collection Trust/© Her Majesty Queen Elizabeth II.

FIG. 63 A detail from the *Perspective View of the Building for the Fireworks in the Green Park,* by Paul Angier after P. Brookes, 1749. Yale Center for British Art, Paul Mellon Collection.

FIG. 64 *A View of the Fireworks and Illuminations at his grace the Duke of Richmond's at Whitehall and on the River Thames, on Monday 15th May 1749.* Private Collection/Bridgeman Images.

FIG. 65 *Windsor on a Rejoicing Night,* by Paul Sandby, 1768. Royal Collection Trust/© Her Majesty Queen Elizabeth II.

FIG. 66 A detail from *The Dinner in Mote Park, Maidstone, after the Royal Review of the Kentish Volunteers,* William Alexander, c.1799. Yale Center for British Art, Paul Mellon Collection.

FIG. 67 *View from the North Portico of Stowe House, Feb. 1818, showing the celebrations for the coming of age of the heir of the Duke of Buckingham & Chandos at Stowe, including Morris dancers,* by an unknown artist, 1818. Reproduced with the permission of the Buckinghamshire Archaeological Society

FIG. 68 The Folly at Doddington. Photo: author.

FIG. 69 The upper room inside The Folly at Doddington. Photo: author.

FIG. 70 The Temple at Bignor Park. Photo: author.

FIG. 71 The interior of Professor Middlemas's Gazebo. Photo: author.

Index

References to images are in *italics*; references to notes are indicated by *n*

Adam, Robert 93, 194, 195, 197
agriculture 14–15, 223 n10
Aislabie, John 96
Aislabie, William 44–5, 161–2
alcohol 179, 180–81
Alnwick (Northumberland) 32
Amelia, Princess 34, 83–5, 152, 153, 197, 210
America *see* United States of America
amorous liaisons 127, 133–4
Ancaster and Kesteven, Peregrine Bertie, 3rd Duke of 72
angling 82–90
    and buildings 90–93
    see also fishing
animals 116–17, 118–20, 121–4
Anne, Queen 4, 9, 170
annual calendar 26–7
Anson, Admiral George 41, 62
Anson, Lady Elizabeth (*née* Yorke) 41–2, 68, 69, 167, 177, 192
Archer, Thomas 176, 215
archery *139*, 140, 142–4
Archery shooting at Hatfield House (Rowlandson) *143*
architecture 3, 4, 118
aristocracy 5, 21, 22, 57
Arklington Hall (Lancashire) 142
art 2–3, 5–6, 51
Ashmolean Museum 116
astronomy 113–15
Audley End (Essex) 116–17
Augusta of Saxe-Gotha, Princess 120, 125, 129–30
Austen, Jane 8, 10, 11, 142, 168–9
    and picnics 52–3, 164
aviaries 122–4
Aylesford, Heneage Finch, 4th Earl of 143

Badeslade, Thomas 178
badminton 142
balls 193–4
Bampfylde, Coplestone Warre 40–41, 108, 216
banqueting houses 4, 44, 45–6, 147
Barrells (Warwickshire) 95
Barrett, Thomas Lennard (later Lord Dacre) 75
Batchacre Hall (Staffordshire) *64*, 65–6, *67*
Bates, Henry 184
Bath 73–4
bathing 73–81, 135
Battie, Catherine 145–6, 148, 149–50
battledore and shuttlecock 142
Beachborough (Kent) 87–8, *89*
Beckford, William 24–5, 94–5, 205
bedding 126–9
Bedford, John Russell, 6th Duke of 15, 122, 162–3
Belhus (Essex) 75
belvederes 109, 112–13, 219, 220
Beresford Hall (Staffordshire) 90
Bignor Park (West Sussex) 217–19
billiards 232 n67
birds 117, 118–19, 120, 121–4
Blenheim (Oxfordshire) 37–8
Blunt Children, The (Zoffany) *137*
boats 12, 29, 56–64, 66–72
bonfires 203–4
botany 116, 117–18, 124–5, 162–3
bowling 140–41
Bradley, Martha 159, 160
Brett, Piercy 174
Bretton Hall (Yorkshire) 203
Bridgeman, Charles 9
Bristol, Frederick Hervey, Lord Bishop of

Derry and 4th Earl of 104
Bristol, John Hervey, 1st Earl of 184–5
Brown, Lancelot 'Capability' 4, 9, 10, 11, 18, 214
    and drives 36, 37
    and kitchen gardens 125
    and Miller 41
    and walks 33
    and water 57, 61, 69
Burdon, John 106, 127
Burke, Edmund 36–7
Burlington, Richard Boyle, 3rd Earl of 73, 127, 185–6
Burney, Fanny 142, 181
Bute, John Stuart, 3rd Earl of 57–8, 59, 129–30
Byng, John (later 5th Viscount Torrington) 143–4
Byron, William, 5th Lord 62–5

Calwich (Staffordshire) 90–91
camera obscuras 109–10
Cannons (Middlesex) 186
Caroline of Ansbach, Queen 20, 100–101
carriages 22, 32, 37–40; see also chaises
Carshalton House (Surrey) 102
cartography 108–9, 112–13
Cascade and Water House at Calwich, Staffordshire, The (Delany) 91
Castell, Robert 73
Castle at Edgehill (Warwickshire) 108, 111, 112, 182–3
Castle Cary (Somerset) 209
Castle Howard (Yorkshire) 206
Castletown (County Kildare) 98
Catherine the Great, Empress of Russia 19, 20
chairs 50–51, 179
chaises 34, 35–6
Chambers, William 200–201
Chandos, James Brydges, 1st Duke of 186
Charlotte, Queen 141, 197
Chartley Hall (Staffordshire) 114, 115
Chatsworth (Derbyshire) 206–7
Chawton (Hampshire) 53, 164
Cheyne, George 74–5
children 29, 85–6, 136–40
Chilham (Kent) 10
Chinese Junk afloat on Virginia Water, The (Sandby) 71
chinoiserie 3, 12, 68, 69–71, 173–5, 215
Chiswick (Middlesex) 73, 127, 207, 209
Christian VII of Denmark, King 197, 200
Claremont (Surrey) 109
class 5, 20–22

Clumber Park (Nottinghamshire) 59, 87
Cobham, Richard Temple, 1st Viscount 24, 59, 131–2, 165–6, 167
coffee 179
Coke, Edward (later Viscount Coke) 202
Coke, Jane 70
Coke, Lady Mary (née Campbell) 34, 83–5, 96, 140–41, 153
Coke, Thomas (later 1st Earl of Leicester) 14–15
coming-of-age celebrations 204–7, 208, 209
Compleat Angler, The (Walton) 90, 228 n2
Conolly, Lady Louisa (née Lennox) 98
Copley, Sir Godfrey 76–7
Corbet, Edward 134
Corelli, Arcangelo 183, 237 n53
Cotton, Charles 90
country houses 22, 24–5, 26–9
countryside 12–13
Coventry, Barbara, Lady (née St John) 124
Coventry, George, 6th Earl 22, 23
Cowper, William 106, 156–8
cricket 141
Croome (Worcestershire) 22, 158, 197
Cumberland, William Augustus, Duke of 70, 127
curricles 39–40

daily routine 27–9
dairies 20, 147, 168
Dashwood, Sir Francis 60–61, 130
Davidson, Duncan 216
deer parks 13–14
Derby, Edward Smith-Stanley, 12th Earl of 194
Devis, Arthur 51
Devonshire, Georgiana, Duchess of (née Spencer) 29, 207, 209
Digby family 26–7
Dinner in Mote Park, Maidstone, after the Royal Review of the Kentish Volunteers, The (Alexander) 206
Discourse on Fish and Fishponds, A (North) 85
Doddington Place (Kent) 216–17, 218
Downhill (County Londonderry) 104–5
Drake Brockman family 87–8
Drayton (Northamptonshire) 127
dress 16, 18–19, 97
drives 36–8
Duncombe Park (Yorkshire) 44
Dunster Castle (Somerset) 217

Eales, Mary 170
Edgcumbe, Richard, Baron 96

Edgehill (Warwickshire), 105, 108, 111, 112, 231 n46
education 136–7
Elizabethan age 3–4, 195
Eltham Lodge (Kent) 47, 48–9, 50
Emma (Austen) 52–3, 164, 168–9, 173, 174–5
English Civil War 44, 94, 156–8, 159
entertainments 6, 24–5, 29, 146, 148–55
and night-time 193–7, 200–13, 238 n9
Enville (Staffordshire) 91–2, 113
Esher Place (Surrey) 28, 150–52, 156
etiquette 159
Europe 19–20
Evelina (Burney) 181
Evelyn, John 13, 94
exercise 31–3
Exeter, Brownlow Cecil, 9th Earl of 184
Experienced Angler, The (Walton) 82–3
Exton (Rutland) 186–7
eye-catchers 1, 3, 12, 215–21, 222 n2

Faerie Queene, The (Spenser) 133
Family of Anglers: the Swaine Family of Laverington Hall in the Isle of Ely, A (Devis) 86
Feeding the Ducklings (Rowlandson) 123
Ferrers, Washington Shirley, 5th Earl 114–15
fête champêtre nocturne 195, 210
fêtes 6, 194, 203
fireworks 6, 29, 190–91, 196–7
Fisher, Paul Hawkins 175–6
Fisher's Hall at Hackfall (Swete) 163
fishing 29, 82–93, 153; see also angling
fish ponds 87
Floyer, Sir John 74
Foley, Lady Ann (née Coventry) 134–5
Fonthill (Wiltshire) 24, 77–8, 205
food 6–7, 43–4, 146–7, 158–60, 167–8, 177–80
and desserts 170–72
and mealtimes 27–8, 29
and picnics 51–3, 164–5
and preparation 160–64
and venison 165–7
see also fruit
Fowler, Ann 42, 97–8
Fox, Lady Caroline (née Lennox) 141
Fox, Henry, 1st Baron Holland 16
Fox-Strangways family, Earls of Ilchester 26, 33, 96–7, 137–8, 209
Fox-Strangways, Lady Elizabeth, see Talbot, Lady Elizabeth
Fox-Strangways, Lady Louisa 137–8

Fox-Strangways, Lady Mary 96–7; see also Talbot, Mary
France 2, 20, 159–60, 195
Frederick, Prince of Wales 58–9, 129, 226 n36
Frederick the Great of Prussia 183
Fremantle, Betsey (née Wynne) 211, 212
French horns 80, 182
Frogmore House (Berkshire) 141
fruit 125, 126, 147, 168–70

Gainsborough, Baptist Noel, 4th Earl of 186
games 140–42
Garden at Hampton House with Mr and Mrs David Garrick taking tea, The (Zoffany) 180
gardens 8, 40–42, 158–9
and class 21–2
and Europe 19–20
and history 2–5, 8–13
and modern day 214–21
and solace 94–104
and walks 31–5
Garrick, David 179
gazebos 220–21
George I, King 4, 9, 20–21
George II, King 21
George III, King 16, 17, 115, 129, 197, 200
George IV, King 207, 209, 210–12
Germany 19–20
Gibside (County Durham) 187–8
Gilpin, William 10
glasshouses 125, 126
Glorious Revolution (1688) 21, 26
Godmersham (Kent) 10, 53, 204
Goodwood (West Sussex) 55–6, 118–20, 141
Gosfield (Essex) 184
Grand Tour 73, 195
Granville, Bernard 90
Great Packington (Warwickshire) 143
Great Storm (1987) 2, 118, 218
Gregory, Dr John 32
Grenville, George 89, 203–4
Grenville, Mrs George 66–7
Grey, Jemima Yorke, Marchioness 23, 29, 68–9, 73, 176–7, 192–3
and children 85–6, 138, 140
and education 113–14
and retreat 98–9, 102–3
Grey, Mary 113
Griffin, Sir John Griffin 116–17
Grimsthorpe Castle (Lincolnshire) 72
Grotto at Stowe, The (Medland) 153

grottoes 78–80, 127, *153*, 154–5
Gunnersbury (Middlesex) 197

ha-has 9–10, 11
Hackfall (Yorkshire) 44–5, 162, *163*
Hagley (Worcestershire) 111
Halifax, George Montagu Dunk, 2nd Earl
    of 120, 121
Halswell (Somerset) 43, 160
Hamilton, Charles 104
Hampton (Middlesex) 179
Handel, George Frideric 185–7
Hanoverian dynasty 4, 20–21
Hanway, Jonas 79–80
Hardwick (County Durham) 106–7, 127
Hardwick Hall (Derbyshire) 207
Hartington, William Cavendish, Marquess
    of 206, 207
hautboys 181–2
haymaking *15*, 16, *17*, 88, 137
Haytley, Edward 87
health 74–5
Heard, Sir Isaac 24–5
Hellfire Club 60, 130
Hellier, Sir Samuel 188–9
Henry I, King 117
Hermitage at Selborne, The (Grimm) *149*
hermitages 100–101, 103–4
hermits 100, 104, 148, 149, 150
Hervey, George (later 2nd Earl of Bristol)
    192
Hestercombe (Somerset) 41
Heveningham (Suffolk) 37
Hoare, Henry 78, 80–81, 189
Holkham (Norfolk) 14–15, 26, 67, 159, 202
Holland House (London) 16, *17*, 141
horses *14*, 15–16
Horton (Northamptonshire) 120–22
Houghton Hall (Norfolk) 24
hunting 27, 182, 222 n6
Hurlstone Tower (Northumberland)
    215–16

ice houses 147, 168, 170–71, 236 n31
Ickworth (Suffolk) 185
illuminations 200–202, 210
Italy 195

jardin anglais 2, 19

Kedleston (Derbyshire) 92–3
Kent, Henry Grey, 1st Duke of 112, 113,
    121, 167
Kent, Sophia Bentinck, Duchess of 113, 167
Kent, William 9–10, 58–9, 132, 195

Kew Gardens (Surrey) *119*, 120, 125,
    129–30, 215
kitchen gardens 125–6, 168
kitchens 160–63
kites 142
Knight, Fanny Austen 53
Knyvett, Charles 212

Lacock (Wiltshire) 192
lakes 3, 12, 57, 65–6, 87–9; *see also* boats
land ownership 12–13, 14–15
landscape design 2–5, 8–13
Landscape Style 2–3, 18
Lawrence, John 14
Leasowes, The (Shropshire) 95, 103
Leigh Park (Hampshire) 11–12
Leinster, Emily, Duchess of (*née* Lennox)
    136–7, 141
Lemon, Lady Charlotte (*née* Fox-
    Strangways) 40
Lennox, Lady Sarah 16, *17*
Leopold Friedrich Franz of Anhalt-Dessau,
    Prince 19–20
Lever, Sir Ashton 142
libraries 104–8
Lincoln, Henry Pelham Clinton, 9th Earl
    of 155
Linley the Younger, Thomas 72, 185
Linnaeus, Carl 117
livestock 13–14, 15
London 26–7, 96, 56–7, 195–6, 197
Longleat (Wiltshire) 51, *52*, 147
Lorrain, Claude 2
Louis XIV of France, King 195
love, buildings associated with 129–33
Luton Hoo (Bedfordshire) 36, 57–8, 59, 143
Luxborough, Henrietta Knight, Lady 95–6,
    110
Lyttleton, George, 1st Baron 164

Mansfield Park (Austen) 10
Marie-Antoinette of France, Queen 20
'maskers' 211–12
mealtimes 27–8, 29, 51, 146
Melbury (Dorset) 26, 28, 40
Melliar, Joanna 209
melons 149, 170
Menagerie at Woburn, The (Repton) *121*, 122
menageries 116–24
Mersey, Richard Bigham, 4th Viscount
    218–19
Michell, John Henry 46
Middlemas, Professor Keith 221
Middleton, Clara Louisa 135–6
Miller, Sanderson 41, 75, 91, 96, 105–6

buildings 91–2, 105, 111, *112*, 174, 230 n18
and food 164, 165–6, 167, 170–72
and music 182–3, 184, 189
and vistas 108, 109, 110
Misses Van, The (Salisbury) *99*
moonlight 191–2
Moor Park (Hertfordshire) 41
Morpeth, George Howard, Lord (later 6th
Earl of Carlisle) 206
morris men *208*, 211–12
Mount Edgcumbe (Cornwall) 96, 110, *178*,
182, 189
Mozart, Wolfgang Amadeus 72
music 29, 80, *111*, 122, 151–2, 156, 181–9,
204, 205, 207, 208, 209, 212, 237
nn53, 54
buildings for 115, 122, 182, 189
Mussenden Temple 104–5

National Maritime Museum 59, 63
National Trust 1, 44
Nattes, Jean Claude 6
naumachia 60–61, 66, 227 n40
Newstead Abbey (Nottinghamshire) 62–5
Newton, Sir Isaac 110
night-time 6, 190–93
Noel, John 186
North, Francis, 1st Earl of Guildford 174
North, Roger 85, 87
*North-west View of Wakefield Lodge in
Whittlebury Forest, Northamptonshire*
(Sandby) *38–9*
Northumberland, Elizabeth Percy, Duchess
of (*née* Seymour) 32, 64

Oaks, The (Surrey) 194, 238 n9
Oare House (Wiltshire) 215
Oatlands (Surrey) 155
O'Brien, Lady Susan (*née* Fox-Strangways)
27, 33
Observations on Modern Gardening (Whately)
3
observatories 113, 115
Oldfield, Richard 216
opera 181, 186, 187–8
Orchard Side, Olney (Buckinghamshire)
106, *107*
Ordnance Survey 109

Painshill (Surrey) 47, 104
Painswick (Gloucestershire) 75
Pamela (Richardson) *132*
Park Place (Oxfordshire) 34, 83, 140–41
Parker, Theresa (*née* Robinson) 86, 182
parks 2–5, 8, 13–16

Parliament 26, 27
parties *see* entertainments
Peace of Aix-la-Chapelle (1749) 195–6, 197
Pei, I.M. 215
Penrice Castle (Glamorgan) 31, 97
*Perspective View of the Building for the
Fireworks in the Green Park* (Angier)
196
*Perspective View of the Menagerie and its
Pavilion* (Sandby) *119*
*Perspective View of Newstead Abby and Park,
A* (anon.) *63*
Peterborough, Charles Henry Mordant, 5th
Earl of 134–5
Petton Hall (Shropshire) 134
Petworth (West Sussex) 13
phaetons 38–40
Phelps, Richard 41
picnics 6–7, 51–3, 164–5
Picturesque style 4, 10
Pitt the Elder, William, 1st Earl of Chatham
24, 41, 96, 182
plants 118, 124–5
pleasure grounds 6, 32, 154; *see also*
Vauxhall, Ranelagh
Pliny the Younger 73
politics 4, 24, 96, 194; *see also* Parliament
ponds 87
Pope, Alexander *58*, 127, *186*, 228 n1
Poussin, Nicolas 3
Pride and Prejudice (Austen) 8, 32–3
Prince of Wales *see* George IV, Frederick
Prior Park (Somerset) 35
privies 54–6
Purnell, Bransbury 133

quoits 141

Radway Grange estate (Warwickshire)
105–6, 165–6, 182, 189, 230 n28
Rand, Reverend Conway 131, 140
Ranelagh Pleasure Gardens (Chelsea) 154
Raynham Hall (Norfolk) 15
Redlynch (Somerset) 26, 28
refreshment stops 43–7, *48–9*, 50–51
Repton, Humphry 9, 10, 12, 122, 125–6,
141
and drives 39–40
and food 52, 162
and water 58, 67
retreats 8, 11, 12, 222 n4
Richmond (Surrey) 20, 100–101, 115, 185,
196–7, 200–201
Richmond, Charles Lennox, 2nd Duke of
118, 120, 122, 141

Riders on an Avenue in the Park at Luton (Sandby) *36*
riding 32
Rievaulx (Yorkshire) 44, 163–4
roads 22–3, 36–8
Robins, Thomas 169
Robinson, Anne 86, 164–5
rococo style 12
Roman Empire 3, 60, 73–4
root houses 99–104, 157
Roslin Castle (Midlothian) *110*, 169
Rouchfoucauld, François de la 158, 159
Rousham (Oxfordshire) 10, 75
Rousseau, Jean-Jacques 100, 136, 137
Royal Navy 57, 59, 62; *see also* naumachia
royalty 5, 20–21
Rufford Abbey (Nottinghamshire) 77
Russia 2, 19, 20

Saltram (Devon) 86, 164–5, 182
Sandby, Paul 108
Sayes Court (Kent) 94
Scarsdale, Nathaniel Curzon, 1st Baron 93
scholarly pursuits 5–6, 104–8
science 116, 117
Seat near the Terrace, with a View of the Adjacent Country to the North-east, The (Sandby) *128*
Selborne (Hampshire) *46*, 47, 115, 145–6, 148–50
Senesino (Francesco Bernardi) *186*, 187
Senex, John 113
Sense and Sensibility (Austen) 11, 56, 164, 168
Sense of Taste, A (Mercier) *171*
Servandoni, Giovanni Niccolò 195, 200
servants 156, 158, 223 n6, 236 n9
sexual liaisons 129–30, 134–6
Shaw family 47, *48–9*, 50
Shenstone, William 95–6, 103
Sherborne (Dorset) 26–7, 28, 71–2, 89–90
shooting 27, 222 n6
Shugborough (Staffordshire) 174
singing 183–4, *186*, 212
Sketches and Hints on Landscape Gardening (Repton) 58
sleep 126–9
Sloane, Hans 76
Southill (Bedfordshire) 127
Spence, Joseph 155
sport 27, 140–44, 222 n6; *see also* fishing
Sprotborough Hall (Yorkshire) 76–7
Stancombe Park (Gloucestershire) 133–4
Staunton, Sir George 12
Stockeld Park (Yorkshire) 135–6

Stoke Edith (Herefordshire) 134–5
Stourhead (Wiltshire) 78–81
Stowe (Buckinghamshire) 1, 6, 10, *14*, 41, 221
  and amorous liaisons 130–33
  and beds 127–9
  and boats *58*, 59
  and bowling 140
  and entertainments 152–5, *208*
  and fishing 83–4
  and music 184, 187, 188
  and night-time 192, 202, 203–4
  Palladian Bridge *34*, 35
  and royalty 209–12
  Temple of Friendship 23, 24
  Temple of Venus 130, 132
Strangways Horner, Elizabeth 40
strawberries 147, 168–9
Strawberry Hill (Middlesex) 23
Stroud (Gloucestershire) 175
Stuart, Lady Louisa 72, 169
Stubbs, George 51
studies 93–4, 104–8
Studley Royal (Yorkshire) 45, 96, 161
swimming 73–81
syllabub 148, 152, 168, 171–2
Sylva: A Discourse of Forest Trees (Evelyn) 13

tables 50–51, 179
Talbot, Catherine 177
Talbot, Lady Elizabeth (*née* Fox-Strangways) 192
Talbot, Lady Mary (*née* Fox-Strangways) 42
Talbot, Thomas Mansel 31, 97
tea 172–5, 176–7, 179
telescopes 109, 110–11, 113–14, 232 n59
Temple, Richard Grenville, Earl 24, 26, 59, 152–3, 154–5, 210
Temple Newsam (Yorkshire) 33
Temple Pond, Beachborough, Kent, The (Haytley) *88, 89*
Temple Pool at Enville, The (anon.) *92*
temples 1, 3, 12, 44, 218–19
  and Chartley *114*, 115
  and Mussenden 104–5
  and Stowe *14*, 24
tents 46–7, *48–9*, 50
Thames, River 56–7, 58–9, 198–9
Three Sons of John, 3rd Earl of Bute (Zoffany) *139*
timber 13
topography 108–9, 112–13
tourism 23, 73, 120

Townshend, Charles 'Turnip', 2nd Viscount 15

Tradescant, John, Elder and Younger 116

travel 22–3

trees 13, 118

Tyers, Jonathan 201, 202

United States of America 2, 19

Vanbrugh, John 9, 109

Vauxhall Pleasure Gardens (London) 29, 154, 182, 201–2

venison 165–7

Victoria, Queen 4, 209–10

victory celebrations 203–4

View of Esher in Surrey the Seat of the Rt. Hon. Henry Pelham Esq., *A* (Sullivan) *151*

View of Foots-Cray Place in Kent, the Seat of Bourchier Cleeve Esq.r, *A* (Woollett) *111*

View of the Fireworks and Illuminations at his grace the Duke of Richmond's at Whitehall and on the River Thames, on Monday 15th May 1749, *A* (anon.) *198–9*

View from the Head of the Lake at Stowe, The (Baron) 58

View from Heaven's Gate at Longleat, The (Repton) 51, 52

View of the Hermitage in the Royal Garden at Richmond, A (Gravelot) *101*

View from the Island Seat of the Lake [to] the Temple of Venus and the Hermitage, Stowe, A (Course) 84

View of such parts [of Stowe] as are seen from the building at the head of the lake (Rigaud) *186*

View of the Walton Bridge, Venus's Temple, etc. in the Garden of Sir Francis Dashwood Bart at West Wycomb (Woollett) *61*

vistas 108, 109–13, 148, 223 n15

Vinery, The (Rowlandson) *124*

Virginia Water (Surrey) 70–71, 87, 127

Wakes, The 46, 115; *see also* Selborne

walks 31–5, 192

Wallbridge (Gloucestershire) 175–6

Walpole, Horace, 4th Earl of Orford 9, 16, 23, 28, 129, 172
  and entertainments 150, 151, 152–3, 154, 156, 191

Walpole, Sir Robert, 1st Earl of Orford 24, 96

Walton, Izaak 82–3, 90, 93, 228 n2

Wardour Castle (Wiltshire) 44, 54–5, 125

waterside buildings 90–93

Wedgwood, Josiah *18*, 19

Wentworth, Sir Thomas 203

West, Gilbert 128, 131

West Wycombe (Buckinghamshire) 59, 60–61, 130
  Temple of Venus 130

Weston Underwood (Buckinghamshire) 157–8

Whately, Thomas 3

White, Gilbert 47, 115–16, 145–6, 148–50, 169–70, 183–4, 220

Whitworth, Admiral Richard 65

William IV, King 4

William Berry Introduced as the Heir to Raith (Zoffany) 50

Wilton (Wiltshire) 35

Wimpole (Cambridgeshire) 193

Windsor Great Park (Berkshire) *35*, 141

Windsor on a Rejoicing Night (Sandby) 200

Wise, Henry 9

Woburn (Bedfordshire) 15, 59, *121*, 122, 125–6, *126*, 162

Wodehouse, The (Staffordshire) 188–9

women 19, 32–3, 40, 42
  and archery 142, *143*
  and gardening 96–8
  and haymaking 16
  and menageries 123–4

Woodforde, James 47, 72, 168, 180

Woodstock Park (Oxfordshire) 117

Wooton Hall (Staffordshire) 100

Wörlitz (Germany) 19–20

Wotton (Buckinghamshire) 61–2, 66, 89, 226 n43, 229 n16

Wotton (Surrey) 94

Wrest Park (Bedfordshire) 56, 68, 73, 85, 98, 192, 215, 230 n39, 240 n1
  and belvedere (Hill House) 112–14
  and boat 68–70
  and children 138–40
  and food 161, 167
  and root house 101–3
  and tea 176–7

Wright, Thomas 69, 113–14, 121, 233 n80

Wroxton (Oxfordshire) 174

Wynne, Harriet 211, 212

Yorke, Philip, 2nd Earl of Hardwick 73, 192

Zoffany, Johan 51, 179

zoology 116, 117–18